DESCRIBING MUSIC MATERIALS

Soldier Creek Music Series

Richard P. Smiraglia, Series Editor

DESCRIBING MUSIC MATERIALS

A Manual for Descriptive Cataloging of Printed and Recorded Music, Music Videos, and Archival Music Collections

For Use with AACR 2 and APPM

Richard P. Smiraglia

Third Edition, Revised and Enlarged
with the assistance of Taras Pavlovsky

Printed in the United States of America

ISBN 0-936996-75-7
ISSN 1056-0041

Library of Congress Cataloging-in-Publication Data

Smiraglia, Richard P., 1952-
    Describing music materials : a manual for descriptive cataloging of printed and recorded music, music videos, and archival music collections : for use with AACR2 and APPM / Richard P. Smiraglia. -- 3rd ed., rev. and enl. / with the assistance of Taras Pavlovsky.
      p. cm. -- (Soldier Creek music series, ISSN 1056-0041 ; no. 5)
    Includes bibliographical references and index.
    ISBN 0-936996-75-7 (paper)
    1. Cataloging of music--Handbooks, manuals, etc. 2. Cataloging of sound recordings--Handbooks, manuals, etc. 3. Cataloging of video recordings--Handbooks, manuals, etc. 4. Cataloging of archival material--Handbooks, manuals, etc. 5. Cataloging of music manuscripts--Handbooks, manuals, etc. 6. Cataloging of interactive media--Handbooks, manuals, etc. 7. Descriptive cataloging--Rules--Handbooks, manuals, etc. 8. Anglo-American cataloging rules. 9. Hensen, Steven L, 1944- Archives, personal papers, and manuscripts. I. Pavlovsky, Taras. II. Title. III. Series.
ML111.S633 1997
025.3'488--dc21

                                     97-2150
                                         CIP
                                       MN

Soldier Creek Press

Nancy B. Olson, President
Edward Swanson, Editor-in-Chief
Sharon Olson, Managing Editor

P. O. Box 734, Lake Crystal, Minnesota 56055-0734 USA

ACKNOWLEDGMENTS

I wish to thank all those who have contributed to the shaping of this book, beginning of course with the readers of the first two editions. I owe a large debt of gratitude to my music cataloging students at the Palmer School of Library and Information Science (Long Island University), who in the summer of 1994 worked with an incomplete version of this text and helped me to understand its shortcomings. I'd also like to thank Leonard J. Lehrman, who, as my graduate assistant at the Palmer School, searched online for all of the catalog copy in this book so I could see what sorts of problems needed to be addressed herein.

Finally, readers will note that Taras Pavlovsky is included on the title page. Without Taras's assistance this project might never have gotten completed. Taras was responsible for reconciling all of the variant versions of LCRIs and MCDs to assure that the latest text appears here. Taras also updated all of the bibliographic apparatus in this book, including the list of thematic catalogs. Finally, on several occasions, Taras and I sat together as we vetted the entire text—much of the rewriting in this edition came at his suggestion.

Chelsea Square
July 12, 1996

TABLE OF CONTENTS

INTRODUCTION

This book is about how to create descriptive cataloging for printed music, musical sound recordings, music videorecordings, and archival music collections. Cataloging music materials for any library can be a challenge. Chief sources of information can be deceptive in appearance (for example, "list" title pages on printed music, or sound recording labels), and sometimes the information they provide is insufficient for one to be able to establish an intelligible entry. Establishing access points can be complicated and confusing for those who are not well grounded in music bibliography. No matter how detailed the rules in the Anglo-American Cataloguing Rules, second edition (AACR 2), special knowledge or special techniques might be required to construct a "correct" bibliographic record for a musical item.

Nevertheless, cataloging is, after all, cataloging. The music cataloger begins by examining an item, and then proceeds to record a transcription of title and statement of responsibility, and details of publication from integral sources of information. A physical description is formulated, and notes are made where needed to further clarify the content of the item. Once the description is completed, access points are formulated to serve as index entries in the catalog. For music materials, access points are made under headings for composers (usually in conjunction with a uniform title) and performers, as well as under the usual headings for editors, compilers, titles, and series.

AACR 2 provides an integrated approach to descriptive cataloging of all types of materials. General rules appear in chapter 1 and in chapters 21-26, which apply to all kinds of materials cataloged by libraries. Special rules for music materials appear in chapters 5 (Music) and 6 (Sound Recordings), and in special sections of chapters 21 (Choice of Access Points) and 25 (Uniform Titles). For videorecordings, musical expertise must be applied to the rules in chapter 7 (Motion Pictures and Videorecordings)—music videos often mimic the bibliographic features of sound recordings, but the cataloger must not lose sight of the fact that the item in hand contains a moving visual image. The music cataloger must be familiar with the general rules as well as with the special rules for music.

Archival processing of collections of materials has become more prevalent in both archives and libraries since the second edition of this book was written. Therefore, in this edition a chapter on the creation of collection descriptions has been added. The basic provisions contained in AACR 2 chapter 4 (Manuscripts) have been expanded and clarified by the archival community. Their manual, *Archives, Personal Papers and Manuscripts* by Steven Hensen, has become the national standard for the creation of archival collection descriptions that appear online in bibliographic networks and local catalogs.

Cataloging practice in the United States is heavily influenced by the policies of the Library of Congress. Rule Interpretations are isssued by the Cataloging Policy and Support Office and provide clarification of many rules as well as examples of their application. Music Cataloging Decisions are issued by the Music Section of the Special Materials Cataloging Division at the Library of Congress and further elucidate specific provisions of the rules as they apply to music cataloging.

Finally, any cataloger of special materials must be familiar with the literature and bibliography of that body of material, and music is no exception. Specialized reference sources must be consulted during the cataloging process to determine how best to relate a particular description to the catalog in general and to the entire body of music literature in particular. This book is one attempt to bring together in one place information about and instruction in the use of all of these aspects.

Cataloging is a dynamic profession, changing by adopting new techniques as new information and new technologies become available to the profession. Probably the most difficult aspect of descriptive cataloging is decision-making. The rules and standards can provide only general guidance. The cataloger must apply rules in a generic way based on personal understanding of both musical materials and the context of bibliographic control. The next segment of this introduction is about the concept of musical documents (scores and recordings) as cultural and artistic artifacts. That is followed by an introduction to procedures for descriptive cataloging of music materials.

MUSICAL DOCUMENTS AS ARTIFACTS

Almost all of the materials that will be described using this book were not created as or intended to be items in libraries. That is, they all were created with other purposes and other audiences in mind. Understanding this fact, and contemplating the use to which the items would normally be put, will help the cataloger grasp the divergent sources of information encountered. Also, understanding the ways in which the items will be used by library clients will help the cataloger make decisions about levels of detail in the description and also about the extent of access that will be useful in the catalog.

PROCEDURES: GENERAL

Most catalogers seem to catalog instinctively, and probably they accomplish all steps of the cataloging process at once. Some catalogers batch their work, doing a large batch of similar descriptions at once, then handling the authority work later. Still others are provided with finished descriptions and authority work along with the items; in these cases catalogers make decisions about the final shape of the bibliographic record and turn their work over to others who key the final records in to bibliographic utilities.

In any event, several steps must be accomplished in the process of creating the descriptive cataloging for an item. Beginning catalogers might benefit from following the steps in this order:

1. Technical reading—Musical documents and bibliographical forms
2. Chief and prescribed sources of information
3. Transcription to create item surrogate
4. Annotation, and identification of works
5. Access points
6. Record formatting

ABOUT THIS BOOK

The first edition of this book grew from a set of eighteen cataloging examples used in a music librarianship practicum in the music library at the University of Illinois at Urbana-Champaign. Eventually the examples were expanded into a workshop outline used in continuing education programs that began with the implementation of the second edition of the Anglo-American Cataloguing Rules in 1980-81. I incorporated Library of Congress published policy statements because of the need for a single source of basic information on how to apply AACR 2 to music materials.

The second edition updated the original text and expanded quite a bit with new examples and material to fill in the gaps noted by my students. This third edition not only updates the second edition, but also includes quite a bit of new material. I have separated the chapters on description of printed music and sound recordings, and I have added chapters on description of music videos, archival music materials, and multimedia products. The examples have been updated as well, with many of the original LP sound recording examples removed and replaced with examples of CD recordings. Where the first two editions had all cataloging examples in one chapter, this edition has them incorporated throughout the text so as to better illustrate specific rules.

A secondary goal of this book is to serve as a handbook for the beginning music cataloger. I do not explain either the basic principles of cataloging or the basic tenets of music librarianship, which are better dealt with elsewhere. This manual does presuppose a thorough understanding of AACR 2, as well as a familiarity with certain basic source material for cataloging.

CHAPTER 1: DESCRIPTION OF PRINTED MUSIC

INTRODUCTION: THE PROCESS

The steps in description of printed music are as follows:

1. Technical reading of the music, to determine the format and use of the item and to select the chief and prescribed sources of information;

2. Transcription of the title and statement of responsibility area from the chief source of information;

3. Consideration of transcription of data into the edition and material-specific details areas to indicate the presentation format of the music;

4. Transcription of the publication, distribution, etc., data, often found in several parts of the item;

5. Physical description of the music;

6. Transcription of series data;

7. Making notes as appropriate.

TECHNICAL READING OF PRINTED MUSIC

Technical reading of a musical document involves careful examination of all parts of the item to comprehend all potential sources of information. Printed scores often have title pages, much like book title pages, and these may be used as chief sources of information. But there is a long history of decorative title pages on printed music (for commerical purposes—the artwork is intended to influence impulse buying). Decorative title pages often do not provide title information adequate to identify the musical work. When this is the case, fuller information from elsewhere in the item will have to be transcribed in notes. Another typical publishing practice is to wrap a piece of music in a "list" or "passe-partout" title page, on which appears title and statement of responsibility data for several related works. In such cases, the cataloger will need to know whether fuller information appears elsewhere on the item. Caption titles—the title data that appear at the top of the first page of the printed music—frequently provide the only source of title and statement of responsibility data. Finally, in sets of scores and parts both must be examined to see whether the title and statement of responsibility data that appear on the each are the same.

Data on edition and musical presentation statements should be sought in the item. These will be closely linked to the nature of the item—in other words, the sort of musical document in hand will determine the style of presentation of the music. Commercial influences as well as the potential use of an item determine how the item is put together physically, which in turn has an influence on how bibliographic data will appear. For instance, a miniature score (intended for study or to be carried along to a concert) fundamentally will be a different physical entity from a conductor's full score. In fact, music intended for study is likely to be bound and have a title page (in other words, look like a book), while music intended for performance probably will be unbound, tall, and able to lie flat on a music stand (therefore there will be less room for bibliographic data, which might in turn be briefer than that found on items intended for study).

Publication and distribution data might be found in several places in the item. Title page, title page verso, bottom of the first page of music, and colophon (bottom of the last page of music or the last page of the item) are all common sites for these data. Also, it is important to browse through all parts of the item to determine whether plate and publisher's numbers appear, and if they do, whether they differ from place to place within the item.

A cursory glance at the music at this stage also can be helpful. The cataloger should determine whether the parts actually are the parts for the work in score, for example, or the opposite, whether the score reflects all of the parts accurately. A glance at the music itself also will confirm whether the piece is likely to be what it says it is—is it a work by J.S. Bach for tuba and celeste? If so, it probably is a transcription or arrangement that will need to be compared to editions of the original work. It is important to look over the notation to see whether it is unique in any way—if so, a note might be required to that effect. In Baroque works does a figured bass appear? If so, has it been realized? If so, by whom? In orchestral music, is the item a full score or a conductor score? Also, if there are plate numbers do they seem to reflect the publisher's name? If not, the item probably is a reprint of an earlier edition that will need to be identified.

CHOOSING THE CHIEF SOURCE OF INFORMATION

Determining which of the potential sources of the information in the item is to be preferred as the *chief* source from which title and statement of responsibility data will be transcribed is the first step in description of printed music. Some music materials have title pages, but others do not, and therefore the cataloger must use a title page substitute.

Printed music often is issued without a title page. In other cases the title page will consist of a list of titles and other title information (a "list" or "passe-partout" title page), frequently with the title of the particular publication underlined.

When a monograph-style title page is present it is used as the chief source of information. When there is no typical title page, but a "list" title page is present, the cataloger should choose whichever of the "list" title page, cover, or caption provides the fullest information, as instructed in 5.0B1. In some cases, the caption is chosen because the cover has no information about the work and because it gives a fuller description of the work than the "list" title page.

When there is no "list" title page, the cataloger should choose a title page substitute according to the instructions in rule 2.0B1. The part chosen as substitute must be the part that supplies the most complete information. Possible substitutes are the cover, half-title page, caption, colophon, running title, etc. The part used as title page substitute must be identified in a note.

If the prescribed source of information is the chief source of information, but the information is not available from the chief source, take it from one of the following sources (in this order of preference): caption, cover, colophon, other preliminaries, other sources.

Bear in mind that decorative title pages are not the same as covers. A cover must be printed on material (usually heavier paper or card stock) that is different from the material on which the music is printed. A colorful title page is not necessarily a cover.

TITLE AND STATEMENT OF RESPONSIBILITY AREA

TITLE PROPER

The first step in description will be transcription of the title of the item. The purpose of transcription in this area is to create for the user a surrogate of the item. That is, the purpose is not necessarily to give information about the musical *work*—that will be handled later, in the notes area, if necessary. Therefore, do not be concerned that the transcribed title is not necessarily fully informative about the work. Transcribe what you see, so that the user who has consulted the catalog description will recognize the item when it is encountered.

The initial step in the transcription of the title information requires that the cataloger make a judgment about the nature of the title itself. For example, if the title is "generic" (i.e., if it consists primarily of the name(s) of one or more types of composition), statements of other identifying elements such as medium of performance, opus number, etc., should be transcribed as part of the title proper.

The reason for this exception is to prevent confusion in title indexes in which only the title proper is displayed. Without the identifying elements many titles would be indistinguishable. Consider, for example, two symphonies by Johannes Brahms. The titles in full are *Symphony 1, C minor, op. 68* and *Symphony 4, E minor, opus 98*. If the identifying elements are not included in the title proper, each title would display in the bibliographic record as "Symphony." To prevent this problem, such statements are transcribed as part of the title proper when the title consists of the name(s) of one or more types of composition, as instructed in rule 5.1B1.

To make this determination the cataloger should first consider the title as a whole, then strip away all statements of medium of performance, enumeration, key, and date of composition. If what remains consists of the name of a type of composition, the title can be considered "generic." The following are "generic" titles (the essential element is in bold type):

> **Symphony** no. 3, A major, op. 56
> String **quintet** no. 1, A major, opus 18
> Zwei **Praeludien und Fugen** für Orgel, op. posth. 7

In case of doubt about whether the term is the name of a type of composition, the cataloger should consult a dictionary of musical terminology (see bibliography). If the term is not defined there, it is unlikely that it is the name of a type of composition.

Names of types of compositions that are modified adjectivally are considered "distinctive." This means, quite simply, that the title is considered sufficient to identify the work without the addition of other identifying elements. The following would be considered "distinctive" titles (again the essential element is in bold type):

> **Easter fresco** for soprano, flute, horn, harp, and
> piano
> **Sinfonia mazedonia** Nr. 4, für grosses Orchester
> **Little suite** for 5 cellos (1956)

The instruction in rule 5.1B1 is to consider other identifying elements as part of the title proper when the title is generic and to consider such elements as other title information when the title is distinctive. The following are proper transcriptions of the preceding examples:

```
    Symphony, no. 3, A major, op. 56
    String quintet no. 1, A major, opus 18
    Zwei Praeludien und Fugen für Orgel, op. posth. 7
    Easter fresco : for soprano, flute, horn, harp,
and piano
    Sinfonia mazedonia : Nr. 4, für grosses Orchester
    Little suite : for 5 cellos (1956)
```

5.1B1 MCD In applying this rule, be governed by the definition of "name of a type of composition" in 25.27A1, footnote 9.

Apply the second sentence of this rule to titles consisting of the names of two or more types of composition only when each of the types named constitutes a more or less distinct part of the work or item. (In such cases the names of types are usually connected by a conjunction or other linking word.)

> Zwei Praeludien und Fugen für Orgel, op. posth. 7
> Sonatas and partitas for solo violin, BWV 1001-1006

When a title consists of two words each of which alone would be the name of a type of composition, but the combination of the two words produces a distinctive title (cf. LCRI 25.27A), apply the third sentence of this rule ("In all other cases ...").

> Fantaisie-impromptu : in C sharp minor, op. 66
> Humoresque-bagatelles : op. 11

Note, however, that "trio sonata" (cf. 25.29C1) and "chorale prelude" are each the name of *one* type of composition. (rev. May 1989)(*MCD* 9)

SERIAL NUMBERS

5.1B1 LCRI Transcribe as part of the title proper a serial number (whether it appears as arabic or roman numerals or spelled out) appearing in conjunction with the title but without the designation "no." or its equivalent, regardless of the nature of the title.

> Antiphony II : variations on a theme of Cavafy
not   Antiphony : II : variations on a theme of Cavafy

Multiple Parallel Data
When succeeding statements of key, etc., are broken up in the source rather than grouped together by language, transcribe the statements so that all elements in one language are together. Treat the first group of elements in one language as part of the title proper and precede each one after the first by an equals sign. Thus,

Concerto
D-Dur/D Major/Ré Majeur
für Horn und Orchester
for Horn and Orchestra
pour Cor et Orchestre

would be transcribed as:

Concerto, D-Dur, für Horn und Orchester = D major, for horn and orchestra = ré majeur, pour cor et orchestre

(Record all the parallel elements; do not omit any of them according to 1.1D2.)

Adopt the following solutions for data that are other title information or statements of responsibility and that are only partially repeated from language to language. For such a problem with a statement of responsibility, rule 1.1F10 provides a solution in the third paragraph ("If it is not practicable ...") by saying to give the statement that matches the language of the title proper and to omit the other statement(s).

... [Czech title proper]
Revidoval — Revidiert von Antonín Myslík

... / revidoval Antonín Myslík.

There is no comparable "If it is not practicable ..." provision in the rule for other title information, yet the same difficulty of transcription arises with partial repetition of other title information. Nonetheless, apply the same idea to other title information.

Sonata a velocità pazzesca
per   for
cembalo

The transcription would be:

Sonata a velocità pazzesca : per cembalo

If no real match in languages is possible, then give the first of the language forms, matching at least the other title information with the statement of responsibility if possible.

Chief source

Gregor Joseph Werner
Concerto per la camera à 4
für   for
Violoncello & Piano
Herausgegeben und bearbeitet von   Edited and arranged by
Richard Moder

Transcription

Concerto per la camera : à 4 : für Violoncello & Piano / Gregor Joseph Werner ; herausgegeben und bearbeitet von Richard Moder

(*CSB* 55: 16-17)

STATEMENTS OF RESPONSIBILITY

Statements of responsibility should be transcribed following the title proper and should be preceded by a space-slash-space, according to 5.1F. As with the title, it is important to remember that the purpose of this transcription is to create a surrogate of the chief source of information for the purposes of matching the bibliographic description that the user encounters in the catalog to the item that the user will subsequently encounter. Therefore, do not be concerned about the form of the name transcribed, or even whether all relevant names appear in the chief source of information. Transcribe what you see. Later, in the notes area, the work will be fully identified if necessary.

Rule 5.1F1 refers catalogers to rule 1.1F; 1.1F14 instructs catalogers to transcribe statements of responsibility even though no person or body is named. Such statements appear frequently on music publications. It is easy to confuse such statements as "vocal score with piano," or "edition for 2 pianos" with edition statements, or musical presentation statements (see below). Statements indicating an arrangement or version of the musical work are statements of responsibility because they imply the work of a person who has altered the musical content of the work for the publication.

```
    My fair lady / music by Frederick Loewe ; book
and lyrics by Alan Jay Lerner ; vocal score ...
    Symphonien / Beethoven ; Klavierauszug von Franz
Liszt ...
```

POPULAR MUSIC FOLIOS

Popular music folios (sometimes referred to as "pop-folios") are usually transcriptions of recordings, sold as scores for voice and piano with guitar chord diagrams and chord symbols. These are primarily commercial products, but they can be used by an ensemble that wants to perform in the style of the popular music group represented. Because these often mirror popular sound recordings (CDs), their covers or title pages are often the same as the front of the container of the corresponding recording. This presents a problem because the featured name on the title page (hence the chief source of information) is usually that of the performer, which might not be the composer(s) of the music represented within. Transcribe such names as statements of responsibility, according to LCRI 5.1F1:

> **5.1F1 LCRI** When the performer's name featured on the chief source of information on a popular music folio does not appear within the title proper, transcribe it as a statement of responsibility.

> 40 hour week / Alabama
> Once upon a time / Donna Summer

(*CSB* 46: 23)

EDITION AREA

Because of widespread colloquial misuse of the word "edition" and its foreign equivalents in, it can be confusing to determine which information should be included in the edition area for printed music. An "in case of doubt" clause in rule 1.2B3 is of little help, because a wide variety of statements including the word "edition" can appear on music materials.

In this area of the bibliographic record the distinction between the item cataloged and the work contained therein is crucial. (This will also be of importance in formulating notes and is vital in the formulation of uniform titles.) The cataloger must remain aware of the difference between the aesthetic (the musical idea that constitutes the work) and the corporeal (the physical manifestation of that idea).

Data about the production history of a specific physical manifestation are recorded in the edition area. A musical work can be presented in an infinite and bewildering array of altered states. That is, it can be arranged for any medium of performance, such as a symphonic work arranged for two pianos, an organ prelude arranged for concert band, a vocal work arranged for different voice ranges, a violin concerto arranged for flute and piano, etc. Because arrangements have undergone human intervention (that is, a person has rewritten the work), they actually constitute versions of the original work. The problem is that the word "edition" might be used in a chief source of information where "version" or "arrangement" perhaps would be more appropriate. Statements such as "Edition for 2 pianos" or "Klavierausgabe" ("Piano edition") are descriptive of the work contained (i.e., they mean "arranged for two pianos" or "arranged for piano," respectively) and thus are not edition statements and should not be transcribed in the edition area.

To complicate matters further, the word "edition" can be used in a statement of responsibility to indicate a form of subsidiary authorship. Statements such as "Busoni edition" are statements of responsibility and should not be transcribed in the edition area unless they are accompanied by information indicative of their relationship to a specific physical manifestation. Such statements usually refer to the process of recording elements of interpretation such as fingerings, bowings, pedal marks, phrasing, breath indications, etc., and can be considered statements of responsibility relating to all editions (i.e., versions).

Last, but not least, are statements such as "Wilhelm-Hansen edition," "Edition Breitkopf," or "Harmonia-Uitgave." Despite the use of the word "edition," such statements (which always include the name of the publisher or one of its subsidiaries, and usually are found in conjunction with a stock number) are referred to as "publisher's numbers" (see 5.7B19 below) and are not edition statements.

Just what, then, should be transcribed in the edition area? Quite simply, those statements that refer to the production history of the physical item, all those copies of an item produced from substantially the same type image or master copy and issued by the same publishing entity (to paraphrase AACR 2, p. 617). Such statements are those that are common in monographs, such as "2nd ed.," "New ed.," "Rev. ed.," etc. However, with the exception of scholarly publications, such statements are uncommon on printed music. An LCRI further clarifies this point:

> **5.2B1 LCRI** Focusing on the concept of "edition" for music publications, note the following points: care must be taken to distinguish between edition statements of the book type, which are found in music publications, and the very common musical presentation statements that should not be taken as edition statements. A musical presentation statement is one that indicates the version, the arrangements, etc., of a work or the form in which a work is presented in the item (i.e., the music format). Unfortunately, these statements frequently include the word "edition." Even so, they should not be regarded as edition statements.

> Musical presentation statements go in the statement of responsibility when the music itself is meant: a *version* of the music, an *arrangement* of the music, even a *transposition* of the music. In all these cases an "author" is responsible for a changing of the original work. In other cases, when the music format is meant (e.g., edition in score format, edition as a set of parts), then the musical presentation statement should be transcribed according to 5.3. (*CSB* 33: 32)

1.0 MCD LCRI 1.0 gives guidance in determining when a new manifestation of an item is to be considered a new edition, and enumerates those areas of the bibliographic description in which differences signal an edition rather than a copy. In addition, for printed music and sound recordings, consider that different editions exist whenever two items have different publisher's or plate numbers. (rev. December 1991)(*MCB* 23:2:2)

VOICE RANGE FOR SONGS

The single exception is the Library of Congress' decision to include statements of voice range in the edition area in some cases. Those cases are spelled out in the following Music Cataloging Decision:

> **5.2B2 MCD** When a song, song cycle, or set or collection of songs bears a statement designating the voice range (as distinguished from a statement of medium of performance) that is not grammatically linked to the title, other title information, etc., transcribe the statement as an edition statement, whether or not it includes the word "edition" or its equivalent.
>
> > Lieder / Franz Schubert ; herausgegeben von Walther Durr. -- Hohe Stimme (Originallage). --
> > Schubert-Album. -- Neue, kritisch durchgesehene Ausg. / von L. Benda, Ausg. für hohe Stimme. --
> > Roadways / words by John Masefield ; music by Edith Rose. -- High key in F. --
>
> *but*
>
> > Lieder : eine Auswahl für hohe Stimmlage und Klavier ...
> > Drei Lieder für eine hohe Stimme mit Klavierbegleitung ...
>
> (March 1982)(*MCD* 11)

Option decisions in LCRI 5.2B3 and 5.2B4 (*CSB* 47 and 34 respectively; not reproduced here) are to apply the option to give an interpolated edition statement when the work being described is known to be a subsequent edition, but not to transcribe parallel edition statements.

MUSICAL PRESENTATION STATEMENT AREA

A musical presentation statement is a word or phrase that appears in the chief source of information that indicates the format of the printed music in the item. Such statements are common on music publications and are transcribed in area 3 of the bibliographic description according to 5.3. Care must be taken not to confuse musical presentation statements with either edition statements or statements of responsibility (see discussions above). If the statements appear in more than one language, transcribe the statement that is in the language of the title proper, or if that does not apply, transcribe the first statement.

```
    Classical symphony : op. 25 / Prokofieff. --
Score. -- New York : ...

    4 quartets for flute, violin, viola, and cello /
Mozart ; [edited by] Jean-Pierre Rampal. -- Parts.
-- New York : ...
```

LC option decisions in LCRI 5.3 (*CSB* 34; not reproduced here) are to apply area 3 (which is designated as optional in the rules) and not to transcribe parallel musical presentation statements.

PUBLICATION, DISTRIBUTION, ETC., AREA

Information for this area is recorded according to the general provisions of AACR 2 chapter 1, by reference to the rules at 1.4 from those appearing at 5.4. Publication data are transcribed from the prescribed source of information, which might be the bottom of the first page of music, or the colophon if the data do not appear on a title page. Place, publisher, and date of publication are transcribed, following the general provisions of AACR 2.

PLACE OF PUBLICATION; NAME OF PUBLISHER

Transcribe the place of publication from the chief source of information or from one of the prescribed sources of information for area 4 (preliminaries, colophon, first page of music). Follow the general instructions at 1.4. LCRI 5.4D1 (*CSB* 8; not reproduced here) instructs catalogers to apply the option at 5.4D1 and give the name of the distributor as well as the name of the publisher. LCRI 5.4E and 5.4G2 (*CSB* 47; not reproduced here) instruct the application of the optional provisions to give a statement of function for publisher or distributor, and to give the place and name of manufacturer according to the general provisions of LCRI 1.4E and LCRI 1.4G4.

PUBLISHER'S ADDRESS

The Library of Congress applies the option in rule 1.4C7 for music scores, adding the address of the publisher, distributor, etc., if it is given in the item according to the following Rule Interpretation:

> **1.4C7 LCRI** Give the address of a publisher, etc., following the name of the place of publication, etc., only for a monograph cataloged according to chapter 2 or chapter 5 that meets these three conditions:
>
> > a) it was issued by a U.S. publisher, distributor, etc., whose address is given in the item being cataloged;
> > b) it was issued in the current three years;
> > c) it does not bear an ISBN or ISSN.
>
> Do not apply 1.4C7 if two or more publishers, distributors, etc., are being recorded in the publication, etc., area. *Exception*: If one of the entities is a U.S. distributor for a monograph published outside of the U.S., give the address of the U.S. distributor if the item meets these four conditions:

a) the U.S. distributor is the only entity being recorded with the distributor's place of publication;

b) the U.S. distributor's address is given in the item;

c) the item was issued in the current three years;

d) the item lacks an ISBN or ISSN.

Apply 1.4C7 also to items in which the name of the publisher, distributor, etc., is unknown and the name of the U.S. manufacturer is being given in the publication, etc., area (1.4G1) if the monograph meets these three conditions:

a) the manufacturer's address is given in the item;

b) the item was issued in the current three years;

c) the item lacks an ISBN or ISSN.

When applying 1.4C7, routinely repeat the name of the city in the address. For street addresses, abbreviate such words as "street," "avenue," "place," etc., according to normal usage. Omit unnecessary elements from the address (e.g., the name of the building when the street address or post office box is given). Do not bracket any of the elements given in the address. (*CSB* 15:3)

DATES OF PUBLICATION, DISTRIBUTION, ETC.

Copyright Dates

Rules for transcribing or supplying dates of publication appear at 5.4F and make reference to the general rules at 1.4F. The prescribed source of information for this area includes the first page of music. Because music publishers rarely indicate dates of publication, catalogers of printed music make great use of copyright dates. These dates more often than not appear at the bottom of the first page of music. (This handy practice allows the publisher to reissue a title from time to time with new covers for boosting sales without making any alterations in the original printing surface.) Because the first page of music is a prescribed source in this area of the description, the copyright date need not be bracketed.

It will often happen that printed music will carry neither a date of publication nor of copyright. In these cases the cataloger must supply an approximate date of publication. Several hints follow.

Hidden Dates

A good idea is to check the first and last pages of music to see if a printing date is present. If so, it can be used in lieu of a date of publication (see figure 1.5). Care must be exercised in this regard. Frequently the date of composition or of the completion of the manuscript will be inscribed at the end of a score. Occasionally items reproduced photographically from manuscripts will carry a date that indicates the date of the printing of the staff paper. Such dates can be regarded as "hints" to estimate dates of publication (that is, if the work was completed in 1973 we know it could not have been published before then), but should not be transcribed as dates of publication.

East European publications from the Soviet-bloc era often carried colophons that supplied a date of publication. Also, East German publications indicated a "Lizenz Nummer." As a rule of thumb, the final digits of the "Lizenz Nummer" indicated the year of publication.

Popular Music Folios

These collections usually are reprinted from a variety of individual sheet music publications. Copyright dates might appear at the foot of the first page of each song. Comparing the various copyright dates will give a hint as to the approximate date of publication of the collection, although care should be exercised that the information given in the bibliographic record is accurate. For example, if the span of copyright dates runs from 1974 to 1985, and the item is being cataloged in 1986, it is probable that the folio was published in 1986. Unfortunately, it is only probable; it could have been published in 1985.

There are at least three ways to express the probable date of publication in a case such as this:

1) If it really seems probable that 1986 represents the year of publication it may be expressed as a questioned date:

[1986?]

2) If there is any doubt on the cataloger's part about the reliability of the more specific estimate (for example, if the item were being cataloged early in 1986 it would seem more likely that it had been published in 1985) it may be expressed as follows:

[1985 or 1986]

3) Finally, if the span between the last copyright date in the collection and the date the item is cataloged is greater than one year (for example, if the item above were being cataloged in 1987) the date may be expressed as:

[between 1985 and 1987]

Publishers' Catalogs, National Bibliographies, Etc.

It also is possible to determine approximate dates of publication by consulting publishers' catalogs or published bibliographies. For example, late nineteenth-century European publications often can be located in Pazdirek's *Universal-Handbuch der Musikliteratur* (Hilversum: F. Knuf, 1967). Such efforts, however, require a great deal of time and bibliographic skill. For most library catalogs the results do not justify the effort.

Early Printed Music

For advice on the use of plate numbers, publisher's addresses, etc., in dating early printed music, see Krummel's *Guide for Dating Early Published Music* (Hackensack, N.J.: J. Boonin, 1974).

PHYSICAL DESCRIPTION AREA

The elements of the physical description area are: 1) a statement of extent of item; 2) a description of other physical details; and 3) the size of the item. For printed music, the statement of the extent begins with an arabic numeral indicating the number of items present and is followed with the specific material designation that identifies the type of musical document in hand:

```
1 score ...
1 vocal score ...
```

If the document in hand is music for one instrument or voice and cannot be described as a type of score, the number of pages of music is used:

```
12 p. of music.
```

LCRI 5.5B1 (*CSB* 47; not reproduced here) refers catalogers to LCRI 1.1C for application of the optional provision. Because the general material designation for music is not used, the optional provision is not followed.

Specific instructions for choosing specific material designations for types of scores and part, and for arraying the descriptive data for sets of scores and parts may be found below.

TYPES OF SCORES

Given below are the definitions from the AACR 2 "Glossary" for the types of scores and parts most commonly found in library collections. One should bear in mind that the bibliographic use of terminology as advocated in AACR 2 does not necessarily coincide with the colloquial use of the same terms. For example, the word "score" is commonly used in everyday speech to indicate any type of printed music.

When attempting to choose the appropriate term keep in mind the basic definition of the word "score" as given below. The most basic requirement is that the score represent all of the different parts, that is, more than one instrument or voice. A work for one instrument or one voice cannot be rendered in score.

> SCORE. A series of staves on which all the different instrumental and/or vocal parts of a musical work are written, one under the other in vertical alignment, so that the parts may be read simultaneously.

> CONDENSED SCORE. A musical score giving only the principal musical parts on a minimum number of staves generally organised by instrumental sections.

> CLOSE SCORE. A musical score giving all the parts on a minimum number of staves, normally two, as with hymns.

> MINIATURE SCORE. A musical score not primarily intended for performance use, with the notation and/or text reduced in size.

PIANO [VIOLIN, ETC.] CONDUCTOR PART [SCORE]. A performance part for a particular instrument of an ensemble to which cues have been added for the other instruments to permit the performer of the part also to conduct the performance.

VOCAL SCORE. A score showing all vocal parts, with accompaniment, if any, arranged for keyboard instrument.

PIANO SCORE. A reduction of an orchestral score to a version for piano on two staves.

CHORUS SCORE. A score of a vocal work showing only the chorus parts, with accompaniment, if any, arranged for keyboard instrument.

PART (MUSIC). The music for one of the participating voices or instruments in a musical work; the written or printed copy of such a part for the use of a performer, designated in the physical description area as *part*.

(AACR 2, (1988), p. 615-24)

The term "short score" also is defined there for use with composer's sketches; these are not commonly encountered in routine library cataloging. LC advises further on the uses of "chorus score" and "vocal score":

5.5B1 MCD For clarifications of the definitions of the terms "chorus score" and "vocal score," see MCD Appendix D.

If neither "chorus score," "close score," nor "vocal score" applies to a vocal publication, use "score" or "miniature score" (for an unaccompanied solo voice or unaccompanied unison voices).

While the specific material designation terms listed following the first paragraph of this rule (score, condensed score, etc.) are to be applied to entire physical units, this is not true of the phrase "of music" in the third paragraph. When "of music" is used, apply the phrase only to those sequences (for the definition of "sequence" see 2.5B2, footnote 2) which are, or consist primarily of, music, and not to sequences which are primarily text.

       1 score (vi, 27 p.)
       (Only p. 1-27 are music)

but   xxv p., 55 p. of music
       (Only p. 1-55 are music)

       129 p. of music, [7] p.
       (Only p. 1-129 are music)

       46, 39 p. of music
       (Both sequences are music)

Do not use "sheet" in describing music. Describe leaves printed on one side only in terms of leaves, whether they are bound, folded, or separate. (rev. August 1981)(*MCD* 13)

POPULAR MUSIC FOLIOS

Notice that "vocal score" applies only when the music was originally written for orchestra and now appears in a version for piano and voice(s). Because music in the popular idiom cannot be said to have been written for any particular medium of performance (let alone voice(s) and orchestra), a popular music folio (or a single song for that matter) cannot be said to be a "vocal score." Describe such publications as "1 score."

EXTENT OF ITEM

Extent of item is described by giving the number of pages in the item, following the general instructions at 1.5B and the specific instructions for printed materials at 2.5B.

The following Library of Congress Rule Interpretation gives instruction for providing the pagination of a single part, and for indicating the extent of scores and parts in volumes:

5.5B2 LCRI When there is only one part, include its pagination. (Disregard the second example under 5.5D1.)

1 score (20 p.) + 1 part (3 p.)

When parts are issued in two or more "volumes," include the number of volumes.

1 score (2 v.) + 1 part (2 v.)
1 score (3 v.) + 2 parts (3 v.)
4 parts (6 v.)

(*CSB* 52: 16)

The volume designation would be applicable to a situation where a collection of works in score and part format is issued in multiple volumes. In the first two examples each volume has a score (probably bound) and parts (at the back or in a pocket). In the third example four parts are issued in each of the six volumes (probably contained in a pocket in each volume).

Other configurations are possible. A single string quartet, issued as parts for the violins, viola, and violoncello would be described as:

```
4 parts
```

A piano trio, with a score for the pianist, and one part each for the violin and violoncello, would be described as:

```
1 score (32 p.) + 2 parts
```

Note that no pagination is given when more than one part is present.

If the item being cataloged is a score and set of parts for orchestral performance, only the number of unique parts is given. For example, a symphony for string orchestra, with multiple copies of parts for violin, viola, violoncello, and double bass, would be described as:

```
1 score (79 p.) + 5 parts
```

The number of multiple copies of each part would be considered local holdings information and could be noted in the local bibliographic record (rule 5.7B20). More often, such information is given in the library's local circulation and holdings records.

LCRI 5.5B3 (*CSB* 47; not reproduced here) refers the cataloger to LCRI 1.1C for instructions on the use of specific material designations for braille or other tactile materials.

OTHER PHYSICAL DETAILS

"Other physical details" for printed music is limited to a statement about the presence of illustrations, given according to the instructions at 2.5C. Therefore, the LCRI for 2.5C2 applies to printed music as well.

> **2.5C2 LCRI** Describe an illustrated printed monograph or serial as "ill." in all cases unless there are maps present or 2.5C6 is applicable.

> *N.B.* The Library of Congress applies the LCRI as written, which results in a reduction of data given in the bibliographic record. Other libraries may wish in certain or indeed in all cases to give the fuller data without this reduction. In this respect bibliographic records must be considered equally valid or "correct," no matter which of the two practices is followed. This policy is especially important in the context of LC's handling records originally created by other libraries when LC is using them in its own cataloging; the fuller data should be left "as is." (*CSB* 51: 29)

DIMENSIONS

Dimensions of musical scores and parts are given by measuring the spine, following the instructions for other printed materials at 2.5D.

> 1 score (29 p.) : ill. ; 31 cm.

SERIES AREA

Series found on music materials are not substantially different from those found on other types of publications. A minor caveat applies, however. Do not confuse a publisher's number on a printed music publication with a series statement (see PLATE AND PUBLISHERS' NUMBERS, below).

> **1.6H MCD** The Library of Congress classifies collected works of composers (Gesamtausgaben) as collected sets in M3. Many such publications are divided into subseries by medium of performance or genre, and individual volumes are numbered only within each subseries. In such cases LCRI 1.6H requires that each subseries be established separately (cf. the "Progress in nuclear energy" example in LCRI 1.6H). This would preclude making a collected set record for the set as a whole and would therefore require classifying each subseries according to its content (Piano music in M22, Operas in M1500, etc.). To avoid this the Music Section has been given permission to deviate from LCRI 1.6H for access points for Gesamtausgaben.

For Gesamtausgaben that are issued in numbered (or alphabetically designated) subseries, with individual volumes numbered only within the subseries, make only one series authority record and only one collected-set bibliographic record—for the set as a whole. In bibliographic records for analyzed volumes (cf. MCD 13.3), transcribe series statements as instructed in the LCRI, but in series added entries omit the subseries title and consider the numerical designation of the subseries to be part of the series numbering. Include an explanatory note in the series authority record.

> *Series statement:* (Neue Ausgabe sämtlicher Werke. Serie II, Messen, Passionen, oratorische Werke / Johann Sebastian Bach ; Bd. 8)
> *Series authority record:* Bach, Johann Sebastian, 1685-1750. Works. 1954.
> *Note (667) in series authority record:* Issued in 9 numbered "Serien." Do not include the title of the "Serie" in the series tracing, but include the number of the "Serie" in the series numbering.
> *Series tracing:* Bach, Johann Sebastian, 1685-1750. Works. 1954 ; Ser. 2, Bd. 8.

In contents notes in collected-set records for Gesamtausgaben treated in this way, list only the numerical designations and the titles of the subseries, not the numbers and titles of individual volumes.

> Contents: Ser. 1. Kantaten -- Ser. 2. Messen, Passionen, oratorische Werke ...

(rev. January 1994)(*MCB* 25:8:2)

NOTES AREA

Notes are made to amplify details about the musical work (such as the medium of performance, the format of the score and parts, the language of the words, etc.) that are not apparent from the transcribed data that appear in areas one through six. Notes also are made to establish the bibliographic identity of the item described (such as the original publication details for a work that is a reprint). Notes also can be made to identify uniquely the *work* contained in the item being described (such as the date of composition, first performance, etc., or the original medium of performance if the work in hand is an arrangement). All notes serve to allow users to select likely candidates for retrieval from among otherwise similar or identical bibliographic descriptions. This is especially important in music cataloging, because music libraries are likely to contain more than one edition of the works by the most commonly encountered composers.

ORDER OF NOTES

The list below is intended to serve as a guide for the order of notes in bibliographic records for music materials. Remember that many of these notes are used only to explain or otherwise elucidate information contained in the preceding areas of the description. Note that the order is essentially the order in which the rules appear in chapter 5.

Form of composition and medium of performance (5.7B1)
Text (language of sung or spoken text) (5.7B2)
Source of title proper (5.7B3)
Variations in title (5.7B4)
Parallel titles and other title information (5.7B5)
Statements of responsibility (5.7B6)
Edition and history (5.7B7)
Notation (5.7B8)
Publication, distribution, etc. (5.7B9)
Duration of performance (5.7B10)
Accompanying material (5.7B11)
Series (5.7B12)
Dissertation note (5.7B13)
Audience (5.7B14)
Other formats (5.7B16)
Contents (5.7B18)
Publishers' numbers and plate numbers (5.7B19)
Copy being described, library's holdings, and restrictions on use (5.7B20)

FORM OF COMPOSITION AND MEDIUM OF PERFORMANCE

5.7B1 MCD Do not name the medium of performance in a note if it is implied by the title or other title information (e.g., "Chorale prelude", "Manfred : symphonie en 4 tableaux") or by the musical form stated in a note made under this rule (e.g., "Opera in two acts"; "Ballet").

If an item is described in the physical description area as "chorus score" or "vocal score" (cf. MCD 5.5B1), give in a note the original medium of performance and the instrument for which the accompaniment is arranged (or indicate that the accompaniment is omitted) if this information is not clear from the rest of the description.

> For solo voices (SATB), chorus (SATB), and orchestra; acc. arr. for piano.
> For chorus (TTBB) and band; without the acc.

(rev. March 1984)(*MCD* 16)

Also apply this provision to other works that are arrangements.

```
Originally for string quartet
Acc. arr. for piano
```

5.7B1 LCRI Consider the form and medium of performance of a musical work or collection of works as given in the uniform title in the main entry as well as from the description in determining whether to make the note. (*CSB* 55: 17)

LANGUAGE OF SUNG OR SPOKEN TEXT

The language of the words of a vocal work should be indicated in a note made according to 5.7B2 whenever it is not clear from the content of the preceding description. This note is governed by a general Library of Congress Rule Interpretation.

1.7B2 LCRI *General Application*

Generally restrict the making of language and script notes to the situations covered in this directive. (Note: In this statement, "language" and "language of the item" mean the language or languages of the content of the item (e.g., for books the language of the text; [for music the language of the words that are to be sung or spoken]); "title data" means title proper and other title information.)

If the language of the item is not clear from the transcription of the title data, make a note naming the language unless the language of the item has been named after the uniform title used as or in conjunction with the main entry. Use "and" in all cases to link two languages (or the final two when more than two are named). If more than one language is named, give the predominant language first if readily apparent; name the other languages in alphabetical order. If a predominant language is not apparent, name the languages in alphabetical order ....

Form of Language

For the form of the name of the language, use the latest edition of the *USMARC Code List for Languages. Note*: For an early form of a modern language that appears in inverted form (e.g., French, Old; English, Middle), use the direct form in the note (e.g., Old French, Middle English). *Exception*: For some dialects that cannot be established separately, the Subject Cataloging Division supplies a specific language name for the use in the note area. (*CSB* 56: 11-12)

When all of the words of a vocal work appear in more than one language, use "and" to link the languages in the note.

```
French and English words
English, German, and Russian words
```

If the words are in more than one language (e.g., one verse in French, and the rest in English), use "or" to link the languages in the note.

```
English or French words
```

If desired, indicate in a note the words that are also printed separately in textual format (usually in addition to being printed between the staves in the score).

```
German words; English translation printed also as
text
```

NOTES ON TITLE PROPER

The Library of Congress does not follow the option in rule 5.7B4 of giving a romanization of the title proper (LCRI 5.7B4, *CSB* 47; not reproduced here).

EDITION AND HISTORY

> **5.7B7 MCD** Since conventions of music publishing have varied widely in the past, it is bibliographically significant to note that an item is photographically reproduced from an earlier edition.
>
> If a recent publication of printed music reproduces a previously issued edition, make a note beginning with an appropriate term ("Reprint"; "Photographic reproduction"; "Reproduces the ed. ..."; etc.) followed by the details of the original publication if available. Observe the restrictions concerning the use of the terms "photoreproduction" and "photocopy" in LCRI 2.7B7. (October 1991)(*MCD* 18)

DURATION OF PERFORMANCE

Durations are given according to rule 5.7B10 when they are stated in the item being cataloged. Such statements may occur at the beginning or ending of the music, on the title page, in the preliminaries, or on the cover. Sometimes the duration of each movement will be printed at the end of each movement. These may be added together to derive the note. Do not attempt to infer the duration of performance from metronome markings, etc.

> **5.7B10 MCD** In a statement of duration in the note area, separate the digits representing hours, minutes, and seconds by colons. If a duration is expressed in seconds only, precede it by a colon.
>
> > Duration: 15:30
> > Duration: 1:25:00
> > Duration: :45
>
> Precede a statement of duration in the note area by "ca." only if the statement is given on the item in terms of an approximation.
>
> > Duration: ca. 27:00
> > Duration: ca. 1:10:00

(May 1982)(*MCD* 19)

CONTENTS

Full contents notes can be very important to catalog users seeking a particular work (especially a song) in a collection. The instructions at rule 5.7B18 cover the specific case of a collection of works all in the same musical form that is named in the title area of the description. In such cases, give only the other details (opus or thematic catalog numbering, key, etc.) in the contents note.

```
     Flute concertos / Wolfgang Amadeus Mozart ...
     Contents: No. 1 in G, K. 313 -- No. 2 in D, K.
314
```

It is especially important to give complete contents for popular music folios.

```
     Vocal selections from Hair ...
     Contents: Aquarius -- Donna -- Ain't got no --
Air -- I got life  -- Hair -- Easy to be hard --
Frank Mills -- Where do I go? -- What a piece of
work is man -- Good morning starshine -- Let the
sunshine in
```

```
     Separate lives, Burning heart & 10 knockout hits
...
     Contents: Separate lives / words and music by
Stephen Bishop -- Burning heart / words and music
by Jim Peterik and Frankie Sullivan -- Lonely ol'
night / words and music by John Mellencamp -- You
belong to the city / words and music by Glenn Frey
and Jack Tempchin -- Crazy for  you / words and
music by Jon Lind and John Bettis -- Broken wings /
words and music by Richard Page, Steve George, and
John Lang -- Girls  are more fun / words and music
by Ray Parker, Jr. -- Never / words and  music by
Holly Knight, Gene Bloch, Ann Wilson, and Nancy
Wilson -- Can't fight this feeling / words and
music by Kevin Cronin -- Never ending  story /
words and music by Giorgio Moroder and Keith Forsey
-- Saving all my love for you / words by Gerry
Goffin ; music by Michael Masser -- The search is
over / words and music by Frank Sullivan and Jim
Peterik
```

It is also traditional to make a contents note for a work in many movements if the movements have distinctive titles (e.g., a suite).

```
     La mer / Claude Debussy ...
     Contents: De l'aube -- Midi sur la mer -- Jeux de
vagues -- Dialogue du vent et de la mer
```

5.7B18 MCD For special provisions for contents notes in collected-set records for collected works of composers (Gesamtausgaben) see MCD 1.6H. (January 1991)(*MCD* 20)

PLATE AND PUBLISHERS' NUMBERS

Plate numbers and publishers' numbers can be crucial for bibliographic identification of editions and states, and sometimes for dating printed music. Publishers' numbers are also critical information for ordering printed music, because few music publishers participate in the ISBN program. The following Library of Congress policy statements define plate and publishers' numbers and clarify the provisions of rule 5.7B19.

> **5.7B19 LCRI** Transcribe a publisher's number even if a plate number is also transcribed. Transcribe the statement as it appears, even if this means giving again a publisher's name already transcribed in the publication, distribution, etc., area.
>
> > Publisher's no.: Edition Peters Nr. 8444

When transcribing two or more distinct numbers, give each in a separate note. (Follow the rule as written for the transcription of numbers for an item in multiple volumes.) Transcribe a publisher's number before a plate number. (*CSB* 52: 17)

5.7B19 MCD When a designation such as "no.," "Nr.," "cat. no.," "Ed. Nr.," etc., appears with a publisher's number or plate number, do not consider it to be part of the number and do not transcribe it. If, however, initials, abbreviations, or words identifying the publisher also appear with the number, follow the instructions in LCRI 5.7B19 and transcribe the entire statement as it appears.

> *On item:* Cat. no. 01 6510
> *Note:* Publisher's no.: 01 6510
>
> *On item:* Nr. 3892
> *Note:* Publisher's no.: 3892

but   *On item:* Edition Peters Nr. 3891.
       Note: Publisher's no.: Edition Peters Nr. 3891.

(September 1985)(*MCD* 20)

COPY BEING DESCRIBED AND LIBRARY'S HOLDINGS

5.7B20 MCD For notes on special feature[s] of imperfections of the copy being described (e.g., if the LC set has fewer or more parts than the number recorded in the physical description area according to 5.5B2), follow the instructions in LCRI 1.7B20.

> LC has 24 parts.

(rev. May 1989)(*MCD* 21)

STANDARD NUMBER AND TERMS OF AVAILABILITY AREA

It is rare but not unheard of for printed music to carry an International Standard Book Number (ISBN). If one appears, it should be transcribed in this area

```
      Bagatelles, rondos, and other shorter works for
piano / Ludwig van Beethoven. -- New York : Dover,
1987.
      124 p. of music ; 31 cm....
      ISBN 0-4862-5392-9.
```

More recently, an International Standard Music Number (ISMN) system has been created and is increasingly being employed for printed music materials. These numbers take the form "M-xxx-xxxxx-x" ("M" eight digits, check digit; in barcode form 979 0 is substituted for "M"), and should be transcribed in this area.

```
      Moz-art : für Oboe, Harfe, Cembalo, Violine,
Violoncello und Kontrabass = for oboe, harp,
harpsichord, violin, violoncello and double bass /
Alfred Schnittke. -- Partitur. -- Hamburg :
Sikorski, c1995.
      1 score (20 p.) + 6 parts ; 31 cm....
      ISMN M-003-02773-9.
```

5.8D1 MCD When cataloging a rental score or rental performance materials received through copyright deposit, give the note "Rental material" in the standard number and terms of availability area, to indicate to other libraries that the item is not available for purchase. (rev. May 1989)(*MCD* 22)

Example 1

```
                MOZART

            SYMPHONY No. 40
            G MINOR (K 550)

        M BARON, Inc., NEW YORK

            PRINTED IN U.S.A.
```

On cover: No. 17

At the foot of each page: MB 17

On verso back cover: *Baron Orchestra Scores*

From respective captions:

I.	*Allegro molto*	6 min.	Page 3
II.	*Andante*	9 min	Page 21
III.	*Allegretto*	4 min	Page 32
IV.	*Allegro assai*	7 min	Page 35

51 pages ; 21 cm.

```
        Symphony no. 40, G minor, K 550 / Mozart. -- New York
    : M. Baron, [19-]
        1 miniature score (51 p.) ; 21 cm. -- (Baron orchestra
    scores ; no. 17)
        Duration: 26:00.
        Pl. no.: MB 17.
```

This miniature score is bound pamphlet-style, and has a title page that can serve as chief source of information. "Symphony" is the name of a type of composition, so the statements of serial and thematic index enumeration and the key are transcribed as part of the title proper.

The publisher's name is shortened slightly, by dropping the "Inc.," but the initial is retained so that the publisher's name in area 4 will correspond to the initialism in the plate number. There is no date of publication—indeed, there are no dates anywhere on the item. The best guess that can be made is that the score must have been published sometime in the twentieth century, so the date "19—" is given in square brackets. The musical notation is printed in a reduced format so this item is described as "miniature score" in the physical description area. The series statement is transcribed from the back cover, and the series number is found on the front cover; the cover is a prescribed source of information for series in printed music.

The total duration is attained by adding together the durations of the individual movements. The number "MB 17", which appears at the foot of each page (i.e., on each plate) of music, is a plate number.

Example 2

CARMEN
Opera in Four Acts
By
GEORGES BIZET
Words by
H. MEILHAC and L. HALEVY
Adapted from the Novel by
PROSPER MÉRIMÉE
English Version by
DR. TH. BAKER

G. SCHIRMER, Inc., NEW YORK

On cover: *G. Schirmer's Vocal Scores of Grand and Light Operas*
Also on cover: "With French and English texts."

Portrait of Bizet faces the title page.

At bottom of first page of music: *Copyright, 1895, by G. Schirmer, Inc.*

"12117" appears at the foot of each page of the score.

391 pages ; 28 cm.

```
    Carmen : opera in four acts / by Georges Bizet ; words
by H. Meilhac and L. Halévy ; adapted from the novel by
Prosper Mérimée ; English version by Th. Baker. -- New
York : G. Schirmer, c1895.
    1 vocal score (391 p.) : ill. ; 28 cm. -- (G.
Schirmer's vocal scores of grand and light operas)
    French and English words.
    Pl. no.: 12117.
```

This vocal score also has a title page that serves as chief source of information. The title "Carmen" is not the name of a type of composition, so all extraneous title page data are transcribed as other title information. There is no date of publication, so the copyright date is transcribed. Because the first page of music is a prescribed source of information for area 4, the date is not bracketed. The original orchestral accompaniment has been arranged for the piano, so this item is described as "1 vocal score." The portrait of Bizet is described with the generic "ill." according to LCRI 2.5C2. The series statement is transcribed from the cover.

The presence of words in both French and English (which is not clear from the title transcription) is indicated in a note. The plate number is given in the final note.

Example 3

```
┌─────────────────────────────────────────────┐
│             Boris Blacher                     │
│                Op. 58                         │
│               Requiem                         │
│         Klavierauszug mit Text                │
│             BOTE & BOCK                       │
│          BERLIN • WIESBADEN                    │
│   Imprimé en Allemagne    Printed in Germany  │
└─────────────────────────────────────────────┘
```

On verso title page: Copyright 1959 ...

On contents page: Spieldauer: ca. 45 Minuten

In caption on first page of music: für Sopran- und Bariton-Solo, gemischten Chor und Orchester.

At bottom of first page of music: © Copyright 1959 by Bote & Bock, Berlin

"B & B 21529" appears at the foot of every page of the score.

104 pages ; 31 cm.

```
    Requiem op. 58 / Boris Blacher ; Klavierauszug mit
Text. -- Berlin : Bote & Bock, c1959.
    1 vocal score (104 p.) ; 31 cm.
    For solo voices (SBar), chorus (SSAATTBB), and
orchestra; acc. arr for piano.
    Duration: ca. 45:00.
    Pl. no.: B & B 21529.
```

Again, this is an example of a score that is bound, and there is a title page to serve as chief source of information. "Requiem" is the name of a type of composition, so the opus number is included as part of the title proper. The statement "Klavierauszug mit Text" (i.e., "piano version with words") implies responsibility because it indicates that the accompaniment has been arranged for piano. Therefore, it is transcribed in the statement of responsibility area, even though no name is associated with it.

The first-named place of publication is given according to rule 1.4C5; Wiesbaden is disregarded. The copyright date is transcribed from the first page of music in lieu of a date of publication. The orchestral accompaniment has been arranged for piano, so this item is described as "1 vocal score" in the physical description area.

A precise formulation of voices is given in the note—this is potentially of use to conductors in selecting the piece from the catalog. The duration is given as an approximation ("ca.") because that is how it appears on the item.

Example 4

On cover:

LEUCKERTIANA
Alte Musik
KLASSISCHE BLÄSERMUSIK
In Erstausgabe und praktischen Einrichtungen

Nr. 115 **Danzi, Franz** (1763-1826) Bläserquintett F-Dur, op. 56,3 Für Flöte, Oboe, Klarinette (B), Horn (F) und Fagott (Original) nach dem Erstdruck herausgegeben von Fritz Kneusslin

Nr. 116 **Danzi, Franz** (1763-1826) Bläserquintett G-Dur, op. 67, 1 Für Flöte, Oboe, Klarinette (A), Horn (D) und Fagott (Original) nach dem Erstdruck herausgegeben von Werner Rottler

Nr. 117 **Mozart, Wolfgang Amadeus** (1756-1791) Quintett c-moll (K.V. 406) nach dem Streichquartett (K.V. 406) für Flöte, Oboe, Klarinette (B), Horn (F) und Fagott übertragen von Werner Rottler

Nr. 118 **Mozart, Wolfgang Amadeus** (1756-1791) Divertimento Nr. 12 Es-Dur (K.V. 252) Für Flöte, Oboe, Klarinette (B), Horn (F) und Fagott übertragen von Werner Rottler

Nr. 119 **Mozart, Wolfgang Amadeus** (1756-1791) Divertimento Nr. 16 Es-Dur (K.V. 289) Für Flöte, Oboe, Klarinette (B), Horn (F) und Fagott übertragen von Werner Rottler

Nr. 120 **Gebauer, François-René** (1773-1845) Bläserquintett Nr. 2 Es-Dur Für Flöte, Oboe, Klarinette (B), Horn (Es) und Fagott herausgegeben von Udo Sirker

Nr. 121 **Gebauer, François-René** (1773-1845) Bläserquintett Nr. 3 c-moll Für Flöte, Oboe, Klarinette (B), Horn (Es) und Fagott herausgegeben von Udo Sirker

Verlag von F. E. C. Leuckart • München - Leipzig

There is no score; there are five parts, one for each of the instruments on the list title page.

At the bottom of each page of each part: F.E.C.L. 10553.

At the bottom of the first page of each part: Copyright 1970 F. E. C. Leuckart

All parts are 31 cm. in height.

Example 4

```
    Bläserquintett Nr. 3, c-moll, für Flöte, Oboe,
Klarinette (B), Horn (Es), und Fagott / Gebauer,
François-René ; herausgegeben von Udo Sirker. -- München
: F.E.C. Leuckart, c1970.
    5 parts ; 31 cm. -- (Alte Musik.  Klassische
Bläsermusik ; Nr. 121) (Leuckartiana)
    Title from cover.
    Pl. no.: F.E.C.L. 10553.
```

The cover of this set of parts presents a "list title page" that contains more complete information than any of the captions of the parts, so it will serve as chief source of information. The entire title is transcribed as title proper because "Bläserquintett" ("wind quintet") is the name of a type of composition. The composer's name is transposed into the statement of responsibility (1.1F3) exactly as it appears in the chief source; it is followed by the subsequent statement of responsibility for the editor.

The first-named place of publication is given in area 4. The initials in the publisher name are retained to correspond to the form in the plate number. The copyright date is transcribed from the first page of music in lieu of a date of publication.

Area 5 contains the number of parts and their dimensions. Series information is transcribed from the chief source.

No note is made for the medium of performance because it is clear from the title transcription. It would be rare for musicians not to be able to recognize the names of their instruments in common West European languages so no exception is made because the title page is in German. The fact that the title is transcribed from a cover is noted, as is the plate number.

Example 5

On cover:

```
┌─────────────────────────────────────┐
│                                      │
│              Kantate                 │
│               Nr. 78                 │
│        Jesu, der du meine Seele      │
│        Jesus, my beloved Saviour     │
│              (BWV 78)                 │
│          Breitkopf & Härtel          │
│               Leipzig                │
│                                      │
└─────────────────────────────────────┘
```

List title page:

JOH. SEB. BACH
KIRCHENSONATEN
KLAVIERAUSZÜGE

Nr.
51. Jauchzet Gott in allen Landen
52. Falsche Welt, dir trau ich nicht
53. Schlage doch, gewünschte Stunde
54. Widerstehe doch der Sünde
55. Ich armer Mensch, ich Sündenknecht
[...]
75. Die Elenden sollen essen
76. Die Himel erzählen die Ehre Gottes
77. Du sollst Gott, deinen Herrn lieben
78. Jesu, der du meine Seele
79. Gott der Herr ist Sonn und Schild
[...]

Caption:

Kantate Nr. 78
am vierzehnten Sonntage nach Trinitatis
"Jesu, der du meine Seele"
Für Sopran-, Alt-, Tenor-, Bass-Solo und Chor

English Version by J. Michael Diack

Cantata No. 78
for the fourteenth Sunday after Trinity
"Jesus, my beloved Saviour"
For Soprano-, Alto-, Tenor-, Bass-Solo and Chorus

Joh. Seb. Bach (BWV 78)
Klavierauszug von Günter Raphael

Colophon:

Lizenz-Nr. 472-155'332/57
Gesamtherstellung
VEB Messe- und Musikaliendruck, Leipzig III/18/157

At the foot of every page: "J. S. B. I. 78"

At the foot of the first page: Copyright 1933 by Breitkopf & Härtel, Leipzig

37 pages ; 27 cm.

Example 5

```
    Kantate Nr. 78 : am vierzehnten Sonntage nach
Trinitatis, Jesu, der du meine Seele, für Sopran-, Alt-,
Tenor-, Bass-Solo und Chor (BWV 78) = Cantata no. 78 :
for the fourteenth Sunday after Trinity, Jesus, my
beloved Saviour, for soprano-, alto-, tenor-, bass-solo
and chorus / Joh. Seb. Bach ; English version by J.
Michael Diack ; Klavierauszug von Gunter Raphael. --
Leipzig : Breitkopf & Härtel, [1957], c1933.
    1 vocal score (37 p.,) ; 27 cm. -- (Kirchenkantaten /
Joh. Seb. Bach ; Klavierauszüge ; Nr. 78)
    Title from caption.
    Pl. no.: J.S.B.I.78.
```

The caption is chosen as chief source of information in this case because it provides fuller information than the cover or the "list" title page. Notice that the complete parallel title is transcribed. Notice also that the title proper as it appears in the chief source is the name of a type of composition; the remainder of the title information is transcribed as other title information. The order of names in the statement of responsibility is somewhat arbitrary—Raphael could precede Diack.

The place of publication and publisher name are transcribed from the title page. The date of publication "1957" is estimated from the Lizenz Nummer in the colophon. Because the date of publication differs from the copyright date both are given.

Example 6

ERIK SATIE
CHEZ LE DOCTEUR
PIANO et CHANT

EDITIONS SALABERT
22, rue Chauchat - PARIS
575 Madison Avenue and 57th Street - NEW YORK
Printed in France

In caption: "Paroles de Vincent Hyspa"

At foot of p. 1:

©1976 by Editions Salabert - Paris   E.A.S. 17209
International Copyright secured all rights reserved
EDITIONS SALABERT S.A. 22 rue Chauchat - Paris

At foot of p. 2:

E. A. S. 17209
Janvier 1976 Imp par E M P I 93 NOISY LE SEC

3 pages ; 32 cm.

The melody ranges from C to D[1].

Example 6

```
     Chez le docteur : piano et chant / Erik Satie ;
[paroles de Vincent Hyspa]. -- Paris ; New York :
Editions Salabert, c1976.
     1 score (3 p.) ; 32 cm.
     For medium voice and piano.
     Pl. no.: E.A.S. 17209.
```

This song folio (one large sheet of paper folded once to make four pages) utilizes the first page as a title page; the music appears on the other three pages. The name of the author of the words is interpolated into the statement of responsibility because it appears prominently in the caption (rule 1.1F1).

Both Paris and New York are transcribed as place of publication—Paris because it is first named and New York because it is in the United States (the country of the cataloging agency). The copyright date is transcribed from the bottom of the first page of music.

The note on medium of performance is added to specify the voice range.

Example 7

GOSPEL BELLS
A
CHOICE COLLECTION
of
Gospel Songs and Standard Hymns
for
Church, Sunday School, Endeavor
and Evangelist

Edited by
E. O. EXCEL AND W. E. M. HACKLEMAN

Published by

CHRISTIAN BOARD OF PUBLICATION
2712-2716 Pine Street
ST. LOUIS, MO.

HACKLEMAN MUSIC COMPANY
416-419 Majestic Building
INDIANAPOLIS, IND.

Consists of four-part choral music written on two staves (two voices per staff).

Caption of each selection has a copyright date for that piece.

Page 254-256: "Index, titles in Roman, first lines in italics."

256 pages ; 20 cm.

Example 7

```
     Gospel bells : a choice collection of gospel songs and
standard hymns for church, Sunday school, endeavor, and
evangelist / edited by E.O. Excell and W.E.M. Hackleman.
-- St. Louis, Mo. : Christian Board of Publication ;
Indianapolis, Ind. : Hackleman Music Co., [191-?]
     1 close score (256 p.) ; 20 cm.
     Index of titles and first lines: p. 254-256.
```

The title page is the chief source of information for this hymn collection. Both publisher's names are transcribed in this example because it is likely that the two companies performed different functions in the publication process. The date of publication is at best an estimate, although a more precise date might be arrived at by investigating the editors and the publishers. The item is described as "1 close score" because the separate vocal parts are written on two staves throughout.

Example 8

THE THEATRE GUILD
presents
OKLAHOMA!
A Musical Play
Based on the play
"Green Grow the Lilacs" by Lynn Riggs
Music by
RICHARD RODGERS
Book and Lyrics by
OSCAR HAMMERSTEIN, 2nd

———————

Production directed by ROUBEN MAMOULIAN
Production under the supervision of
Theresa Helburn and Lawrence Langner
Musical Director   *Costumes by*   *Settings by*
Jay S. Blackton   Miles White   Lemeul Ayers
Dances by Agnes de Mille
Orchestrations by Russsell Bennett
Price, $12.00
VOCAL SCORE
(edited by Albert Sirmay)

Copyright 1943 by WILLIAMSON MUSIC, INC.
DE SYLVA, BROWN & HENDERSON, INC., New York, N. Y.
International copyright secured   Printed in U.S.A.
ALL RIGHTS RESERVED Including public performace for profit
Any arrangement or adaptation of this composition without the
consent of the owner is an infringement of copyright

At the foot of first page of music:

Williamson Music Inc. New York, N. Y.
DeSylva, Brown & Henderson, Inc., Sole Selling Agent

In lower left corner of each page: C-523-

208 pages ; 30 cm.

Example 8

```
    The Theatre Guild presents Oklahoma! : a musical play
based on the play "Green grow the lilacs" by Lynn Riggs /
music by Richard Rodgers ; book and lyrics by Oscar
Hammerstein, 2nd ; vocal score edited by Albert Sirmay.
-- New York, N.Y. : Williamson Music : sole selling
agent, DeSylva, Brown & Henderson, c1943.
    1 vocal score (208 p.) ; 30 cm.
    Pl. no.: C-523-.
```

Note that the title proper includes the words that precede the actual title "Oklahoma!" on the title page. The statements of responsibility that pertain to the staged production but not to this item have not been transcribed. The price is not included because it is not current.

Example 9

GUNS N' ROSES
THE SPAGHETTI INCIDENT?
The Authorized Edition

Cherry Lane Music, Port Chester, New York
Exclusively distributed by **Hal Leonard Corp.**, Milwaukee, Wisconsin

---

On verso title page:

©1994, Cherry Lane Music
Due to licensing restrictions, "Ain't it fun' and 'Attitude' do not appear in this collection.

On cover:

PLAY IT LIKE IT IS™:
GUITAR-VOCAL WITH TABLATURE

On back cover:

ISBN 0-89524-826-3
$22.95

Also on back cover:

Cherry Lane Music Company, PO Box 430, Port Chester, NY 10573
exclusively distributed by:
Hal Leonard Corporation, 7777 W. Bluemound Rd. Milwaukee, WI

On p. [94-95]: "Tablature explanation : Notation legend."

Contents page lists song titles only; full attributions are found in the caption of each song.

93 pages, 2 unnumbered pages ; 31 cm.

Example 9

> The spaghetti incident? / Guns n' Roses. -- The
> authorized ed. -- Port Chester, N.Y. : Cherry Lane ;
> Milwaukee, Wis. : Exclusively distributed by Hal Leonard
> Corp., c1994.
> 1 score (93, [2] p.) : ill. ; 31 cm.
> Rock music, as recorded by the musical group Guns n'
> Roses; voice and guitar tablature with chord symbols.
> "Tablature explanation : Notation Legend," p. [94-95].
> "Due to licensing restrictions 'Ain't it fun' and
> 'Attitude' do not appear in this songbook"--T.p. verso.
> Contents: Since I don't have you / words and music by
> Joseph Rock, James Beaumont, and the Skyliners -- New
> rose / words and music by Brian James -- Down on the farm
> / words and music by Charlie Harper, Alvin Gibbs, and
> Nicky Garrett -- Human being / words and music by Johnny
> Thunders and David Johansen -- Raw power / words and
> music by Iggy Pop and James Williamson -- Buick McKane /
> words and music by Marc Bolan -- Big dumb sex / words and
> music by Christopher J. Cornell -- Hair of the dog /
> words and music by Dan McCafferty, Darrell Sweet, Pete
> Agnew and Manuel Charlton -- Black leather / words and
> music by Steve Jones -- You can't put your arms around a
> memory / words and music by Johnny Thunders -- I don't
> care about you / words and music Lee Ving.
> ISBN 0-89524-826-3 ; $22.95

This example is also more like a sound recording than a score. In fact, it is what is referred to as a "pop-folio" and is really a printed manifestation of a sound recording. A title page is present to serve as chief source of information. Note that the name of the rock group is given as a statement of responsibility because it appears in the chief source (not because the statement identifies the composer necessarily). The phrase "guitar-vocal with tablature" appears on the cover, so it is not transcribed as area 3 data because it does not appear in the chief source. The publisher and distributor names are given according to option decisions for 5.4 (1.4, etc.). The trademark "Play it like it is" appears on the cover but is not transcribed.

Note the description includes the term "guitar tablature" as well as "chord symbols." Also, three contents notes are given to elucidate the contents of the volume: the tablature explanation (so users will know that exact fingering, etc., can be expected); the licensing statement (so users will know those two songs from the corresponding recording are not present); and the complete contents with attributions.

Example 10

On cover:

> **NIGHT SCENES**
>
> *for speaker, flute, clarinet, two*
> *percussionists, piano and celesta*
> *(1985)*
>
> Prologue:
> *The Night*
>
> Scenes:
> *Evening and Nighttimes blues*
>
> Epilogue
> *Sunday Night in the City*
>
> *Poetry by LOU LIPSITZ*
> *Music by CHANDLER CARTER*

On caption:

> Night Scenes
> *Poetry by Lou Lipsitz*   *by Chandler Carter*

At the bottom of each page: **Judy Green Music   T-62**

At the bottom of p. 29: *C.C., Boston, 2/85*

On back cover:

> Works for Voice and Piano by Chandler Carter
> ...
> Works for voice and instrument
> ...
> for information concerning purchase of scores and parts, contact:
> Chandler Carter
> 632 East 11th St., Apt. 16
> ...

20 pages; 28 cm.

Example 10

```
     Night scenes : for speaker, flute, clarinet, two
percussionists, piano and celesta (1985) / poetry by Lou
Lipsitz ; music by Chandler Carter. -- New York, N.Y. :
C. Carter, [1985?]
     1 score (29 p.) : 28 cm.
     Title from cover.
     Xerographically reproduced from holograph.
     Contents: Prologue : The night -- Scenes : evening and
nighttimes blues -- Epilogue : Sunday night in the city.
```

Music publishing has often been a risky business because of the high cost of production, and there is quite a tradition of self-publishing as well as of on-demand publishing (copies are produced as they are ordered to limit production costs). This score appears to be self-published xerographically by the composer. There is no imprint on it (the "Judy Green Music" legend at the bottom of each sheet is for the score paper), but a list of works by the composer is printed on both sides of the rear cover along with the composer's address (presumably for inquiries).

The cover is the chief source of information (there is no title page, and the cover is more detailed than the caption). We assume the composer is the publisher, and we give only his name in abbreviated form in area 4 because it already appears in area 1 (rule 1.4D4); the address, which appears on the rear cover, is not given because publication is not assumed to be within the current three years. A physical description note is added to convey to users the notion that the music is not typeset and therefore might be a bit difficult to read; the term "holograph" is used because the composer's initials appear at the end of the score indicating that this is in his own hand.

Example 11

SCHIRMER'S LIBRARY
OF MUSICAL CLASSICS

**Twenty-Four Italian Songs
and Arias**
of the
Seventeenth and Eighteenth
Centuries

FOR MEDIUM HIGH VOICE
→ FOR MEDIUM LOW VOICE

G. SCHIRMER, *Inc.*
distributed by
Hal Leonard Publishing Corporation
7777 West Bluemound Road PO Box 13819 Milwaukee, WI

Copyright © 1948 (Renewed) by G. Schirmer, Inc (ASCAP) New York, NY

On cover: Schirmer Library Volume 1723-B

Glued to the cover is a compact disc bearing the same titles and numbering as the score

On the compact disc: Recorded accompaniments: John Reene, piano

At the foot of every page: 41573

On back cover: **About the recorded accompaniments...**

Also on back cover: **U.S. $14.95**
ISBN 0-7935-1514-9
HL50481593

100 pages; 31 cm.

Example 11

```
    Twenty-four Italian songs and arias of the seventeenth
and eighteenth centuries. -- For medium low voice. -- New
York, NY : G. Schirmer ; Milwaukee, WI: distributed by
Hal Leonard, [1986?], c1948.
    1 score (100 p.) ; 31 cm. + 1 sound disc : digital ; 4
3/4 in. -- (Schirmer's library of musical classics ; vol.
1723-B)
    With piano acc.
    Italian words with English translations, mostly by
Theodore Baker.
    Recorded acc. by John Keene, attached.
    Pl. no.: 41573.
    G. Schirmer: HL50481593.
    ISBN 0-7935-1514-9.
```

Song albums are a mainstay of teaching music collections, and these Schirmer albums have introduced a new wrinkle into music cataloging—how to handle the accompanying compact disc that contains recorded accompaniments. The recorded accompaniments certainly could make the album more useful to singers. As issued by the publisher, the CD is attached with adhesive to an extra cover wrapped around the cover of the score. Because the CD is clearly meant to accompany the score (not the other way around), we catalog the score and add details of the CD in area 5 and 7.

The title page of the score is the chief source of information. Notice that the phrase identifying the version "for medium low voice" is transcribed as an edition statement according to MCD 5.2B2.

In the publication, distribution, etc. area (area 4) the publisher's name (G. Schirmer) is given before the distributor's (Hal Leonard). Addresses are not given, because this score is not published within the current three years. The date of publication is inferred. The score has a copyright date of 1948 but obviously the presence of the CD makes it clear that publication is more recent than that. The CD has a copyright date of ℗1986 on it, so we assume that the package could not have been published before that. Thus we estimate the publication date as 1986, given in square brackets because it is supplied and given with a question mark because it is questionable (i.e., we really don't know when this was published). We disregard the various copyright dates that appear at the foot of each song. Also, we disregard the *design* copyright dates that appear on the covers.

In area 5 we give physical description of the score, then using rules 5.5E1, 1.5E1, and 6.5 we give a physical description of the recording following the plus sign.

The series statement is transcribed from the chief source, but the series number is supplied from the cover.

In notes it is important to indicate that the words of all the songs appear in both Italian (which could have been inferred from the title) and English; browsing through the volume we see that all but two of the songs state that the English versions are by Theodore Baker, so that attribution is included in the note. The recorded accompaniments also are noted, as is the pianist. The plate number for the score is followed by label name and number for the recording. No contents note is given, partially because these collections are ubiquitous and their content is analyzed in reference sources, and partially because it would take a great deal of time to transcribe all of the title and statement of responsibility data. Some libraries might find it useful to have included the contents note.

SUMMARY

Description of printed music begins with technical reading of the item, including all captions on score and parts and the foot of the first page of music, to select the chief source of information, to get a sense of the type of music present, and also to comprehend the physical form of the item. Title pages are common in music, but captions and covers also often are utilized as chief sources.

Description begins in a manner quite similar to book description with the transcription of title and statement of responsibility data from the chief source of information. A distinction is made about the type of title given—titles that consist of the name of a type of composition will have more detail recorded as part of the title proper. In most cases the date of copyright will be transcribed into area 4 in lieu of a date of publication, but for older items research might be required to establish an approximate date.

Physical description begins with a specific material designation for the type of printed music document (score, part, etc.), but pagination, illustrations, and dimensions are recorded in much the same way they would be for printed books.

Notes on chief source of information, medium of performance, and plate numbers are commonplace. If the work has not been fully identified in the process of title transcription, fuller detail—such as medium of performance, original medium (if the work is an arrangement), language of sung words, etc.—is added in the notes. Contents notes are frequently made for works with several distinctively titled movements and for collections.

CHAPTER 2: DESCRIPTION OF SOUND RECORDINGS

INTRODUCTION: THE PROCESS

The steps in description of a sound recording are as follows:

1. Technical reading of the disc and container, to select the chief source of information;

2. Transcription of the title and statement of responsibility area from the chief source of information; only some statements may be transcribed into area 1 of the description;

3. Transcription of the publication, distribution, etc., data; this will include the label name, which is not necessarily the same as the name of the publisher; this also will include transcription of the dates of release or copyright of the *sound*;

4. Physical description of the recording;

5. Transcription of series data if appropriate;

6. Creation of the label name and number note;

7. Making other notes as appropriate.

TECHNICAL READING OF A SOUND RECORDING

Technical reading of a sound recording involves careful examination of all potential sources of information. Typically, title and statement of responsibility data will be found on the disc itself (or on a paper label attached to the disc in the case of LPs and older recordings), on the container, and in a booklet or pamphlet enclosed in the container alongside program notes, printed texts of vocal works, etc. At this point the cataloger must compare the various sources to see whether there are any differences in the data that appear on them. Because the data printed on the disc itself (or its paper label) probably will be the data transcribed for the basis of the description, it is important to see whether title or statement of responsibility data are given in fuller form elsewhere (in which case notes may be used to flesh out the description). Also, it is important to check all of the potential dates of performance, release, copyright, etc., as well as the recording history (analog to digital, direct to disc, etc.) to develop an understanding of the "bibliographic history" of the recording, which might be reflected in different ways in different parts of the description. Finally, it is important to discover at this stage what, if any, information will need to be sought elsewhere (in reference sources)—for example, dates of release must sometimes be inferred from information about the performance recorded.

CHOOSING THE CHIEF SOURCE OF INFORMATION

For sound recordings the chief source of information is generally the label or labels as specified in rule 6.0B1. Note that for compact discs, the data printed on the disc are considered to constitute a "label."

An exception is made for collections, in which the accompanying textual matter of the container is preferred if it provides a collective title and the label or labels do not. In Figure 2.1 the labels do not provide a collective title. Because the container does, it is preferred as the chief source of information. This substitute must be identified in a note.

MCD 6.0B1 For compact discs and cassettes, consider information which can be read through the closed container (including information on the front cover of a booklet inserted in the container) to be on the container.

For sound recordings containing two works of the same type by one composer without a collective title on the label(s), do not consider as a collective title a title on the container or accompanying material that is made up of the name of the type plus one or more of the following identifying elements for the two works: serial number, opus number, thematic index number, key.

Do not transcribe as collective title:

> *On container:* Piano concertos no. 25, K. 503, no. 26, K.537
> *On container:* Sonatas no. 4, op. 7, and no. 11, op. 22
> *On container:* Symphonies nos. 88 and 104 (London)

Transcribe as collective title:

> *On container:* The violin concertos / Serge Prokofiev
> *On container:* Les deux sonates pour violoncelle et piano
> *On container:* Ballets / Igor Stravinsky
>   (*Contains Apollo and Orpheus*)

(rev. May 1989)(*MCD* 23)

TITLE AND STATEMENT OF RESPONSIBILITY AREA

Transcribe the title proper from the label. If the title consists of musical terms, use the instructions at rule 5.1B. Remember that the purpose of transcription in this area is to create for the user a surrogate of the item. That is, the purpose is not necessarily to give information about the musical content of the recording; that will be handled later, in the notes area, if necessary. Therefore, do not be concerned that the label title is shorter or less informative than the title on the container. Transcribe what you see, so that the user who has consulted the catalog description will recognize the item when it is encountered.

6.1B1 LCRI If the chief source shows the name of an author or the name of a performer before the titles of the individual works and there is doubt whether the publisher, etc., intended the name to be a collective title proper or a statement of responsibility, treat the name as the title proper. *Exception*: If the works listed are musical compositions and the name is that of the composer of the works, treat the name as a statement of responsibility in cases of doubt.

If the chief source being followed is the label of a sound recording and the decision is to treat the name as a title proper but one name appears on the label of one side and another name on the second side, transcribe the two names as individual titles (separated by a period-space). (*CSB* 44: 25)

COLLECTIVE TITLES

The name of a performer that appears in the chief source of information may, in fact, be a collective title. The cataloger's decision should be based on the prominence, wording, and typography of the labels, container, and accompanying textual matter of the recorded collection (also consult rule 1.1B3). Generally, when the name of the performer is in bolder type or a more prominent position than either composer or title, it may be considered a collective title.

Rule 6.1G1 gives the cataloger a choice when describing a sound recording that has no collective title. According to the rule, one may describe such a recording as a unit or one may make a separate description for each separately titled work on the recording. The Library of Congress describes all sound recordings with unit descriptions whether the recording has a collective title or not (according to LCRI 6.1G1, which is not reproduced here).

GENERAL MATERIAL DESIGNATION (GMD)

The GMD "sound recording" is used by the Library of Congress according to LCRI 1.1C, 6.1C (not reproduced here). The GMD is given in square brackets immediately following the first iteration of title proper in area one of the description.

```
Symphony no. 25, D major [sound recording] / ...
Partita in F [sound recording] ; Partita in G ...
```

STATEMENT OF RESPONSIBILITY

The statement of responsibility area for sound recordings is used in a somewhat limited way. The rule requires, of course, the transcription of names of composers of music, authors of texts, and collectors of field recordings. These names are transcribed because they identify the persons or bodies responsible for the material that has been recorded. This usage is consistent with the instructions for printed materials.

Sound recordings also have performers, and rule 6.1F1 makes a distinction between performers of highly improvisational music, whose names are to be transcribed in the statement of responsibility area, and other performers, whose names are transcribed in a note. A Library of Congress Rule Interpretation adds this caveat:

6.1F1 LCRI The rule allows performers who do more than perform to be named in the statement of responsibility. Accept only the most obvious cases as qualifying for the statement of responsibility. (*CSB* 11: 15)

The point here is to recognize as a type of author those performers who play a creative role in the performance of music. The point of view reflected in the rules is that in traditional Western "classical" music, the performer recreates a composer's musical idea (performance), adding nuance and perhaps ornamentation (interpretation). Other types of music, however, do not tend to be as strictly composed. In these cases the performer adds musical ideas to the preconceived sketch (for example, the jazz musician who improvises on a set of chord changes). In the latter case the name of the performer should be transcribed in the statement of responsibility.

Occasionally, when one is describing as a unit a sound recording that has no collective title, placement of the performer's statement of responsibility can be confusing. The problem arises chiefly in the description of older 45 or 78 rpm popular music recordings. Typically there will be two musical works, one on each side, each with a different composer, but both performed by the same artist. Because there is rarely a container supplying a collective title, the cataloger must use the two labels together as the chief source of information. Note that the Library of Congress advises against editorial emendations to such statements of reponsibility:

6.1F3 MCD For recordings of those types of music for which it is possible for performers' names to appear in the statement of responsibility (cf. 6.1F1), use bracketed words or phrases under this rule only when it is not clear from other parts of the description (e.g., the performer note, the contents note, etc.) whether the names in the statement of responsibility are those of composers, performers, or composers-performers. (March 1981) (*MCD* 26)

Instructions in chapter one of AACR 2 direct the cataloger to record the individual titles, together with the statements of responsibility that apply to each, in the order in which they appear in the item.

```
I believe in you (you believe in me) / Don Davis
; [sung by] Johnnie Taylor.  Stop doggin' me / B.
Crutcher, D. Davis, A. Snider ; [sung by] Johnnie
Taylor [sound recording].
```

EDITION AREA

Edition statements are rare on sound recordings. In sound recording manufacture and distribution there is no parallel for the practice of revising or correcting slightly a textual source and printing more copies or issuing a new edition, the print tradition from which edition statements are derived and for the identification of which they are transcribed into bibliographic descriptions. Recordings of specific performances often are reissued, to be sure. However, a reissue will require a new copyright, which alone would probably be sufficient to cause a separate and distinct bibliographic record for a subsequent reissue to be created. At the time of this writing, reissues of recordings originally released on 33 1/3 rpm LP discs are finding their realization in compact digital discs, a difference that would certainly cause the creation of a different bibliographic record, particularly because additional musical works often are added to compact disc releases to take advantage of their greater storage capacity. Further, commercial considerations—sound recordings as cultural objects are designed primarily for entertainment rather than scholarship—make it likely that a reissued recording will have different accompanying textual matter, which could mean that slightly different bibliographic characteristics (titles, for instance) would be transcribed into a bibliographic description.

It is exceedingly unlikely that one would be encountered, so the rules for transcribing edition information usually are disregarded.

Nonetheless, rules for transcribing edition information appear at rule 6.2. LCRIs exist to cover option decisions for rule 6.2B3 (optionally, if necessary add an interpolated edition statement using the instructions in LCRI 1.2B4) (*CSB* 38: 29), and for rule 6.2B4 (do not apply the optional provision for transcribing parallel edition statements) (*CSB* 34: 26). These LCRIs are not reprinted here.

PUBLICATION, DISTRIBUTION, ETC., AREA

Information for this area is recorded according to the general provisions of AACR 2. A few notable exceptions are discussed below.

PLACE OF PUBLICATION

The cataloger should remember that the objective here is the same as for any kind of material, namely to transcribe the information from the item itself. Information to be transcribed in this area may be taken from the labels, the accompanying textual matter, or the container (rule 6.0B1). Despite this generous provision of the rule, it is not unusual for a sound recording to indicate no place of publication. Reference to rule 1.4C will help here. If the place of publication is not indicated, the cataloger supplies it in square brackets, adding a question mark if necessary to indicate uncertainty. Lacking any solid evidence, and following provisions of rule 1.4C6, the country of publication is supplied in square brackets:

```
[United States] : Stax Records ...
```

The point here is not to let the absence of a formally named place of publication cause undue concern. If desired, the cataloger can consult a standard commercial guide such as Phonolog, Billboard ... International Buyers' Guide, or a Schwann product for information on the location of a particular publisher, should the cataloging agency deem this area to be of such importance as to warrant the extra work. Otherwise an estimate ([United States?]) will suffice. As a last resort, when not even the probable country of publication can be inferred, the abbreviation "[S.l.]" (for *Sine loco*) can be given.

PUBLISHER'S NAME

Providing the name of the publisher can be a confusing aspect of descriptive cataloging for sound recordings. The point is to determine the name most useful to the catalog user. A common difficulty is the appearance of several similar terms in the item, thus confusing the cataloger who may be unfamiliar with the vagaries of the entertainment industry. When a recording lists the name of a publisher, a trade name, and a series, all of which appear to be similar in nature, the cataloger must determine which name is to be preferred for this area.

There are two practical approaches. First, examine the item to see if one of the names appears in conjunction with the serial number. This is the "trade name" referred to in rule 6.4D2 and should be transcribed in the publication, etc., area. If confusion still exists because of the layout, the next approach is to consult a listing in Phonolog or Schwann to see how the publisher is listed there.

While sound recording series do exist, they are somewhat less common than those for other types of materials. More often, sound recording companies utilize series titles as sales gimmicks. These names (such as Columbia Masterworks or Immortal Performances) may appear on the label, but more often they appear only on the container, usually in a smaller or different typeface from that used for the other data given. Rule 6.4D3 warns the cataloger about trade names that appear to be names of series as opposed to the name of a publishing subdivision. Care must be exercised. While Columbia Masterworks and Disney Storyteller are series, RCA Red Seal is not. Again, consulting a standard commercial list such as Schwann or Phonolog will help avoid confusion in this area.

An optional provision of rule 6.4D1 allows the additional transcription of the name of a distributor, different from the name of the label. LCRI 6.4D1 instructs us to apply this optional provision (*CSB* 8: 10). Be certain not to confuse a name of a distributor with the label name. Also, LCRI 6.4E allows for the optional provision of an interpolated statement of function of publisher, distributor, etc. (*CSB* 47: 36). Readers are referred to the text of LCRI 1.4E:

> **1.4E LCRI** Apply the rule when there are two entities named, one for publishing and the other for distributing, and the distributing entity's name does not convey an indication of this function. Apply it also when a single entity is named, if it is known that this entity performed only a distributing function and its name does not indicate this function. Do not apply it in other cases. (*CSB* 12: 11).

DATES OF PUBLICATION, DISTRIBUTION, ETC.

The purpose of giving a date of publication is to identify the "edition" of the item in hand. For sound recordings, we are interested specifically in identifying the "release" of the sound contained in the recording. Many dates can appear on sound recordings, including dates of performance, dates of composition of works recorded, copyright of textual matter or artwork on the container, copyright of the sound (which corresponds to the release date), date of re-release, etc.

Copyright Dates

Since 1971 by international convention the symbol ℗ has been used to indicate the copyright date of recorded sound. Because the date used is the year of first release (publication) of the recording, such dates are useful in the absence of formally stated dates of publication (see rules 6.4F and 1.4F6).

Confusion stems from the wide array of dates that might be present on labels, containers, and accompanying texts. Various © dates might be present, indicating copyright protection for the work performed, or for the accompanying visual matter (the art work, program notes, librettos or song texts, etc.).

When a single ℗ date is present it should be transcribed as the date of copyright of the recorded sound. When various ℗ dates appear on a single recording, the cataloger must determine whether they represent a reissue (as would be the case when the recording has only one work), in which case the latest date should be transcribed, or whether each date represents the copyright for a different part of the recording. In the latter instance no ℗ date should be transcribed, because there is none that applies to the recording as a whole. An estimated date of publication can be arrived at by considering the latest ℗ date on the item to be the likely date of publication.

When no ℗ date is present on the item, a © date before 1971 should be transcribed as the date of copyright. For © dates later than 1970, the cataloger should infer an estimated date of publication.

Another situation that might occur is that of the digitally remastered analog recording that has been released on compact disc. For such a recording, the © date (copyright for the textual matter on the container) may be used to infer the date of publication, but the ℗ date should also be transcribed following the instructions at 1.4F5.

When No Copyright Date is Present

AACR 2 requires a date of publication, distribution, release, etc., to be given in every description. When no copyright dates are present on sound recordings, the cataloger, exercising great care, may estimate the date of release.

It is reasonable to assume that a recent recording was released within one year of the date it was recorded, although this is not always a reliable yardstick, because many recordings are released years after their performance. When the date of recording is within the current twelve months it is probably safe to estimate the current year as the date of release.

Another approach is even less reliable, but still worth mentioning. The cataloger can check a manufacturer's number file to see if there is a chronological pattern among recordings within a range of serial numbers. Large files of this type are available in all major network union catalogs. Be advised, however, that many record manufacturers do not assign these so-called "serial" numbers serially, so this approach should be used only as a last resort. A date may be estimated this way only when a clear chronological pattern is present in the file.

Finally, one might consult reviews to infer a date of release (the recording cannot have been released *after* it was reviewed). If all else fails, especially with older recordings, discographies might be of some help.

Data On Manufacture

LCRI 6.4G2 allows the optional transcription of data about place, name, and date of manufacture of a recording in certain circumstances (the data must be present on the item, must differ from data concerning publisher, and must be considered important by the cataloging agency) (*CSB* 47: 36). It is unlikely to be of importance in music libraries to transcribe these superfluous data in the odd cases when they appear.

> **1.4G4 LCRI** Apply the option on a case-by-case basis .... When applying the rule, give both the place of manufacture and the name of the manufacturer even if this means a repetition of data already recorded in the publication, distribution, etc., area.

London : The Society, 1971 (London : Plowshare Press)

(*CSB* 45: 13).

PHYSICAL DESCRIPTION AREA

The elements of physical description for sound recordings are three. The first element is a statement of extent of item, in which the specific material designation is given (sound disc, sound tape, etc.) along with the number of items in the bibliographic entity. The option in rule 6.5B1 to delete the word "sound" is not applied (LCRI 6.5B1, *CSB* 47: 36; LCRI 1.1C, *CSB* 44: 10). Extent is indicated by giving the duration of the recording parenthetically following the specific material designation.

```
1 sound disc (38 min.)
1 sound cassette (75 min.)
```

The purpose of the statement of extent is to give a user an idea of the length of the recording as information for use in selecting from among recordings of different lengths. Note that the cumulative effect of MCD 6.5B1, and MCD and LCRI 6.5B2 (below) is to give a statement of extent only for recordings that contain only one work. This example of the confusion of work and item, caused by the MCD, means that catalogers cannot simply learn a pragmatic rule and apply it in all cases.

6.5B1 MCD For multipart items, give only the number of physical units (e.g., discs) in the physical description area. If the number of containers or discographic units (often called "volumes") differs from the number of physical units, give this information in notes (cf. MCD 6.7B10, MCD 6.7B18).

For multipart items that are not yet complete, give in the physical description area the cumulative number of physical units held in angle brackets (i.e., follow DCM B7.2.2b 4) in all cases. If the holdings are not clear from the contents note (e.g., when there is no contents note), give them in a separate note (cf. 6.7B20, LCRI 1.7B20). (rev. May 1992)(*MCB* 23:8:2)

6.5B2 LCRI When the total playing time of a sound recording is not stated on the item but the durations of its parts (sides, indivudual works, etc.) are, if desired add the stated durations together and record the total, rounding off to the next minute if the total exceeds 5 minutes.

Precede a statement of duration by "ca." only if the statement is given on the item in terms of an approximation. Do not add "ca." to a duration arrived at by adding partial durations or by rounding off seconds.

If no durations are stated on the item or if the durations of some but not all the parts of a work are stated, do not give a statement of duration. Do not approximate durations from the number of sides of a disc, type of cassette, etc. (*CSB* 33: 36)

6.5B2 MCD Apply the "Interpretation" in LCRI 6.5B2 and give the total duration in the physical description area if the recording contains only one work (as defined in Appendix D, "Musical work" (1)), regardless of the number of physical units (e.g., discs) in the recording. State the duration equal to or greater than one hour as hours and minutes or as minutes (in either case with seconds if appropriate), depending on how it is stated in the item being cataloged.

For sound recordings containing more than one work, apply LCRI 6.7B10 and MCD 6.7B10. (rev. January 1990)(*MCD* 28)

The second element is a statement of physical details of the recording. This will include a word to indicate the way in which the sound is encoded on the item and, therefore, the type of playback equipment that will be required.

For grooved discs, for which a turntable with a needle is required for playback, give the term "analog." Also use the word "analog" for standard cassette tapes. Give other physical details as noted in AACR 2, preceded by a comma-space.

```
1 sound disc (38 min.) : analog, 33 1/3 rpm, stereo.
```

For compact discs requiring a laser device for playback, and for DAT (digital audio tape) cassettes, give the word "digital." No playing speed is given for digital discs because it is not a requirement of playback equipment.

```
1 sound disc (59 min.) : digital
```

The third element of physical description is the size of the item. The standard LP is 12 inches in diameter; the standard compact disc is 4 3/4 inches in diameter.

```
1 sound disc (45 min.) : analog, 33 1/3 rpm, stereo.
; 12 in.
1 sound disc (47 min.) : digital ; 4 3/4 in.
```

6.5C3 MCD For tape cassettes, give the playing speed only if it is stated on the item. (April 1984)(*MCD* 29)

6.5C7 MCD When the number of sound channels is not stated explicitly, do not record any term. (January 1981)(*MCD* 29)

6.5C8 MCD Apply this option whenever the information would be needed for selecting playback equipment to get the full audio effect of the recording; e.g., record the quadraphonic process in the physical description area when special equipment is required to listen to the recording in quad., even if it can be listened to in stereo. without the special equipment. (January 1981)(*MCD* 29)

SERIES AREA

Series titles are transcribed into area 6. Care should be taken not to confuse a label name or a sounc recording manufacturer's trade name with a series title (see the discussion above under PUBLISHER'S NAME).

NOTES AREA

Notes are made to allow users to make relevance judgments when looking at descriptions in a catalog. That is, a catalog user who is browsing through a sequence of bibliographic records for sound recordings ought to be able to decide which recordings might be of interest. The simple bibliographical details given according to transcription from the chief source of information in areas 1 through 6 of the description often are quite sketchy for sound recordings (remember that the purpose of this transcription is to create a surrogate in the catalog of the item). Consequently it is commonplace for fairly extensive notes to be used in sound recording cataloging to provide catalog users with the best information possible about the musical works and performances recorded.

ORDER OF NOTES

Make notes about any or all of the following, when applicable, in the order given below. Note that this order corresponds to the sequence of rules in chapter 6 of AACR 2 for making notes, with the exception of the first note (manufacturer's number), which is placed first according to an LCRI (6.7B19).

> Manufacturer's number (6.7B19)
> Nature or artistic form and medium of performance (6.7B1)
> Text (language of sung or spoken text) (6.7B2)
> Source of title proper (6.7B3)
> Variations in title (6.7B4)
> Parallel titles and other title information (6.7B5)
> Statements of responsibility (6.7B6)
> Edition and history (6.7B7)
> Publication, distribution, etc. (6.7B9)
> Physical description (including durations) (6.7B10)
> Accompanying material (6.7B11)
> Series (6.7B12)
> Dissertation note (6.7B13)
> Audience (6.7B14)
> Other formats available (6.7B16)
> Summary (6.7B17) (Spoken word recordings only)
> Contents (6.7B18)
> Copy being described, library's holdings, and restrictions on use (6.7B20)

PUBLISHER'S (I.E., LABEL NAME AND) NUMBER

6.7B19 LCRI When applying rule 6.7B19 to include the label name and number in a note, make this note the first one. Transcribe spaces and hyphens in publisher's numbers on sound recordings as they appear. Separate the first and last numbers of a sequence by a dash.

> Angel: S 37781
> RCA Red Seal: ARL1-3715
> Deutsche Harmonia Mundi: 1C 065-99 615
> Euphonic: EES-101--EES-102

When the item bears both a set number and numbers for the individual items (e.g., discs), give only the set number unless it does not appear on the individual items; in that case give the set number first, followed by the numbers of the individual items in parentheses.

> Philips: 6769 042 (9500 718--9500 719)

Give matrix numbers only if they are the only numbers shown on the item. Follow each matrix number by the word matrix in parentheses.

> Melodiia : C10 06767 (matrix)--C10 06768 (matrix)

(*CSB* 14:17)

6.7B19 MCD   When a publisher's number appears in various forms on a sound recording, its container, accompanying material, etc., transcribe only the form on the recording itself (e.g., the labels of a disc).

> *On disc:* S-37337
> *On container:* DS 37337
> *Note:* Angel: S-37337.

When an item consists of two or more individual units (e.g., discs), do not transcribe numbers which represent in a truncated form the numbers of the individual units.

> *On discs:* LPX 18124
>   LPX 18125
>   LPX 18126
>   LPX 18127
>   LPX 18128
> *On container:* LPX 18124-28
> *Note:* Hungaroton: LPX 18124--LPX 18128.

> *On discs:* HMC 1235
>   HMC 1236
>   HMC 1237
> *On container:* HMC 1235.37
> *Note:* Harmonia Mundi France: HMC 1235--HMC 1237.

When two or more distinct publisher's numbers appear on a sound recording, its container, accompanying material, etc., transcribe each in a separate note. Follow each number other than the first by an indication of its location, if appropriate.

> Pape: FSM 43721
> Pape: POPR 790051 (on container)

If, however, each unit (e.g., disc) in a set bears an individual number but the item also bears a number applying to the set as a whole, follow the instructions in LCRI 6.7B19.

Apply the above principles also when a disc (or discs) bears only matrix numbers but a different or variant number appears on the container.

> *Matrix numbers on disc:* S10-17429
>   S10-17430
> *On container:*   S10 17429 008 (a "set" number)
> *Note:* Melodiia: S10 17429 008 (S10-17429 (matrix)--S10-17430 (matrix)).

> *Matrix numbers on disc:* S10-06513
>   S10-06514
> *On container:*   S10-06513-14 (a truncation of the matrix numbers)
> *Note:* Melodiia: S10-06513 (matrix)--S10-06514 (matrix).

(rev. October 1991)(*MCD* 35).

NOTES ON MEDIUM OF PERFORMANCE

6.7B1 LCRI Consider the form and medium of performance of a musical work (or collection of musical works) as given in the uniform title in the main entry as well as from the description in determining whether to make a note. (*CSB* 55: 17).

6.7B1 MCD Do not name the medium of performance in a note if it is implied by the title or other title information (e.g., "Chorale prelude"; "Manfred : symphonie en 4 tableaux") or by the musical form stated in a note made under this rule (e.g., "Opera in two acts"; "Ballet").

If a work is published for a medium of performance other than the original, give the original medium of performance in a note if it is not clear from the rest of the description or the uniform title and the information is readily available.

If an item is described in the physical description area as "chorus score" or "vocal score" (cf. MCD 5.5B1), give in a note the original medium of performance and the instrument for which the accompaniment is arranged (or indicate that the accompaniment is omitted) if this information is not clear from the rest of the description.

> For solo voices (SATB), chorus (SATB), and orchestra; acc. arr. for piano.
> For chorus (TTBB) and band; without the acc.

(rev. October 1991)(*MCB* 23:1:4)

NOTES ON TITLE PROPER

The Library of Congress does not follow the option in rule 6.7B4 of giving a romanization of the title proper (LCRI 6.7B4, *CSB* 47: 36).

PERFORMER NOTES

Performer notes created according to rule 6.7B6 (in conjunction with rule 1.7B6) are "statements of responsibility" notes. Transcribe them from the item and use prescribed punctuation as outlined for the statement of responsibility area. Do not give a performer note for a multi-performer collection with a collective title. In this case, give the performers' names in the contents note (rule 6.7B18) in parentheses, following titles and statements of responsibility for each work performed.

A memorandum from the Library of Congress Cataloging Policy and Support Office was printed in *MCB* 23:12:3 (December 1992) rescinding the earlier MCD that directed the use of prescribed punctuation in performer notes, while simultaneously noting the usefulness of prescribed punctuation in long notes. The memorandum concludes with the following equivocation:

> Standard punctuation (semicolon-space) or prescribed punctuation (space-semicolon-space) may be used when making the notes called for [in] AACR 2 rules 6.7B6, 7.7B6, 9.7B6.

Because the data are intended to be descriptive, and because they are supplied from the item, my recommendation continues to be to consider performer notes to be like statements of responsibility and to use prescribed punctuation accordingly.

DATA ON RECORDING SESSIONS, EDITION, AND HISTORY

These data are referred to under the heading "Edition and history" in AACR 2. Information on the recording sessions can be used for discographical purposes to identify particular performances that might have been released at different times on different labels or in different physical formats. Whenever information on the recording session is indicated in the item, it should be given in an "edition and history" note.

```
           Recorded Oct. 27, 1955 (1st work), and Sept. 25-
      27, 1956 (2nd work), at Studio Domovina, Prague
```

This note also is used to indicate that recorded material has been issued before.

```
      All selections previously released
```

PHYSICAL DESCRIPTION—TYPE OF RECORDING

6.7B10 MCD Do not make the note "Analog recording" or "Digital recording." ([rev.] October 1991)(*MCB* 23:1:4).

PHYSICAL DESCRIPTION—CONTAINERS

6.7B10 MCD Give a note on the presence of container(s) only when the number of containers is not clear from the rest of the description. (rev. October 1991)(*MCB* 23:1:4)

PHYSICAL DESCRIPTION—DURATIONS

6.7B10 LCRI If the individual works in a collection are identified in the title and statement of responsibility area, list the durations of the works in a note. If the individual works are listed in a contents note (6.7B18), give their durations there.

When recording individual durations in the note area, give them as they appear on the item (e.g., in minutes and seconds if so stated). If only the durations of the parts of a work are stated (e.g., the movements of a sonata), if desired add the stated durations together and record the total for the work in minutes, rounding off to the next minute.

Precede a statement of duration by "ca." only if the statement is given on the item in terms of an approximation. Do not add "ca." to a duration arrived at by adding up partial durations or by rounding off seconds.

If the duration of a work is not stated on the item, or if the durations of some but not all of the parts are stated, do not give a statement of duration for that work. Do not approximate durations from the number of sides of a disc, type of cassette, etc. (*CSB* 13: 14-15)

6.7B10 MCD Generally do not give more than six statements of duration in the note area. If durations of more than six works in a collection are available from the item, generally do not give any durations in the note area. More than six durations may be given, however, if in the cataloger's judgment they are especially important.

In a statement of duration in the note area, separate the digits representing hours, minutes, and seconds by colons. If a duration is expressed in seconds only, precede it by a colon.

> Duration: 45:00
> Durations: 1:25:00; :48; 15:10
> Duration: ca. 1:15:00
> Durations: ca. 27:00; ca. 17:00

For instructions on the use of "ca." preceding durations in the note area, see LCRI 6.7B10. (rev. October 1991)(*MCB* 23:1:4)

ACCOMPANYING MATERIAL

6.7B11 MCD The phrases "neither mentioned in the physical description area nor given a separate description" modify "accompanying material," not "details." For further information see MCD 1.5E1.

Make notes on accompanying program notes, etc., only if they are important, either because of their content or because they are physically separable. Do not, however, make a note for phsyically separable materials accompanying a compact disc unless their content is important. (rev. May 1989)(*MCD* 34)

Program notes are ubiquitous on sound recording containers. Frequently they have little useful information. Consider program notes to be important only when they are substantial (e.g., a separate booklet, score, libretto, etc.) or when they provide information that is unique, such as a discography, or historical or biographical information that cannot be found in standard reference sources. Do not consider the mere presence of textual matter on a container to be sufficiently significant to warrant making a note.

OTHER FORMATS AVAILABLE

6.7B16 LCRI Generally make a note on the availability of the item in another medium or other media, if this is known. Record these notes in the position of 6.7B16 ... and use the term "issued."

> Issued also as motion picture, filmstrip, and slide set

(*CSB* 13: 15)

CONTENTS

Contents notes are very important for musical sound recordings, most of which are collections. Information about the individual selections on a recording is essential when the recording collection cannot be browsed. In particular, for recordings that will not receive analytical added entries for all works on them, a complete contents note can provide a backup source of access to individual titles in an online catalog that allows keyword searching. Therefore, complete contents should always be given when the recording has a collective title.

When contents are given, durations of the individual works (if present on the item) should be given in parentheses following the descriptive information for each work.

```
Pleasure songs for flute [sound recording] ...
  Contents: Passepied from Suite de Ballet /
Vaughan Williams (2:02) -- Greensleeves (4:40) --
Molly on the shore / Grainger (4:13) ...
```

Two Library of Congress policy statements apply to the inclusion of durations in contents notes.

LCRI 6.7B18 For durations of works recorded in a formal contents note, apply LCRI 6.7B10. (*CSB* 13: 14)

MCD 6.7B18 For the forms of durations recorded in a formal contents note, see MCD 2.6B10.

For multipart items, when the number of discographic units (often called "volumes" by publishers) differs from the number of physical units (e.g., discs) or containers, include when necessary the number of physical units or containers in the contents note (cf. LCRI 2.7B18, section 6b).

> Contents: 1. Vom 6. Sonntag bis zum 17. Sonntag nach Trinitatis (6
> discs) -- 2. Vom 18. bis zum 27. Sonntag nach Trinitatis (6 discs) ...

(rev. June 1994)(*MCB* 25:8:2)

The provisions of rule 5.7B18 also apply to sound recordings. That is, if all the works on a sound recording that is a collection are in the same musical form and that musical form is named in the title area of the description, give only the other details in the contents note.

```
Six sonatas for flute and harpsichord [sound
recording] / Carl Philipp Emanuel Bach ...
  Contents: No. 1 in B flat major, Wq. 125 (6:14)
-- No. 2 in D major, Wq. 126 (6:26) -- No. 3 in G
major, Wq. 127 (7:01) ...
```

When each performer on a collective sound recording performs a different selection, each name is given in parentheses following the transcription for the work performed.

```
     A Motown anniversary collection [sound recording]
. . .
     Contents: Heat wave / E. Holland, L. Dozier, B.
Holland (Martha Reeves & The Vandellas) -- You've
really got a hold on me / W. Robinson, Jr. (The
Miracles) -- Signed, sealed, delivered / Stevie
Wonder, S. Wright, L.M. Hardaway, L. Garrett
(Stevie Wonder) ...
```

Example 12

**RUSSIAN
DISC**

Pyotr Ilyich Tchaikovsky
Liturgy of St. John Chrysostom, Op. 41

Leningrad Glinka Choir
Vladislav Chernushenko

RD CD 11 040
AAD Stereo

℗ 1994 Russian Disc

On container verso:

    62:32
    CD Made in U.S.A.
    Printed in Canada

```
     Liturgy of St. John Chrysostom [sound recording] :
op. 41 / Pyotr Ilyich Tchaikovsky. -- [Canada?] : Russian
Disc, p1994.
     1 sound disc (62 min., 32 sec.) : digital, stereo.  ;
4 3/4 in.
     Russian Disc: RD CD 11 040.
     Leningrad Glinka Choir ; Vladislav Chernushenko,
conductor.
     Compact disc.
```

This compact disc recording contains one work by one composer, which makes transcription into area 1 fairly simple. Note that the title proper does not consist of the name of a type of composition, so the GMD appears immediately following the title proper, and the opus number appears as other title information.

The verso of the container says: "CD made in U.S.A; printed in Canada." With no further information than that, the use of "Canada" as place of publication is a guess. The date is based on the copyright date (℗1994); reference within the liturgy to Pimen, Patriarch of the Russian Orthodox Church, indicates that the performance was recorded prior to his death in 1991. Note that the term "stereo" appears on the disc, therefore it is transcribed into the other physical details portion of area 5.

Brief program notes that appear on the booklet in the container are disregarded in this description, because they do not contain any significant information. A contents note could be used to indicate the "movements" of this liturgy, but in this case the cataloger has opted not to do so, as the parts are "ordinary" (fairly standard for this type of setting).

Example 13

Janáček
Sinfonietta
Mša Glagolskaja (Glagolitic Mass)

Troitskaya • Randová • Kaludov • Leiferkus
Chœr et Orchestre symphonique de
Montréal / Charles Dutoit

LONDON

℗ 1994 The Decca Record Company Limited, London
STEREO
436 211-1

On p. 10 of booklet:

>   Recording location: St. Eustach, Montréal, 16 May 1991 (1-8) and 3 October 1991 (9-13).
>   Publisher: Universal Edition AG, Vienna

On cover of booklet:

JANÁČEK
Glagolitic Mass   Glagolitische Messe
Sinfonietta

Troitskaya Randová Kaludov Leiferkus
DUTOIT • MONTRÉAL

On back cover of booklet:

Natalia Troitskaya soprano
Eva Randová mezzo-soprano
Kaludi Kaludov tenor
Sergei Leiferkus bass
Thomas Trotter organ
Choeur et Orchestre Symphonique de Montréal
Chorus director: **Iwan Edwards**
Charles Dutoit

Example 13

```
    Sinfonietta [sound recording] ; Mša glagolskaja =
Glagolitic mass / Janáček. -- London : London, p1994.
    1 sound disc : digital, stereo. ; 4 3/4 in.
    London: 436 211-2.
    Sung in Old Church Slavic (mass).
    Parallel title on container: Glagolitische Messe.
    Natalia Troitskaya, soprano ; Eva Randová, mezzo-
soprano ; Kaludi Kaludov, tenor ; Sergei Leiferkus, bass ;
Thomas Trotter, organ (Mass) ; Choeur et Orchestre
Symphonique de Montréal ; chorus director, Iwan Edwards ;
Charles Dutoit, conductor.
    Recorded at St. Eustache, Montréal, 16 May 1991 (Mass),
and 3 Oct. 1991 (Sinfonietta).
    Editions recorded: Vienna : Universal Edition.
    Program notes, and words of the Mass in Old Church
Slavic and English in booklet.
    Compact disc.
    Contents: Mša glagolskaja (41 min.) -- Sinfonietta (24
min., 14 sec.).
```

This compact disc recording contains two works by the same composer. Note that the titles of the two works are reversed on the chief source of information (the mass actually is the first work on the recording), so it is necessary to make a contents note to clarify the positioning of the two works. Also, in the notes on performers and recording sessions it is necessary to indicate the work to which each element applies, in this case by using "Mass" or "Sinfonietta" in parentheses. The additional German language parallel title for the mass appears only on the container, so it is not interpolated into area 1; rather it is given in a note.

The label of this disc and the copyright statements on the container clearly show the Decca Record Company as the publishing entity, but LONDON is the trademark or label-name that is recorded in the details of publication, distribution, etc., area, and in the note on manufacturer's number.

No statement of extent is given in the physical description area. The durations of each movement are listed on the verso of the container and in the booklet (not reproduced here). Although it would be perfectly feasible to add together the stated durations of the various works, MCD 6.5B2 indicates this should not be done for recordings that contain more than one work. Consequently, statements of extent for each work are created for the contents note by adding the individual durations together.

The program notes are noted in this instance only because they accompany the words of the Mass, which are separately printed in both Slavonic and English. (Note that the Library of Congress uses the term "Old Church Slavic" for "Church Slavonic".)

Example 14

Deutsche
Grammophon

STEREO   419050-2
Ⓟ 1977

LUDWIG VAN BEETHOVEN
Symphonie No. 2 op. 36
Symphonie No. 7 op. 92

Berliner Philharmoniker
Herbert von Karajan

On container:

    Ludwig van Beethoven
    Symphonien Nr. 2 & 7
    Berliner Philharmoniker
    Herbert von Karajan

    GALLERIA
    Digitally Remastered

Program notes (6 pages) in container.

On back cover of booklet: © 1986

Durations on container verso.

Example 14

```
     Symphonie No. 2, op. 36 [sound recording] ; Symphonie
No. 7, op. 92 / Ludwig van Beethoven. -- Hamburg :
Deutsche Grammophon, [1986], p1977.
     1 sound disc : digital, stereo. ; 4 3/4 in. --
(Galleria)
     Deutsche Grammophon: 419 050-2.
     Berliner Philharmoniker ; Herbert von Karajan,
conductor.
     Recorded 1977; "digitally remastered."
     Compact disc.
     Durations: 31 min., 6 sec. ; 35 min., 5 sec.
```

This compact disc contains two works by the same composer. Although the container presents a collective title that the disc itself does not, the MCD for 6.0B1 instructs us to disregard the collective title, thus the label is preferred as the chief source of information for the title transcription. Note that the title consists of the name of a type of composition, so the work numbering is treated as title proper data, not as other title information.

This recording is produced from a digital remastering of a performance originally captured on analog tape, which is noted by quoting from the container.

The durations of the works are stated and could have been added together to produce a statement of extent in the physical description, but once again according to MCD 6.5B2 we are instructed not to give the information there.

Note that a true series statement appears on the container and is transcribed into area 6.

The program notes, which occur in four languages and occupy the accompanying booklet, are disregarded for this description, because they do not contain any substantial or unique information.

Example 15

Contents and durations on container verso.

Also on container verso:

Recorded at the State University of New York at Purchase, Recital Hall, June 1993

Example 15

```
    John Corigliano, Alec Wilder [sound recording]. --
Westbury, NY : Koch International Classics, p1994.
    1 sound disc : digital ; 4 3/4 in.
    Koch International Classics: 3-7187-2HI.
    Oboe music.
    Brooklyn Philharmonic ; Michael Barrett, conductor ;
Humbert Lucarelli, oboe ; Mark Wood, percussion (sixth
work).
    Recorded at the State University of New York at
Purchase Recital Hall, June 1993.
    Compact disc.
    Contents: The winter's past / Wayne Barlow (5:15) --
Concerto for oboe, orchestra and percussion / Alec Wilder
(20:33) -- Requiem ; Narrative / Robert Bloom (6:51 ;
6:31) -- Aria for oboe and strings / John Corigliano
(6:20) -- Piece for oboe and improvisatory percussion /
Alec Wilder (4:16).
```

This recording apparently was produced to emphasize its primary contents, which are oboe works by Corigliano and Wilder. The disc label contains no title information other than the names of these two composers and the performer statements of responsibility. The cover of the booklet (which appears as the container cover, and which is not reproduced here) has some title information but only for the Wilder and Corigliano works. This is a good example of a case where the transcription creates a surrogate of the disc but is not particularly informative about the contents of the recording, which must be spelled out in the notes area.

Once again there is no statement of extent in area 4, according to MCD 6.5B2, because there is more than one work on the recording.

Example 16

john mellencamp   dance naked
dance naked (3:00)
brothers (3:14)
when Margaret comes to town (3:20)
wild night (3:28)
l.u.v. (2:59)
another sunny day 12/25 (3:02)
too much to think about (3:02)
the big jack (3:23)
the breakout (3:38)

MERCURY   314 522 428-2

produced by john mellencamp and michael wanchic
1,2,3,5,7 written by john mellencamp
4 written by van morrison
6,8,9 written by john mellencamp/george green

Around circumference of disc:

℗© 1994 JOHN MELLENCAMP
MANUFACTURED AND MARKETED BY
POLYGRAM RECORDS, INC.,
NEW YORK, NEW YORK

Example 16

```
      Dance naked [sound recording] / John Mellencamp. --
New York, N.Y. : Mercury, p1994.
      1 sound disc : digital ; 4 3/4 in.
      Mercury: 314 522 428-2.
      Rock music.
      John Mellencamp, with accompaniment; produced by John
Mellencamp and Machael Wanchic; works by Mellencamp, Van
Morrison (4th work), and Mellencamp and George Green
(6th, 8-9th works).
      Words printed as text in container.
      Recorded at Belmont Mall Studio, Belmont, Ind., 1994.
      Compact disc.
      Contents: Dance naked (3:00) -- Brothers (3:14) --
When Margaret comes to town (3:20) -- Wild night / with
Me'shell Ndegéocello (3:28) -- L.u.v. (2:59) -- Another
sunny day 12/25 (3:02) -- Too much to think about (3:02)
-- The big jack (3:23) -- The breakout (3:38).
```

This rock recording was quite popular in the summer of 1994, as Mellencamp conducted a national tour to promote it. Notice that the recording really constitutes a work in several movements *produced* by Mellencamp and Wanchin. It also is true, however, that the individual songs have diverse authorship, as is noted directly on the disc.

A minor point: notice that the place is given on the disc and container as New York, New York; therefore, in area 4 we use the approved abbreviation from AACR 2 Appendix B.

No statement of extent is given in area 5.

A great deal of information about the personnel performing each piece appears in the booklet in the container (not reproduced here); a library collection devoted to rock music might warrant a more fulsome description than is given in this example. For instance, performers names could be combined into a statement of responsibility note:

```
Kenny Aronoff, drums & percussion ; John Mellencamp and
Andy York, guitars ; Mike Wanchic and Missy, backing
vocals ; Toby Myers, bass ; Andy York and Mike Wanchic,
organ ....
```

Example 17

MUSIC FROM THE MOTION PICTURE
PHILADELPHIA

1. Streets of Philadelphia (3:51)
Bruce Springsteen
PERFORMED BY BRUCE SPRINGSTEEN

2. Lovetown (5:27)
Peter Gabriel
PERFORMED BY PETER GABRIEL

3. It's in your eyes (3:44)
LeRonald Walker Samuel Waymon
PERFORMED BY PAULETTE WASHINGTON

4. Ibo Lele (Dreams come true) (4:13)
Richard Mores
PERFORMED BY RAM

5. Please send me someone to love (3:42)
Percy Mayfield
PERFOMED BY SADE

6. Have you ever seen the rain   (2:39)
John Fogerty
PERFORMED BY SPIN DOCTORS

7. I don't wanna talk about it (3:36)
Danny Whitten
PERFORMED BY INDIGO GIRLS

8. La Mamma Morta (4:48)
Umberto Giordano
PERFORMED BY MARIA CALLAS

9. Philadelphia (4:03)
Neil Young
PERFORMED BY NEIL YOUNG

10. Precedent (4:04)
MUSIC COMPOSED AND CONDUCTED BY HOWARD
SHORE

EPIC SOUNDTRAX
EK 57624

Around circumference of disc:

Motion Picture Artwork Title: ©1993 TriStar Pictures, Inc. ...
©1993 Sony Music Enterntainment Inc./℗ 1993 Sony Music Enterntainment Inc. ...

Example 17

> Music from the motion picture Philadelphia [sound recording]. -- New York, NY : Epic Soundtrax, p1993.
>   1 sound disc : digital ; 4 3/4 in.
>   Epic Sountrax: EK 57624.
>   Music from the TriStar motion picture.
>   Words for Streets of Philadelphia and Philadelphia printed as text in container.
>   Contents: Streets of Philadelphia / Bruce Springsteen ; performed by Bruce Springsteen (3:51) -- Lovetown / Peter Gabriel ; performed by Peter Gabriel (5:27) -- It's in your eyes / LeRonald Walker, Samuel Waymon ; performed by Paulette Washington (3:44) -- Ibo Lele = Dreams come true / Richard Mores ; performed by RAM (4:13) -- Please send me someone to love / Percy Mayfield ; perfomed by Sade (3:42) -- Have you ever seen the rain? / John Fogerty ; performed by Spin Doctors (2:39) -- I don't wanna talk about it / Danny Whitten ; performed by Indigo Girls (3:36) -- La Mamma Morta / Umberto Giordano ; performed by Maria Callas (4:48) -- Philadelphia / Neil Young ; performed by Neil Young (4:03) -- Precedent / music composed and conducted by Howard Shore (4:04).

Motion pictures and the music used in them can be quite complex. This is the motion picture music from the recent film, released on compact disc. The description is straightforward and all derived from data on the disc itself. Note the detail concerning the complexity of attribution for this music. All of it is recorded in this contents note because it appears on the disc.

Example 18

Label side 1:

angel
Wagner: Wesendonk Lieder
1. Der Engel • 2. Stehe still!
3. Im Treibhaus • 4. Schmerzen • 5. Traume

JANET BAKER (mezzo-Soprano)
LONDON PHILHARMONIC ORCHESTRA,
SIR ADRIAN BOULD, cond.

Recorded in England
℗ 1976 EMI Records Limited
RL-1-32017 (SQ-1-37199)
STEREO 33-1/3

Label side 2:

angel
Richard Strauss:
1. Liebshymnus • 2. Ruhe, meine Seele!
3. Das Rosenband • 4. Muttertändelei
Brahms: 5. Alto Rhapsody, Op. 53

JANET BAKER (mezzo-Soprano)
LONDON PHILHARMONIC ORCHESTRA,
SIR ADRIAN BOULD, cond.
5. with the John Alldis Choir
Recorded in England
℗ 1976, 1971 EMI Records Limited
RL-2-32017 (SQ-2-37199)
STEREO 33-1/3

On container:

Janet Baker
BRAHMS: ALTO RHAPSODY
WAGNER: WESENDONK LIEDER
STRAUSS: FOUR SONGS

SIR ADRIAN BOULT
London Philharmonic Orchestra
*The John Alldis Choir

Enclosed: German texts & English translation

Program notes and durations on container verso.

Example 18

```
     Janet Baker [sound recording]. -- [Los Angeles,
Calif.] : Angel, p1976.
     1 sound disc : analog, 33 1/3 rpm, quad. ; 12 in.
     Angel: RL-32017 (SQ 37199).
     Title from container.
     Janet Baker, mezzo-soprano ; London Philharmonic
Orchestra ; Sir Adrian Boult, conductor ; The John Alldis
Choir.
     Song texts in German with English translations ([4] p.
; 28 cm.) inserted.
     Contents: Wesendonk Lieder / Wagner ; texts by
Mathilde Wesendonk (22:59) -- Liebeshymnus : op. 32, no.
3 (1:59) ; Rühe, meine Seele : op. 27, no. 1 (4:26) /
Richard Strauss ; Klopstock (3:26) -- Muttertändelei :
op. 43, no. 2 / Richard Strauss ; Burger (2:11) --
Rhapsody for contralto, male chorus and orchestra, op. 53
/ Brahms ; Goethe (11:40).
```

This LP recording is an example of the use of the performer's name as presented on the container as a collective title. Because that collective title is not provided by the labels, the container is preferred as chief source of information.

Note also the physical description of this quadrophonic recording—the information about other physical details—is transcribed from the labels. No statement of extent is given.

Example 19

Label side 1:

> **FOLKWAYS Records**
> AND SERVICE CORP., 43 W. 61st ST., NYC 10023
> Long Playing Non-Breakable Micro Groove 33 1/3 RPM
> **EARLY AMERICAN FOLK**
> **MUSIC AND SONGS**
> **by CLARK JONES**
> **Produced by JOHN R. CRAIG**
>
> SIDE 1   FTS 31091 A
>   Stereo
>
> 1. Rhododendron 2:16
> 2. The Rich Lady Over The Sea 2:30
> 3. I Will Give My Love An Apple 4:05
> 4. Under the Magnolia 1:51
> 5. The Holly Bears A Berry 3:44
> 6. Rye Whiskey 2:53
> 7. John Barleycorn 2:54
> 8. The Paw-Paw Patch :30
>
> ℗©1982 Folkways Records and Service Corp.

Label side 2:

> **FOLKWAYS Records**
> AND SERVICE CORP., 43 W. 61st ST., NYC 10023
> Long Playing Non-Breakable Micro Groove 33 1/3 RPM
> **EARLY AMERICAN FOLK**
> **MUSIC AND SONGS**
> **by CLARK JONES**
> **Produced by JOHN R. CRAIG**
>
> SIDE 2   FTS 31091 B
>   Stereo
>
> 1. Watermelon Suite 2:08
> 2. Beans, Bacon And Gravy 2:15
> 3. The Seeds Of Love 4:02
> 4. Aiken Drum 3:16
> 5. The Cherry Tree Carol 4:08
> 6. Young Man Who Wouldn't Hoe Corn 1:30
> 7. The Praties They Grow Small 2:05
> 8. Simple Gifts 1:23
>
> ℗©1982 Folkways Records and Service Corp.

On container verso: ABOUT THE SONGS [...]

5 p ; inserted in container: ABOUT THE ARTIST [...]

Example 19

```
    Early American folk music and songs [sound recording]
/ [performed] by Clark Jones. -- N[ew] Y[ork] C[ity] :
Folkways Records, p1982.
    1 sound disc : analog, 33 1/3 rpm, stereo. ; 12 in.
    Folkways Records: FTS 31091.
    Clark Jones, vocals, hammered dulcimer, banjo,
mountain dulcimer, and guitar.
    Program notes on container; biographical and
descriptive notes (5 p.) in container.
    Contents: Rhododendron (2:16) -- The rich lady over
the sea (2:30) -- I will give my love an apple (4:05) --
Under the magnolia (1:51) -- The holly bears a berry
(3:44) -- Rye whiskey (2:53) -- John Barleycorn (2:54) --
The paw-paw patch (:30) -- Watermelon suite (2:08) --
Beans, bacon, and gravy (2:15) -- The seeds of love
(4:02) -- Aiken drum (3:16) -- The cherry tree carol
(4:08) -- Young man who wouldn't hoe corn (1:30) -- The
praties they grow small (2:05) -- Simple gifts (1:23).
```

This recording is typical of the Folkways series of ethnic LP recordings from the 1970s and 1980s. Note that the word "by" is presented on the label in the sense that the *recording* (i.e., not the music) is by Jones. A simple emendation in square brackets clarifies Jones' role in the statement of responsibility. No statement of extent is given.

Example 20

Label side 1:

**"DEDICATED TO
THE ONE I LOVE"**
(Lowman Pauling, Ralph Bass)

THE TEMPREES
Produced by Jo Bridges & Tom Nixon
Arranged by Lester Snell & Tom Nixon

   **STX-1026**
STX-1026-A

Trousdale Music, BMI
Time: 3:32 (Intro 0:12)
℗1977 STAX Records
DISTRIBUTED BY
FANTASY RECORDS, BERKELEY, CALIFORNIA

Label side 2:

"EXPLAIN IT TO HER MAMA"
(Cleophus Fultz & Leon Moore)

THE TEMPREES
Produced & Arranged by
Jo Bridges & Tom Nixon
Rhythm by
We Produced Band

STX-1026
STX-1026-B

Stripe Musi East/Memphis Music, BMI
Time: 2:57 (Intro 0:08)
℗ 1977 STAX Records
DISTRIBUTED BY
FANTASY RECORDS, BERKELEY, CALIFORNIA

On paper sleeve: *"**Double** HITTER"*

45 rpm. ; 7 in.

Example 20

```
     Dedicated to the one I love [sound recording] / Lowman
Pauling, Ralph Bass ; [performed by] The Temprees ;
arranged by Lester Snell & Tom Nixon.  Explain it to her
Mama / Cleophus Fultz & Leon Moore ; arranged by Jo
Bridges & Tom Nixon ; [performed by] The Temprees ;
rhythm by We Produced Band. -- [United States] :  Stax
Records ; Berkeley, Calif. : distributed by Fantasy
Records, p1977.
     1 sound disc : analog, 45 rpm ; 7 in. -- (Double
hitter)
     Stax: STX-1026.
     Soul music.
     Durations: 3:32; 2:57.
```

This 45 rpm recording illustrates the difficulties of transcription and the potential complexity of entry for popular music recordings. Note the recurrence of the statement of responsibility for the performing group, which appears in conjunction with each title on each label. No statement of extent is given.

Example 21

Label side 1:

BRAHMS PROGRAM 1
1. First Movement: Allegro non troppo
2. Second movement: Andante moderato

Critics Choice
STEREO   QUINTESSENCE   P4C-7094

Label side 2:

BRAHMS PROGRAM 2
1. Third Movement: Allegro giocoso
2. Fourth movement: Allegro energico e passionato

Critics Choice
STEREO   QUINTESSENCE   P4C-7094

On container:

Critics Choice

BRAHMS
SYMPHONY NO. 4 IN E MINOR, OP. 98
DIETRICH FISCHER-DIESKAU CONDUCTING
THE CZECH PHILHARMONIC ORCHESTRA
P4C-7094
DOLBY SYSTEM
QUINTESSENCE

On container verso:

QUINTESSENCE
BRAHMS: SYMPHONY NO. 4 IN E MINOR, OP. 98
DIETRICH FISCHER-DIESKAU CONDUCTING
THE CZECH PHILHARMONIC ORCHESTRA

P4C-7094
STEREO
Made in U.S.A.

BRAHMS PROGRAM 1
1. First Movement: Allegro non troppo
2. Second movement: Andante moderato

BRAHMS PROGRAM 2
1. Third Movement: Allegro giocoso
2. Fourth movement: Allegro energico e passionato
DIETRICH FISCHER-DIESKAU CONDUCTING
THE CZECH PHILHARMONIC ORCHESTRA

1 "standard" cassette tape.

Example 21

```
    Symphony no. 4 in E minor, op. 98 [sound recording] /
Brahms. -- [Minneapolis, Minn.] : Quintessence, [197-?]
    1 sound cassette : analog, stereo., Dolby processed.
-- (Critic's choice)
    Quintessence: P4C-7094.
    Title from container.
    Czech Philharmonic Orchestra ; Dietrich Fischer-
Dieskau, conductor.
```

This is a typical cassette recording. Note that there is no title information on the cassette itself.

Example 22

Label side 1:

LINDA RONSTADT • WHAT'S NEW

Side One: WHAT'S NEW • I'VE GOT A CRUSH ON YOU •
GUESS I'LL HANG MY TEARS OUT TO DRY • CRAZY HE
CALLS ME • SOMEONE TO WATCH OVER ME

Produced by PETER ASHER
Arranged & conducted by NELSON RIDDLE
Recorded & mixed by GEORGE MASSENBURG

DOLBY STEREO
60260-4
asylum

Label side 2:

LINDA RONSTADT • WHAT'S NEW

Side Two: I DON'T STAND A GHOST OF A CHANCE
WITH YOU • WHAT'LL I DO • LOVER MAN (OH
WHERE CAN YOU BE) • GOOD-BYE

Produced by PETER ASHER
Arranged & conducted by NELSON RIDDLE
Recorded & mixed by GEORGE MASSENBURG

DOLBY STEREO
60260-4
asylum

On container insert:

WHAT'S NEW
ARRANGED & CONDUCTED BY NELSON RIDDLE
PRODUCED BY PETER ASHER
RECORDED & MIXED BY GEORGE MASSENBURG
Assisted by **Barbara Boosey** & **Robert Spane**
Recorded at The Complex (L.A.) June 30th, 1982 — March 4th, 1983
Mastered by **Doug Sax** *at the Mastering Lab (L.A.)*
Photography by **Brian Aris**
Art direction and design by **Josh** *with* **Ron Larson**
Album coordination by **Gloria Boyce**
Special thanks to George for his help with the vocals, and to
John Neal for his advice during the recording

Piano: **Don Grolnick**
Guitar: **Tommy Tedesco** *or* **Dennis Budimir**
Bass: **Ray Brown** *or* **James Hughart**
Drums: **John Guerin**
Concertmasters: **Leonard Atkins** & **Nathan Ross**

Verso container insert: ℗ 1983
1 "standard" cassette

Example 22

```
    What's new [sound recording] / Linda Ronstadt ;
arranged & conducted by Nelson Riddle. -- [New York,
N.Y.] : Asylum, p1983.
    1 sound cassette : analog, stereo., Dolby processed.
    Asylum: 60260-4.
    Linda Ronstadt, vocals ; Nelson Riddle Orchestra ;
Nelson Riddle, conductor.
    Recorded at the Complex, Los Angeles, June 30, 1982-
Mar. 4, 1983.
    Contents: What's new -- I've got a crush on you --
Guess I'll hang my tears out to dry -- Crazy he calls me
-- Someone to watch over me -- I don't stand a ghost of a
chance with you -- What I'll do -- Lover man (oh where
can you be) -- Good bye.
```

A cassette issue of this popular music recording. Note that Riddle's name is transcribed in the statement of responsibility because he is given credit for the arrangements (orchestrations) of these songs. The physical description is limited because this is a standard cassette.

SUMMARY

Description of sound recordings begins with technical reading of the disc and container in order to select the chief source of information and to gain a clear understanding of the commercial aspects of the recording. This will help in decision-making about the level of detail to be recorded in contents notes, and in the number and type of access points to be made.

Most data that appear in the description are transcribed from the disc itself, except for rare instances of containers that provide collective titles. This appears to be less of a problem with compact discs than it was in the past with LP or 78 rpm discs. Only some statements of responsibility may be transcribed into area 1 of the description (e.g., composers of Western art music; performers whose work is considered improvisatory). The label name, which is not necessarily the same as the name of the publisher, is given in area 4 of the description. The date given in area 4 should be the date of release of the recording, usually represented with the phonogram copyright symbol ℗.

Physical description is rote, with the exception of recordings containing one work in several movements, for which the durations of the movements are to be added together to produce a statement of extent of item. No such statement is given for other recordings unless it appears on the item and can be transcribed.

Extensive notes usually will be called for to record the label name and number, identify the performers, describe the works performed and the performance recorded, and then to describe the contents of the recording in detail.

CHAPTER 3: DESCRIPTION OF MUSIC VIDEORECORDINGS

INTRODUCTION: THE PROCESS

The steps in description of music videorecordings are as follows:

1. Technical reading of the videorecording (usually a cassette) and its container, to determine the musical and visual content of the video and to select the chief and prescribed sources of information; if a videocassette recorder is available the video should be viewed;

2. Transcription of the title and statement of responsibility area from the chief source of information, preferably the title frames and credits;

3. Transcription of the publication, distribution, etc., data, usually found on the container;

4. Physical description of the videocassette;

5. Transcription of series data;

6. Making notes as appropriate.

TECHNICAL READING OF MUSIC VIDEOCASSETTES

Music videorecordings are first and foremost videorecordings. Many are issued by divisions of record companies, many take on the appearance of sound recordings, and, indeed, many relate themselves to similar audiorecordings. However, the cardinal principle of description in AACR 2 is to *describe the item in hand* (0.24); therefore it is important that the music cataloger approach music videos not just from the point of view of their musical value, but primarily from their true nature as motion pictures.

Therefore, technical reading of videorecordings must incorporate thorough examination of the container, and the cassette label, and visual examination of the videorecording. Sources of information will be diverse—similar but often variant details will be given in the different sources—and will not necessarily be sequential. That is, title data might occur in title frames at the beginning of a recording, or it might be dispersed throughout the recording. Occasionally it occurs only in credits at the end of the recording. As the recording is examined it is wise to make judicious use of the pause button and jot down the relevant data as they appear in the source.

Videorecordings in music collections fall into four categories that affect the way in which the musical content is reflected and is to be treated in the catalog. First, the video might be a recording of a staged performance. If so, it is possible that there will be a corresponding audiorecording of the same performance. While the basic bibliographic descriptions for the two would differ greatly because they are fundamentally different items, the same musical information would be useful to create access to both recordings. Also, the bibliographic details will be focussed more on the staged performance (the performers and the music) than on the visual aspects per se. A second major category of music video is the musical film, produced for theatrical release or perhaps for television. In this case, bibliographic details will be more like those of a motion picture and will be focussed more on the visual aspects of the production (the producer, director, screenplay, etc.). A third category is the field recording, produced for educational purposes to record indigenous music. Finally, the fourth category common in music collections is the locally produced, unpublished, recording of a performance.

In general, videos that fall into the first and fourth categories tend to bear few or no inherent bibliographic details. Certainly this is the case for the locally produced, unpublished, recording of a staged performance. Whatever is known about the production will be supplied primarily from accompanying materials. This is often true of field recordings as well. However, professionally produced motion pictures will be quite different—title and statements of reponsibility concerning the production, direction, and screenplay probably will appear in sequential title frames, while cast and crew as well as other contributors will be identified in credit frames at the end. Also, professional motion picture productions often are quite fanciful or at least artistic in their display of bibliographic data so the cataloger must use common sense and judgment, particularly in the "transcription" of titles.

CHOOSING THE CHIEF SOURCE OF INFORMATION

Basically, rule 7.0B2 makes it clear that the chief source of information for a videorecording may be the entire package, although a table of preference is given in the rule that establishes an order in which title frames are preferred, but cassette labels (or data imprinted on laserdiscs) are acceptable as secondary sources. Accompanying textual material and the container also may be used to provide bibliographic data that are not available from title frames or a cassette label.

TITLE AND STATEMENT OF RESPONSIBILITY AREA

The title and statement of responsibility should be transcribed, preferably from title frames with reference to the examples at 7.1B1 and the instructions at 1.1B. Words preceding the title proper may be omitted following the LCRI for 7.1B1.

7.1B1 LCRI When credits for performer, author, director, producer, "presenter," etc., precede or follow the title in the chief source, in general do not consider them as part of the title proper, even though the language used integrates the credits with the title. (In the examples below the [italicized] words are to be considered the title proper.)

> Twentieth Century Fox presents *Star wars*
> Steve McQueen in *Bullitt*
> Ed Asner as *Lou Grant*
> Jerry Wald's production of *The Story on page one*
> *Ordinary people* starring Mary Tyle Moore and Donald Sutherland
> *Thief*, with James Caan

This does not apply to the following cases:

> 1) the credit is *within* the title, rather than preceding or following it;

> > CBS special report
> > IBM--close up
> > IBM puppet shows

2) the credit is actually a fanciful statement aping a credit;

> Little Roquefort in Good mousekeeping

3) the credit is represented by a possessive immediately preceding the remainder of the title.

> Neil Simon's Seems like old times

(*CSB* 13: 15)

If the item lacks a title, rules 7.1B2 and 1.1B7 may be used to supply a title. The option in 7.1B2 directs the cataloger to supply description of the action and length of each shot in an unedited film (such as a newsfilm) in a note.

> **7.1B2 LCRI** *Option Decision*. Apply the optional provision of the rule on a case-by-case basis. (*CSB* 8: 11)

GENERAL MATERIAL DESIGNATION (GMD)

The Library of Congress uses the general material designation "videorecording" for all videos. The GMD should immediately follow the title proper.

> **7.1C LCRI** *Optional addition*. General material designation. See LCRI 1.1C. Optional addition. General material designation. (*CSB* 47: 36)

STATEMENT OF RESPONSIBILITY

Statements of responsibility concerning the video's production—producer, director, writer of screenplay, etc.—are transcribed in the statement of responsibility in area 1 according to rule 7.1F1. Performers (i.e., the stars of the film) are identified in a note.

> **7.1F1 LCRI** When deciding whether to give names in the statement of responsibility (7.1F1, 8.1F1) or in a note, generally give the names in the statement of responsibility when the person or body has some degree of overall responsibility; use the note area for others who are responsible for only one segment or one aspect of the work. Be liberal about making exceptions to the general policy when the person's or body's responsibility is important in relation to the content of the work, i.e., give such important people and bodies in the statement of responsibility even though they may have only partial responsibility. For example, the name of a rock music performer who is the star of a performance on a videorecording may be given in the statement of responsibility even if his/her responsibility is limited to the performance.

> > Ain't that America / John Couger Mellencamp

> Normally the Library of Congress considers producers, directors, and writers (or, in the case of slides and transparencies, authors, editors, and compilers) as having some degree of overall responsibility and gives [their names] in the statement of responsibility. (*CSB* 36: 12)

ITEMS WITHOUT A COLLECTIVE TITLE

7.1G1 LCRI Describe the item as a unit or make a description for each separately titled work, whichever solution seems better in the particular situation. (*CSB* 38: 32)

7.1G4 LCRI Option Decision. See LCRI 7.1G1. (*CSB* 47: 36)

EDITION AREA

Edition statements are rare in videorecordings; if encountered they should be transcribed into area 2 using the rules at 7.2.

7.2B3 LCRI *Optional addition.* Apply the option according to the statements in LCRI 1.2B4. (*CSB* 47: 37)

7.2B4 LCRI *Option Decision.* Do not apply the optional provision of the rule. (*CSB* 34: 26)

PUBLICATION, DISTRIBUTION, ETC., AREA

Record the place of publication, publisher name, and date of publication (usually a copyright date) as instructed in 7.4 and 1.4. Give neither a place name nor the abbreviation *s.l.* for an unpublished videorecording. If a distributor is named in the prescribed source of information in addition to a publisher, give both, and if it isn't clear how each named entity functions add a term in square brackets to clarify their functions.

7.4C LCRI Do not apply the option stated in 1.4C7 for adding the full address of a publisher, distributor, etc., when cataloging materials covered by chapters 7 and 8. (*CSB* 13: 16)

7.4D1 LCRI *Option Decision.* Apply the optional provision of the rule. (*CSB* 47: 37)

7.4E LCRI *Optional addition.* Statement of function of publisher, distributor, etc. See LCRI 1.4E. Optional addition. Statement of function of publisher, distributor, etc. (*CSB* 47: 37)

7.4F2 LCRI Give a date of original production differing from the dates of publication/distribution or copyright, etc., in the note area (see 7.7B9 and 8.7B9). Apply the provision if the difference is greater than two years.

> Santa Monica, CA : Pyramid Films, 1971.
> *Note*: Made in 1934.

(When dealing with different media, see 7.7B7 and 8.7B7.) (*CSB* 33: 37)

7.4G2 LCRI Optional addition. See LCRI 1.4G4. Optional addition. (*CSB* 47: 37)

PHYSICAL DESCRIPTION AREA

Three common elements are used to create a physical description of a videorecording: specific material designation and extent of item, other physical details, and dimensions.

Begin the physical description area using an arabic numeral and the specific material designation "videocasette" or "videodisc" (see also other specific material designations for visual materials at 7.5B1). Give the duration of the video, if it is stated on the item, as a statement of extent of item. The LC option decision (not reproduced here) is not to apply the option in 7.5B1; therefore, use the terms videocassette, videodisc, etc. Give a statement of extent by giving the playing time as stated on the item.

```
1 videocassette (65 min.)
1 videodisc (105 min.)
```

The options in rule 7.5B2 apply to videodiscs consisting of still images. An LCRI applies:

7.5B2 LCRI *Option Decision.* Apply both options on a case-by-case basis. (*CSB* 47: 37)

The net effect of this LCRI is that if the number of frames of still images on a videodisc is available, give it as a statement of extent when no playing time is stated on the item, or give it in a note if playing time is given in area 5.

The second element of physical description, other physical details, involves indicating whether sound and color are present.

```
1 videocassette (65 min.) : sd., col.
1 videodisc (105 min.) : sd., col. with b&w
sequences
```

The final part of physical description is the statement of dimensions. Describe standard commercial videocassettes as "1/2 in." and give the diameter of a videodisc in inches.

```
1 videocassette (65 min.) : sd., col. ; 1/2 in.
1 videodisc (105 min.) : sd., col. with b&w
sequences ; 12 in.
```

SERIES AREA

Record series statements as instructed in 1.6.

NOTES AREA

Notes are made to amplify details about the musical content, the performance, and the physical characteristics of the videocassette that are not apparent from the transcribed data that appear in areas 1 through 6. Notes also are made to establish the bibliographic identity of the item described (such as the relationship between sound and videorecordings of the same performance or between a motion picture and videocassette release of the same visual material). All notes serve to allow users to select likely candidates for retrieval from among otherwise similar or identical bibliographic descriptions.

ORDER OF NOTES

The list below is intended to serve as a guide for the order of notes in bibliographic records for music videos. Remember that many of these notes are used only to explain or otherwise elucidate information contained in the preceding areas of the description. Note that the order is the order in which the rules appear in chapter 7.

Nature or form (7.7B1)
Language (7.7B2)
Source of title proper (7.7B3)
Variations in title (7.7B4)
Parallel titles and other title information (7.7B5)
Statements of responsibility; cast and credits (7.7B6)
Edition and history (7.7B7)
Publication, distribution, etc., and date (7.7B9)
Physical description (7.7B10)
Accompanying material (7.7B11)
Series (7.7B12)
Dissertation note (7.7B13)
Audience (7.7B14)
Other formats (7.7B16)
Summary (7.7B17)
Contents (7.7B18)
Numbers (7.7B19)
Copy being described, library's holdings, and restrictions on use (7.7B20)

NATURE OR FORM

In this first note identify the performance in musical *and* visual terms as specifically as possible. Imagine that the bibliographic record you are creating will be found among many bibliographic records for non-musical motion pictures—in such a case a user might reasonably assume the video described contained a motion picture unless you indicate otherwise.

```
        Rock music, performed by The Bottle Rockets ....
```

Or, imagine that the bibliographic record you are creating will be found among many bibliographic records for sound recordings—in such a case a user will need information about the visual aspects of the performance.

```
        Rock music, performed by The Bottle Rockets in
        concert at the Mercury Lounge, New York NY,
        December 1994.
            Music video, featuring the band Megadeth.
```

LANGUAGE

7.7B2 LCRI If the videorecording incorporates closed-captioning for the hearing impaired, make the following note:

> Closed-captioned for the hearing impaired.

(*CSB* 32: 14)

SOURCE OF TITLE PROPER

Be certain to identify the source of the title transcription if it is other than the title frames. This will be particularly important in distinguishing variant manifestations in a union catalog.

```
Title from cassette label.
```

VARIATIONS IN TITLE

7.7B4 LCRI *Option Decision.* Do not apply the optional provision of the rule. (*CSB* 47: 37)

STATEMENTS OF RESPONSIBILITY; CAST AND CREDITS

A well-developed LCRI gives details on which names to include in this note. Remember that we have been somewhat circumspect in transcribing names into a statement of responsibility in area 1 of the description. This note is used to identify all other important contributors whose names might be used as added entries for the bibliographic record.

7.7B6 LCRI For audiovisual items, generally list persons (other than producers, directors, and writers) or corporate bodies who have contributed to the artistic and technical production of a work in a credits note (see LCRI 7.1F1).

Give the [names of the] following persons or bodies in the order in which they are listed below. Preface each name or group of names with the appropriate term(s) of function.

> photographer(s); camera; cameraman/men; cinematographer
> animator(s)
> artist(s); illustrator(s); graphics
> film editor(s); photo editor(s); editor(s)
> narrator(s); voice(s)
> music
> consultant(s); adviser(s)

(*CSB* 22: 21)

EDITION AND HISTORY

7.7B7, 8.7B7 LCRI When an item is known to have an original master in a different medium and the production or release date of the master is more than two years earlier than that of the item being cataloged, give an edition/history note.

> Originally produced as motion picture in [year]
> Originally issued as filmstrip in [year]

Make a similar note when an item is known to have been previously produced or issued (more than two years earlier) if in a different medium, but the original medium is unknown.

> Previously produced as motion picture in [year]
> Previously issued as slide set in [year]

If the date of production or release of an original master or an earlier medium is unknown or if the difference between its production or release date and the production or release date of the item being cataloged is two years or less, indicate the availability of the other medium or media in a note according to 7.7B16 and 8.7B16.

> Produced also as slide set.
> Issued also as slide set and videorecording.

Note: The use of production versus release dates is left to the cataloger's judgment. Make the note that seems best to give information about either production or release of other formats on a case-by-case basis. (*CSB* 15: 6-7)

SUMMARY

Summary notes are common in bibliographic records for visual materials, perhaps owing to the influence of educational materials in the compilation of rules for cataloging films and videos. Perusal of bibliographic records for music videos in the bibliographic utilities leads to the conclusion, however, that summary notes are rare on bibliographic records for music videos with the possible exception of those for operatic productions. One rule of thumb might be that if the video tells a story a summary note should be made. Otherwise, if the nature of the performance, together with the title and statement of responsibility area (and perhaps individual song titles in a contents note) are sufficient to identify the *work* (the visual performance) then a summary note probably is superfluous.

CONTENTS

Contents notes are particularly important for all bibliographic records that describe collections and for many bibliographic records that describe musical works, therefore they will be of importance for music videos as well. Whenever more than one musical *piece* (i.e., song, aria, movement, etc.) is performed on a recording, or whenever more than one musical piece is given prominence in the item (e.g., when individual songs begin with individual title frames), give the individual titles in a contents note. However, do not give the titles of the arias in an opera that is complete.

Example 23

Cassette label:

RCA/COLUMBIA PICTURES HOME VIDEO
COLUMBIA PICTURES PRESENTS
Tommy VHS/hi-fi/stereo/mono-compatible
{[the movie] appears inside the 'o' in Tommy}
© 1975 The Robert Stigwood Organisation Limited. Approx. 108 mins.

Title frames:

[1]

COLUMBIA PICTURES
HOME ENTERTAINMENT *PRESENTS*

[2]

ROBERT STIGWOOD
PRESENTS

[3]

A FILM BY KEN RUSSELL

[4]

A FILM BY KEN RUSSELL
TOMMY

[5]

A FILM BY KEN RUSSELL
TOMMY
by "THE WHO"

Example 23

Credits:

[1]

TOMMY

[2]

Directed by
KEN RUSSELL

[3]

Produced by
ROBERT STIGWOOD & KEN RUSSELL

[4]

Executive Producers
BERYL VIRTUE & CHRISTOPHER STAMP

[7]

Screenplay by
KEN RUSSELL

[8]

Based upon the rock opera by
PETE TOWNSHEND
Additional Material by
John Entwistle & Keith Moon

[9]

Oliver Reed
Frank
Ann-Margret
Nora
Roger Daltrey
as Tommy
and Featuring
ELTON JOHN
as the Pinball Wizard

© MCMLXXV by the Robert Stigwood Organisation Limited

Example 23

```
      Tommy [videorecording] / by The Who ; directed by Ken
Russell ; produced by Robert Stigwood and Ken Russell ;
screenplay by Ken Russell. -- [United States] : RCA/
Columbia Pictures Home Video, c1975.
      1 videocassette (ca. 108 mins.) : sd., col. ; 1/2 in.
      Based upon the rock opera by Pete Townshend ;
additional material by John Entwistle and Keith Moon.
      Cast: Oliver Reed (Frank), Ann-Margret (Nora), Roger
Daltrey (Tommy), Elton John (Pinball Wizard).
      Summary: Tommy is a boy who is traumatized by the
death of his father, and becomes deaf, dumb, and blind.
The story has Tommy become a "Messiah" after a
miraculous, if bizarre, cure.
```

There is no lack of title information in this motion picture videorecording; however, the problem becomes *how* to transcribe the title information and which bits of the various statements of responsibility to record in area 1 of the description. LCRI 7.1B1 is applied and the title is transcribed from the title frames; however, "A Film by Ken Russell" is ignored in lieu of transcription of proper statements of responsibility from the credits.

No place of publication is given on the cassette or is recognizable on the videorecording, so "United States" is assumed and given in square brackets. Note that in such a case it is not abbreviated to "U.S." because it is not used as an addition to a place name, but rather it is the place name (cf. AACR 2 rule B.14A). The publisher name is transcribed from the cassette label, as is the copyright date.

Notes are made to identify the work from which the screenplay is derived, and to give the major cast members' names. Only those whose names appeared to be featured in the credits have been recorded. The names of the characters they play are given in parentheses.

Example 24

Cassette label:

440 085 557-3
Approximate running time: 65 mins.

Video:

© 1991 Island Records Limited
PolyGram Video
ISLAND Visual Arts

U2 Achtung Baby

the VIDEOS
the CAMEOS
and a whole
lot of
INTERFERENCE
from ZOOtv

HI-FI
STEREO
DIGITALLY
MASTERED
VHS

[FBI warning]

Manufactured and Marketed by PolyGram Video, a division of PolyGram Records, Inc., New York, New York.

No title frames.

Credits:

[1]

U2

bono
lead vocalist, guitar
the edge
guitar, vocals
adam clayton
bass
larry mullen jnr.
drums, percussion
...
all songs music
bono, U2
...
produced by
ned o'hanlon
directed by maurice linnane

Example 24

```
    Achtung Baby [videorecording] : the videos, the
cameos, and a whole lot of interference from ZooTV / U2 ;
produced by Ned O'Hanlon ; directed by Maurice Linnane.
-- New York, N.Y. : Island Visual Arts ; manufactured and
marketed by PolyGram Video, c1991.
    1 videocassette (ca. 65 min.) : sd., col. ; 1/2 in.
    Rock music from the sound recording of the same title,
interspersed with interviews of the musicians.
    Title from container.
    "All songs and music by Bono, U2."
    U2 is Bono, lead vocalist, guitar; The Edge, guitar,
vocals; Adam Clayton, bass; Larry Mullen Jnr., drums,
percussion.
    440 085 557-3.
```

This rock video contains excerpts from concert performances and interviews with the members of U2. There is no title frame other than an image of the album cover for the sound recording *Achtung Baby*, so the cassette label is used as the alternative chief source of information. A note is made to that effect. However, a clear statement of responsibility does appear in credits at the end of the video; that is transcribed in the statement of responsibility area.

Island Visual Arts is taken to be the publisher, or at any rate the "imprint" for this video. Following the LCRI, PolyGram video is transcribed as well as the "distributor."

Notes are made to relate this video to the corresponding sound recording, to identify the members of the band, and to record the videocassette number.

Example 25

Cassette label:

LONDON

CARRERAS DOMINGO PAVAROTTI
in concert
Orchestra del Maggio Musicale Fiorentino
Orchestra del Teatro dell'Opera di Roma
Zubin Mehta
℗ 1990 The Decca Record Company Limited, London
MADE IN USA

071 223-3 LH   DDD   CC   NTSC   VHS   HI-FI STEREO

Title frames:

[1]

**CARRERAS
DOMINGO
PAVAROTTI
MEHTA**

[2]

from CARACALLA
Rome

[3]

with the Orchestras
of
**Maggio Musicale
Fiorentino**
and
**Teatro dell'Opera
Di Roma**

[4]

*A Mario Dradi
presentation*

[5]

Executive Producer
Gian Carlo Bertelli

[6]

Producer
Herbert Chappell

[7]

Director
Brian Large

Example 25

```
    In concert [videorecording] / Carreras, Domingo,
Pavarotti ; executive producer, Gian Carlo Bertelli ;
producer, Herbert Chappell ; director, Brian Large. --
London : London, p1990.
    1 videocassette : sd., col. ; 1/2 in.
    Three tenors in concert from Caracalla, Rome.
    Title from container.
    "A Mario Dradi production."
    With the Orchestras of Maggio Musicale Fiorentino and
Teatro dell'Opera Di Roma ; Zubin Mehta conducting.
    071 223-3 LH.
```

The first problem with this videorecording is identifying the title. The title frame gives the four names CARERRAS DOMINGO PAVAROTTI MEHTA as though that were to be the title. Even the cassette label gives the three tenors' names more prominently than the words "In Concert." However, it makes bibliographic sense for the transcription of title and statement of responsibility to come from the cassette, giving the tenors' names as a statement of responsibility.

Place of publication is straightforward. The name of the video label, or publisher, is London, which is a division of Decca. The phonogram copyright date is transcribed in lieu of a date of publication.

There is no statement on the item about duration, so none is given in area 5.

Contents may be given; the information would have to be transcribed from the container.

Notes are made to identify the orchestras and conductor, to give details of the performance (place and date), and to record the videocassette number.

Example 26

Cassette label:

RCA/COLUMBIA PICTURES
HOME VIDEO
PRESENTS
KOREA 1
©1975 Smithsonian/Folkways Records   48:26

Title frames:

[1]

COLUMBIA PICTURES
presents

KOREA 1

[2]

Producer
ICHIKAUA KATSUMORI

[3]

Director
NAKAGAWA KUNIHIKO
ICHIASHI YUJI

[4]

Produced in collaboration with
The National Museum of Ethnology (Osaka)
and with Smithsonian/Folkways Records

Program booklet:

1. Hyangak : court music 2. Chongjae mugoch'um : drum dance 3. Salp'uri : dance to exercise evil spirits 4. Chakpop Parach'um : cymbal dance 5. Kayagum pyongch'ang : song with kayagum (zither) 6. Chongak 7. Tal'chum 8. Pompae

Suppliers of visual materials 1-7 NHK Service Center; 8 Mainichi Broadcasting System.

Example 26

```
     Korea. 1 [videorecording] / producer Ichikaua
Katsumori ; director[s] Nakagawa Kunihiko, Ichihashi
Yuji. -- [U.S.] : RCA/Columbia Pictures Home Video,
c1975.
     1 videocassette (48 mins., 26 secs.) : sd., col. ; 1/2
in.
     "Produced in collaboration with the National Museum of
Ethnology (Osaka) and with Smithsonian/Folkways Records."
     Suppliers of visual materials 1-7 NHK Service Center;
8 Mainichi Broadcasting System.
     Contents: Hyangak -- Chongjae mugoch'um -- Salp'uri --
Chakpop Parach'um -- Kayagum pyongch'ang -- Chongak --
Tal'chum -- Pompae.
```

On the face of it, this is a fairly straightforward ethnomusicological videorecording presenting the cataloger with few difficult choices. Title and statement of responsibility data are transcribed from title frames, details of publication are provided from the label. Note that rule 1.1B9 is used to transcribe the number "1" as supplementary to the title proper.

There is a second tape *Korea 2* available as well. Our repository holds only this tape, so this cataloging reflects its inherent bibliographic characteristics. Subsequent issues of this tape appear in the *JVC Video Anthology of World Music and Dance* as part of the subseries *East Asia*. Those data are not included in this description, primarily because they were not on the item in hand, but also because traditionally such relationships are described in reverse chronological order. That is, the subsequent issues should point to the description of this, earlier, manifestation.

The collaboration of the National Museum of Ethnology (Osaka) and Smithsonian/Folkways Records is cited in a note. Individual musical segments are identified using the accompanying textual material; these are noted in a contents note.

Example 27

Cassette has no label.

Title frame:

E.G.

Program booklet:

[p. 1]

E.G.
A musical portrait of **Emma Goldman**
Book and lyrics by Karen Ruoff Kramer & Leonard Lehrman
Music by Leonard Lehrman

[p. 3]

A multimedia work commemorating the 125th birthday of the great
Russian•Jewish•American•Feminist•Anarchist, Emma Goldman

Performed at Hillwood Recital Hall, C.W. Post Campus,
Long Island University, June 27, 1994.

Helene Williams *soprano*
Leonard Lehrman *piano*
Russell Simon *slide projectionist*
Richard Riccomini *dancer*

Example 27

>   E.G. [videorecording] : a musical portrait of Emma
> Goldman / book and lyrics by Karen Ruoff Kramer & Leonard
> Lehrman ; music by Leonard Lehrman. -- 1994.
>   1 videocassette : sd., col. ; 1/2 in.
>   Title from program notes.
>   Performed at Hillwood Recital Hall, C.W. Post Campus,
> Long Island University, June 27, 1994.
>   "A multimedia work commemorating the 125th birthday of
> the great Russian Jewish American feminist anarchist,
> Emma Goldman"--Program notes.
>   Cast: Helene Williams, soprano ; Leonard Lehrman,
> piano ; Russell Simon, slide projectionist ; Richard
> Riccomini, dancer.

This video records a local, not-for-profit performance of an unpublished work. The videorecording itself is noncommercially produced, so elements of the instructions in AACR 2 chapter 4 (Manuscripts) are used in addition to the instructions in chapters 6 and 7 to create this description.

SUMMARY

Description of music videos begins with careful examination of the entire item, as well as viewing of the visual material, to gain comprehension of the *visual* and *musical* natures of the performance recorded. Transcription of basic bibliographic data then will ensue based on the chief source of information—the title frames—and will be supplemented using notes that carry information derived from the other, less formal sources of information. Physical description is rote.

Like sound recordings, notes might be extensive, being used to describe the nature and contents of the recorded performance, to list the cast and credits (especially for those important contributors for whom added entries will be made), and to relate the particular publication to other versions, formats, or editions of the film or videorecording.

CHAPTER 4: DESCRIPTION OF INTERACTIVE MULTIMEDIA PACKAGES

Interactive multimedia packages are increasingly presenting challenges to music catalogers. A number of innovative presentations have been marketed for the purposes of enhancing music education and appreciation. While there are no rules at present specifically designed for use with these packages, a draft set of guidelines does exist. These guidelines can be used together (as it were, "interactively") with the advice in the preceding three chapters to help music catalogers describe musical interactive multimedia packages.

The guidelines were promulgated by the Committee on Cataloging: Description and Access of the Cataloging and Classification Section of the American Library Association and published as: *Guidelines for Bibliographic Description of Interactive Multimedia* (Chicago: American Library Assn., 1994). The guidelines define interactive multimedia thus:

> Media residing in one or more physical carriers (videodiscs, computer disks, computer optical discs, computer audio discs, etc.) or on computer networks. Interactive multimedia must exhibit both of these characteristics: (1) user-controlled, nonlinear navigation using computer technology; and (2) the combination of two or more media (audio, text, graphics, images, animation, and video) that the user manipulates to control the order and/or nature of the presentation. (p. 1)

The guidelines continue with several pages of advice about how to identify interactive multimedia. It is important for the cataloger to be aware of the fact that a *work* of interactive multimedia might have been issued in several pieces over time, and thus the several items that contain it might be assembled in the cataloging process.

INTRODUCTION: THE PROCESS

The steps in description of music interactive multimedia packages are as follows:

1. Assembling the package, to make certain all of the parts are together and to understand how the parts work interactively;

2. Technical reading of the entire package—physical components and intellectual components—to determine the musical and visual content, and identification of the chief and prescribed sources of information;

3. Transcription of the title and statement of responsibility area from the chief source of information, preferably the title screen;

4. Transcription of the publication, distribution, etc., data, usually found on the containers or textual material;

5. Physical description of the components;

6. Transcription of series data;

7. Making notes as appropriate.

TECHNICAL READING

Begin by carefully examining the entire physical package. Particularly if there are several items it is likely that there will be variability in the title data and other details of publication. Before you begin the description you will need to be aware of the several locations where title and publication data are found, and you will need to be aware of how they might vary. Examine containers, computer diskette and audio disc labels, accompanying textual matter, etc.

Also, at this time, attempt to understand the capabilities of the package. That is, find out how the various parts may interact with one another, and how a user can interact with the entire system. Because title data might not be very detailed or revealing, it will be important to summarize the functional aspects of the package in notes.

Finally, examine the package's intellectual content by loading it and playing with it. That is, examine the title screen (or screens) to compare title and publication data there with those on the external surfaces that you already have examined. And also at this time check the functionality of the program by testing its various aspects.

CHOOSING THE CHIEF SOURCE OF INFORMATION

According to the *Guidelines*, the chief source of information for an interactive multimedia package is the entire package. This includes both internal sources (title screens, etc.) and external sources (containers, labels, text, etc.). External data (such as publisher's brochures, etc.) may be used to provide bibliographic data that are not available from title frames or a cassette label. For the purposes of transcription of bibliographic data into areas 1-4 and area 6 of the description, select as the chief source that part of the item that has the fullest information (i.e., the title with the most elucidating information, statements of responsibility, etc.).

TITLE AND STATEMENT OF RESPONSIBILITY AREA

In the event that title information varies in the chief source of information (chosen for fullness, as above) transcribe the fullest title proper. In any event, always make a note on the source of the title proper.

The title and statement of responsibility should be transcribed with reference to AACR 2 rules 5.1 and 6.1. That is, if the title proper is a musical title, transcribe it according to the provisions in rule 5.1B1. For example:

> The Magic flute ...

but

> String quartet no. 14, op. 131 ...

GENERAL MATERIAL DESIGNATION (GMD)

The *Guidelines* recommend use of the general material designation "interactive multimedia." The GMD should immediately follow the title proper.

```
The Magic flute [interactive multimedia] ...
String quartet no. 14, op. 131 [interactive
multimedia] ...
```

STATEMENT OF RESPONSIBILITY

Statements of responsibility concerning the production of the interactive multimedia package are transcribed in the statement of responsibility in area 1. Composers of music and performers are identified in a note. This will occasionally result in some odd-looking transcriptions. The music cataloger must remember that this area of description is intended to represent a surrogate for *the item in hand* and is not a citation for any musical work or performance that might be included (which is provided using properly formulated access points).

EDITION AREA

Transcribe an edition statement relating to the entire interactive multimedia package in the edition area. Frequently these statements will include the word "version."

```
IBM version.
```

Neither supply edition statements when none appear in the chief source of information, nor record doubtful statements. Instead, give such statements in a note.

```
Version 3.3a.
```

Likewise, if various parts of the package contain individual edition statements, transcribe such statements as notes, always giving the source of the statement.

```
Ed. statement on computer disk label: Version
3.3a.
```

PUBLICATION, DISTRIBUTION, ETC., AREA

The *Guidelines* give no instructions for the transcription of publication data into area 4. Give the place and name of the publisher according to the rules in AACR 2 1.4B-1.4FE The *Guidelines* do include brief instructions, however, for the selection of dates of publication. According to them, the cataloger is to consider that any dates found anywhere among the parts of the package apply to the entire work. Therefore, the cataloger's task is to locate the *latest* date that appears (as an indication of the most recent formulation of the whole package) and transcribe it. It will be useful for catalogers of sound recordings to remember that the task here is to identify the date of issue of the entire package. The date of any performance included in the package is to be given later, in a note.

PHYSICAL DESCRIPTION AREA

The *Guidelines* refer the cataloger to AACR 2. If there is a single phyiscal item (the *Guidelines* use the term physical carrier), describe it according to the appropriate rules in X.5B. That is, if it is a videodisc use 7.5B; if it is a computer disk use 9.5B, and so forth. Note that the *Guidelines* instruct the use of the word "disk" for any magnetic computer disk; "disc" is used in all other cases.

If several physical items make up the interactive multimedia package consult AACR 2 rule 1.10C2 and use either method "a"—stringing the separate specific material designations and statements of extent in a single phrase, separated by commas

```
1 videodisc, 1 computer disk (3 1/2 in.), 1 score
(28 p.)
```

—or method "c"—giving separate statements for each item:

```
1 videodisc : sd., col. ; 12 in.
1 computer disk ; 3 1/2 in.
1 score (28 p.) ; 19 cm.
```

If an interactive multimedia package is available only by remote computer access (i.e., there is no physical item in hand), give no physical description in accordance with AACR 2 rule 9.5, footnote 3.

SERIES AREA

The *Guidelines* give no instructions for the transcription of series data. Transcribe information regarding the series according to AACR 2 rules 1.6.

NOTES AREA

Notes are made to amplify details about the entire interactive multimedia package. In addition, notes can be made to identify any musical content, e.g., the work and its performance, that is not apparent from the transcribed data that appear in areas 1 through 6. Notes also are made to establish the bibliographic identity of the item described (such as the relationship between sound or videorecordings of the same performance that appear apart from this package, or between the separately published scores, etc., and the music that accompanies or appears in the interactive package. All notes serve to allow users to select likely candidates for retrieval from among otherwise similar or identical bibliographic descriptions.

ORDER OF NOTES

The *Guidelines* recommend the following notes be made (in the order presented here) for interactive multimedia packages:

System requirements
Mode of access
Language and script
Source of title proper
Variations in title
General material designation
Statements of responsibility
Edition and history
Physical description
Summary
Contents

Additionally, standard numbers (ISBN, etc.) should be transcribed in area 8, following the notes.

Example 28

> Microsoft Multimedia Schubert [interactive multimedia] : the Trout quintet : an illustrated, interactive musical exploration / by Alan Rich and the Voyager Company. -- [Redmond, Wash.] : Microsoft, c1993.
>
>   1 computer optical disc : sd., col. ; 4 3/4 in. + 1 folded instruction sheet ([6] p.)
>
>   System requirements: Multimedia PC (or PC with Multimedia PC upgrade kit) with 386SX microprocessor or higher; 4MB RAM; MS-DOS 3.1 or later; Windows 3.1 or later; MSCDEX 2.2 or later; VGA or VGA+ graphics capabilities (256-color display recommended); MPC-compatible audio board; 30MB hard disk; CD-ROM drive; mouse; headphones or speakers.
>
>   Title from disc label.
>
>   Summary: Multimedia exploration of Schubert's music through text, graphics, and audio samples. Includes biographical and historical information, illustrations of general music concepts, commentary, and an educational game. Features digital recordings of Schubert's Trout quintet and Die Forelle.
>
>   Contents: Track 1-2. Data -- Track 3-7. "The Trout" quintet (38:29) -- Track 8. Die Forelle (2:26) -- Track 9-46. Supplementary audio.

This interactive multimedia package consists of one computer optical disc and one instruction sheet. Note the use of the entire package as chief source of information. The title proper has been transcribed from the disc label, but the statement of responsibility is found on the instruction sheet.

Method "a" of AACR 2 rule 1.10C2 has been used to combine the physical descriptions of the two items that comprise this package.

Example 29

> Exotic Japan [interactive multimedia] : an interactive introduction to Japanese culture and language / by Nikki Yokokura. -- Macintosh/Windows. -- New York : Voyager Co., c1994.
>
> 1 computer optical disc : sd., col. ; 4 3/4 in. + 1 user's guide (7 p. ; 18 cm.)
>
> System requirements (Macintosh): any color Macintosh (25MHz 68030 or faster processor); 3,500K RAM (5000K recommended, 8MB installed); System 7 or later; CD-ROM drive (double-speed recommended); 13 in. (640x480 resolution) or greater color monitor.
>
> System requirements (IBM): IBM-PC or compatible (486SX-25 or faster processor); 8 MB RAM; Microsoft Windows 3.1 or later; MS-DOS 5.0 or later; MPC2-compatible CD-ROM drive; sound card with speakers or headphones; 640x480 256-color display (accelerator recommended).
>
> Textual matter in English, voices in Japanese.
> Title from title screen.
> "CEXOTIH/894"--Disc label. "CDRM1257370"--Disc label.
> Summary: 150 lessons and quizzes, instructive animations, a traditional game, and beautifully reproduced woodcuts provide information on everything from the Bullet Train to the exchange of business cards. Interactive program guides the user through proper pronunciation (including the ability to record and play back the user's voice) with entertaining musical passages and clever sound effects complementing the lessons and game.
> ISBN 1-55940-435-3.

This is a good example of the ways in which interactive multimedia is being used in music education to explore musics other than Western art music. The package is fairly straightforward, consisting of one computer optical disc and one booklet. The title and statement of responsibility, and the edition statement, are transcribed from the internal source—the title screen.

Method "a" of AACR 2 rule 1.10C2 has been used to combine the physical descriptions of the two items that make up this package.

Notes are made on the variations in language in the two sources and on the disc numbers that appear on the disc label (which have been combined into a single note on the basics of rule 1.7A5).

Example 30

> A German requiem [interactive multimedia] : op. 45 :
> the greatest choral work of the romantic era / annotated
> by Warner New Media. -- Burbank, CA : Warner New Media,
> c1991.
>
>   2 computer optical discs : sd. ; 4 3/4 in. + 1 folded
> instruction sheet ([8] p.). -- (Warner audio notes)
>
>   System requirements: Macintosh; 1MB RAM; System 6.0.5
> or later; hard disk with 5MB free space; AppleCD SC or
> compatible CD-ROM drive; audio playback equipment.
>
>   Title from disc label.
>
>   Features the 1983 recording (Telarc CD-80092) of the
> Requiem with Robert Shaw conducting the Atlanta Symphony
> Orchestra and Chorus.
>
>   Summary: A multimedia program that introduces the user
> to A German requiem by Brahms through photographs, music,
> commentaries, diagrams, sounds, historical information,
> glossary, and musical analysis.
>
>   Contents: Disc 1. CD-ROM data -- Selig sind, die da
> Leid tragen -- Denn alles Fleisch -- Herr, lehre doch
> mich -- Extra audio examples -- Disc 2. CD-ROM data --
> Wie, lieblich sind deine Wohnungen -- Ihr habt nun
> Traurigkeit -- Denn wir haben hie -- Selig sind die Toten
> -- Extra audio examples.

Note that, in the statement of responsibility, the urge to transcribe "Brahms" has been resisted. Note also use of two statements of other title information.

Method "a" of AACR 2 rule 1.10C2 has been used to combine the physical descriptions of the two items that make up this package. The series statement is transcribed in area 6.

An edition and history note identifies the specific recording of Brahms's work.

Example 31

> The magic flute [interactive multimedia] / annotated
> by Warner New Media. -- Burbank, CA, USA : Warner New
> Media, c1989.
>   3 computer optical discs : sd. ; 4 3/4 in. + 1 guide.
> -- (Warner audio notes)
>   System requirements: Macintosh computer, System 6.0.2
> or later, 1M RAM; hard disk with 4.5M available; AppleCD
> SC ROM drive or compatible; audio playback equipment.
>   Title from title screen.
>   Includes a recording of Mozart's opera conducted by
> Nikolaus Harnoncourt, previously released by Teldec in
> 1988 (2292-42716-2), and also playable on a CD audio
> player.
>   German libretto by Emanuel Schikaneder, with
> uncredited English translation.
>   Summary: A running commentary offers plot summaries
> and libretto in English and German along with a musical
> analysis and a quiz. Provides information on background
> of composition and numerous related topics.

This opera interactive multimedia package contains three discs and a guide. Its description is fairly straightforward; the transcription of bibliographic data comes from the internal source—the title screen. Once again the urge to transcribe the composer's name into the statement of responsibility has been resisted. The composer, conductor, and librettist are identified in edition and history notes. A series statement appears.

SUMMARY

Interactive multimedia packages are increasingly commonplace in music collections; they make very helpful educational tools. The description of these packages must begin with a very careful examination of the entire product both internally and externally. Probably the trickiest aspect of description will be the selection of the chief source and identification of a unifying title proper.

The music cataloger must resist the urge to ignore the entire package and create a transcription that identifies only the musical work or the audio portion in area 1. These very important aspects must be identified separately, in notes on edition and history.

All of the parts of the package must be included in the physical description and, for each, the system requirements must be clearly identified.

A summary note will be very important to indicate to users the breadth and functionality of the product.

CHAPTER 5: DESCRIPTION OF ARCHIVAL COLLECTIONS OF MUSICAL DOCUMENTS

INTRODUCTION: PRINCIPLES

Archives are collections of the papers of a corporate entity. Like personal papers and manuscripts, they may be treated collectively for preservation and information retrieval. This is done to preserve the collective entity, which is as important a messenger as the content of any given document within the collection itself. Many musical repositories have developed archival collections in the past decade. In this introduction, some brief concepts of archival treatment will be covered. Then, in the remainder of this chapter, guidelines will be presented for the archival processing of musical collections, based on those guidelines found in *Archives, Personal Papers, and Manuscripts* (APPM is the standard set of rules for compilation of archival description, which is based upon the broad guidelines established by the International Standard Bibliographic Description and AACR 2). Citations for additional reading about the use of collection-level or archival cataloging can be found in the bibliography in chapter 8 of this book. Catalog record examples in this chapter have been derived from collection-level records produced by musical repositories—working copies of these records can be found in the Research Libraries Information Network (RLIN).

PROCESSING, FINDING AIDS, CATALOGING

Archival description is unlike library cataloging in a number of ways, most of which have to do with the inherent nature of archival materials and the ways in which archival collections are accumulated, acquired, processed (specific segments of the collection are housed, preserved, physically arranged, and otherwise accounted for), and made available for information retrieval. Archival collections are not static—they may be added to over time. Processing of archival collections often proceeds in stages—a collection-level record may be created at the point of acquisition, but more detailed series- and subseries-level records will be created as processing proceeds and as finding aids become available for the materials in the collection. Item-level description is rare or nonexistent. The catalog record is a pointer, not only in the local catalog but more importantly in the bibliographic networks, not to the material itself (as is the case for library materials) so much as to a finding aid—an index, folder list, database, etc.—that provides detailed information about the specific documents in a collection. Thus archival catalog records may be changed over time as the processing proceeds and finding aids for part or all of a collection are produced.

One consequence of this is that procedures are a bit more difficult to stipulate than is the case for library cataloging. The most important thing to keep in mind is that the catalog record must reflect the sum-total of the collection's provenance (point of origin) and its preserved original order. Therefore, transcription of bibliographic data into the first six areas of ISBD description is a less important task; making of detailed notes is the more important task. These notes will reveal the history and activities of the originators of the records and will include a fairly detailed summary of the contents of the collection.

PROVENANCE, ORIGINAL ORDER, AND THE CONCEPT OF SERIES

Key concepts about archival collections and their use as historical source material inform the management, arrangement, and use (and therefore cataloging) of collections of archival materials. These concepts also should govern the creation of in-house library collections of like materials that will constitute collections over which archival control is exerted. The leading principle is that of *provenance*, the idea that the originator of the collection determines the organic nature of the collection itself. That is, any archival collection can be seen as a reflection of the life and work of the organization or individuals from which it emanates.

The principal of respect for provenance carries with it some very interesting implications for the arrangement, description, and use of archival collections, because there is the implication that the context of the collection is as important as, if not more important than, the content of any document. For example, readers of detective fiction learn quickly that the details of a crime scene must not be disturbed—the detective wishes to examine the entire context as it was at the time of the criminal event. Similarly, the context of a collection of manuscript documents conveys information that no single document itself contains. The fact that a composer wrote hundreds of letters to organizations specializing in ecological issues is more important for what it says about the interests of the composer than is the particular content of any document; further, the proportion of letters written to ecological organizations as compared to those written to other sorts of organizations likewise yields important contextual information about the composer's life and times, and in turn the context in which certain musical works might have been created. So respect for provenance as an organizing principle is very important to users of archival collections, who are presumed to be primarily scholars utilizing historical methods of inquiry.

This leads to the second important principle, *original order*. That is, the order in which the materials were arranged by their creator must be maintained because of the contextual information it can supply to users of the collection. This means, for example, that collections of bound nineteenth-century song sheets must not be disbound to file the music in alphabetical order. To do so is to destroy the message about the socio-economic, artistic, and cultural influences surrounding the collection of the specific sheets in a volume that can be deduced from the collection itself. Or, for another example, a composer's papers must not be reorganized in some way that makes logical sense for information retrieval—for example, pulling all the correspondence from all files into one place—because to do so destroys the message conveyed by the collective grouping of materials *as the composer used them*. Original order must be maintained for what it conveys—therefore other means must be found for facilitating information retrieval, and that is where archival description (descriptive cataloging) comes in to play.

Furthermore, adherence to the principles of provenance and original order will mean ultimately that certain hierarchies, which are implicit within and among collections, also will dictate the way in which the materials will be preserved and described.

THE PROCESS

The steps in description of archival collections are as follows:

1. Examination of (or preparation of) the finding aid;

2. Transcription of the title and statement of responsibility area from the chief source of information, preferably the finding aid;

3. Assignment of the date;

4. Physical description of the collection;

5. Creation of notes as appropriate.

FINDING AID: THE CHIEF SOURCE OF INFORMATION

According to APPM, the finding aid—an index, folder list, database, etc., that provides detailed information about the specific documents in a collection—is used as the chief source of information for the description of an archival collection. Note the presumption that cataloging will not proceed until a finding aid exists. Where in descriptive cataloging, a technical reading is the first step by which the cataloger gets acquainted with the item to be described, in archival description an examination of the collection and preparation or identification of a finding aid is the first step.

In the case where no finding aid has been prepared, and it is desirable to proceed with the creation of a collection-level record, the cataloger may turn to provenance and accession records or the materials themselves as a chief source of information (*APPM* 1.0B1).

Any source may be used—including external reference resources—for the creation of notes about the collection (*APPM* 1.0B2).

FORMAL DESCRIPTION

TITLE AND STATEMENT OF RESPONSIBILITY

In some cases, formal titles and statements of responsibility will appear on finding aids and can be transcribed accordingly. However, for most collections the cataloger will have to formulate a supplied title. APPM rules 1.1 and following provide detailed instructions. Typically the elements that can be considered will be the name of the person or body associated with the collection and the form of material. For musical materials, terms such as "performances," "records of performances," or "field recordings" will be useful.

For collections of materials that require general material designators, add the GMD following the title proper and before the date.

```
Broadcast performances [sound recording] ...
```

DATE

Give an inclusive date or span of dates for the materials in the collection, following a comma, as the last element of the title area. Consult AACR 2 (rule 1.4F) or APPM (rule 1.1B5) for specific instructions and examples.

```
Field recordings [sound recording], 1946-
[ongoing].
```

PHYSICAL DESCRIPTION

Give a statement of the extent of the collection by giving either the exact number of items

    256 sound discs

or give the number of linear or cubic feet the collection occupies (see APPM 1.5B).

    256 linear feet

Give other physical details as appropriate

    256 sound discs : digital ; 4 3/4 in.

NOTES AREA

Notes are made to establish links among the parts of an archival collection (referred to as "series") and to amplify details about the provenance of the collection and the historical context in which it was created. Notes also can be used for musical archival collections to give information about the musical content (e.g., the performances, works performed, etc.) and the physical characteristics of the collection. These notes will be critical for users examining the archival records from remote locations. APPM gives detailed instructions for each of the notes in the list that follows. The order below is that in which the rules appear in APPM (and therefore is the order in which the notes should appear in a bibliographic record).

> Biographical/Historical (1.7B1)
> Scope and Content/Abstract (1.7B2)
> Linking entry complexity (1.7B3)
> Additional physical form available (1.7B4)
> Reproduction (1.7B5)
> Location of originals/duplicates (1.7B6)
> Organization and arrangement (1.7B7)
> Language (1.7B8)
> Provenance (1.7B9)
> Immediate source of acquisition (1.7B10)
> Restrictions on Access (1.7B11)
> Terms governing use and reproduction (1.7B12)
> Cumulative index/finding aids (1.7B13)
> Citation (1.7B14)
> Preferred citation of described materials (1.7B15)
> Publications (1.7B16)
> General note (1.7B17)
> Contents (1.7B18)
> Numbers (1.7B19)
> Copy being described, library's holdings, and restrictions on use (1.7B20)

Example 32

> Eugene Ormandy collection of scores, ca. 1920-1984.
> 497 boxes
>
> Contains approximately 1172 scores, 178 sets of scores
> and parts, and 41 sets of parts. Most of the scores
> contain markings made by Ormandy in preparation for
> performance with the Philadelphia Orchestra, and many of
> the parts contain markings by orchestra personnel. Other
> scores contain inscriptions from the composers to
> Ormandy. Summaries of these markings are entered on the
> cataloging record for each item. The collection includes
> orchestral arrangements made by Ormandy.
> From Ormandy's personal score collection and from the
> library of the Philadelphia Orchestra.
> Location: Special Collections, Van Pelt Library,
> University of Pennsylvania, Philadelphia, Pennsylvania
> 19104-6206.

This large collection of scores from Eugene Ormandy's work is held at the University of Pennsylvania. The supplied title includes Ormandy's name, a precise description of the forms of the materials, and the inclusive dates. Item-level descriptions also have been made for each score in the collection; this is indicated in the scope note.

Example 33

```
     Collection of broadcast recordings [sound recording],
1942-1949.
     ca. 750 sound discs : analog, 33 1/3 rpm ; 16 in.
     The Armed Forces Radio Service (AFRS) was an agency
created in 1942 by the United States government to
produce radio shows for broadcast to troops fighting
overseas in World War II. Created mainly by Jerome
Lawrence and Robert Lee, the AFRS produced and aired a
wide variety of programs-comedy, informational, and
dramatic programs, among others.  The AFRS also aired
edited versions of popular commercial radio programs. The
service was first centered in New York, but soon moved to
Los Angeles, where many of its most famous programs were
produced.  Some of these were: Yarns for Yanks, Command
performance, Mail call, and weekly broadcasts of concerts
of many major American symphony orchestras.  Many of the
shows, such as Command performance and Mail call, relied
on the donation of time and effort by major talent in
show business, who thought of appearances on the programs
as a way to contribute to the war effort.  The Armed
Forces Radio Service continued producing shows after the
end of World War II and was restructured under the
broader title of the Armed Forces Radio and Television
Service in the late 1940's.
     The Armed Forces Radio Service collection of broadcast
recordings consists of electrical transcription discs
that the AFRS distributed for broadcast.  The substantial
portion of the collection consists of concert recordings
of the Boston Symphony, NBC Symphony, New York
Philharmonic, and  other groups, from 1943 through 1945.
Also included are selected episodes of a wide variety of
other AFRS offerings, such as Globe theater, Mail call,
Command performance, Yarns for Yanks, Words with music,
and Music from America.
     Major portions of the Armed Forces Radio Service
collection were donated by the Alan Hewitt Estate.
Portions also donated by Jerome Lawrence and Robert Lee.
     Finding aid available in repository in: *L(Special)
88-31.
     Location: Rodgers & Hammerstein Archives of Recorded
Sound, The New York Public Library, 111 Amsterdam Avenue,
New York, NY 10023.
```

This collection of 750 sound discs contains the record of the Armed Forces Radio Service broadcasts from World War II housed at the Rodgers & Hammerstein Archives at Lincoln Center in New York. Note the extensive historical note about the service, followed by a detailed scope note. The provenance is clearly identified as well. Note also that site information is included in the notes. Finding aids (registers, indexes, etc.) are not always available, so the fact that one exists is noted along with its local call number.

Example 34

> Performance history records of shows about Kurt Weill,
> using his music, or from his world, [192-]--[ongoing].
> <107> folders (ca. <1> linear ft.)
>
> Includes press announcements, programs, and reviews of
> shows and programs either produced by Weill (Lunch hour
> follies, 1942-) or by others; in the latter case, those
> which 1) use, at least in part, his music, 2) take Weill
> and/or Lenya, or aspects of their world as subject
> matter, or 3) which are closely related in some manner to
> their world (e.g., a production by the Berliner Ensemble
> of a work by Brecht with music by Dessau, or a production
> of the Beggar's opera).
> Materials are organized into four subseries: 52A,
> staged productions, primarily revues and pastiches, at
> least partially derived from, or using at least in part,
> Weill's music in arrangements by others; 52B, radio and
> television shows or programs and films about Weill and/or
> Lenya; 52C, ballets choreographed to Weill's music; and
> 52D, solo and duo cabaret shows (i.e., without cast).
> Materials for each production or performance are foldered
> separately. Folders for Subseries 52A-52C are arranged
> alphabetically by title; those for Subseries 52D
> alphabetically by name of performer.
> Primarily in English or German.
> Core collection comes from Lotte Lenya's legacy, with
> additional materials donated by producers, performers,
> and scholars.
> Finding aid available in repository; folder-level
> [i.e., production-level] control in all cases, and item-
> level in some.
> Cite as: Weill-Lenya Research Center, Ser.52.
> In: Kurt Weill Foundation for Music. Weill-Lenya
> Research Center. Repository description. Related Rec. ID:
> (NNWFM)NYWS93-A8
> Location: Weill-Lenya Research Center, Kurt Weill
> Foundation for Music, 7 East 20th Street, New York, N.Y.
> 10003.

This collection, a part of the Kurt Weill Foundation's collections, contains records relating to performances that included Weill's works. Notice the detailed supplied title statement, and the "ongoing" date, which shows that material is still being added to the collection. In addition to the scope note, the note that details the organization of the subseries gives additional information about the scope of the collection. In addition to finding aid and repository information, we are given a "Citation" note. This tells us the format preferred by the repository for citations of this collection (*APPM* 1.7B15).

Example 35

> The Railroad hour, radio program [sound recording],
> 1948-1954.
>   490 sound discs : analog, 33 1/3 rpm ; 16 in.
>   42 sound tapes : analog, 7 1/2 ips, 2 track, mono. ;
> 7 in.
>
>   Transcription discs and tape copies for the radio
> program Railroad hour.
>   The Railroad hour was a program that presented
> excerpts of famous musical comedies, as well as
> original stories, for radio audiences. Each half-hour
> episode of the program presented the highlights of one
> musical. Gordon MacRae was the host and leading man
> for each episode; his leading ladies came from radio
> and the Metropolitan Opera.
>   The program featured works by: Irving Berlin, Henry
> Blossom, Guy Bolton, Noël Coward, B.G. De Sylva,
> Herbert Fields, Rudolf Friml, George Gershwin, Ira
> Gershwin, William S. Gilbert, Fred de Gresac, Clifford
> Grey, Oscar Hammerstein, Otto Harbach, Lorenz Hart,
> Moss Hart, Victor Herbert, Jerome Kern, Fritz Kreisler,
> Jerome Lawrence, Robert E. Lee, Franz Lehar, Alan Jay
> Lerner, Frank Mandel, Joseph McCarthy, Cole Porter,
> Richard Rodgers, Sidney Romberg, Lawrence Schwab, Harry
> B. Smith, Leo Stein, Arthur S. Sullivan, Fred Thompson,
> Harry Tierney, Vincent Youmans.
>   Featured performers: Ann Ayars, Kenny Baker, Marion
> Bell, William Bendix, Mimi Benzell, Ralph Blane, Evelyn
> Case, Nadine Conner, Doris Day, Clark Dennis, Annamary
> Dickey, Dorothy Donnelly, Eileen Farrell, Virginia
> Haskins, Dorothy Kirsten, Frances Langford, Jeanette
> MacDonald, Elaine Malbin, Victor Moore, Patricia
> Morison, Patrice Munsel, Lucille Norman, Jarmila
> Novotna, Walter O'Keefe, Irra Petina, Jane Powell,
> Dorothy Sarnoff, Dinah Shore, Ginny Simms, Jane Stuart
> Smith, Jo Stafford, Risë Stevens, Gladys Swarthout,
> Blanche Thebom, Margaret Truman, Dorothy Warenskjold,
> Margaret Whiting, Eileen Wilson.
>   Gift of Jerome Lawrence and Robert E. Lee.
>   Access to discs restricted; advance notification
> required.
>   Classmarks for individual shows listed in finding
> aid.
>   Preservation copies of 87 programs recorded at The
> New York Public Library. To determine programs
> transferred, consult finding aid.
>   Finding aid available in repository. In: *L(Special)
> 88-1.

```
     Forms part of:  Lawrence and Lee collection of
broadcast recordings.  In: Lawrence, Jerome,1915-
Lawrence and Lee collection of broadcast recordings.
Related Rec. ID: (CStRLIN)NYPW88-A22
     Location: Rodgers & Hammerstein Archives of Recorded
Sound, The New York Public Library, 111 Amsterdam Avenue,
New York, NY 10023.
```

This collection, another radio program, contains recordings of the Railroad hour radio program housed at the Rodgers & Hammerstein Archives at Lincoln Center in New York. The collection consists of both sound discs and sound tapes, so two statements of extent have been given so as to detail the physical characteristics of each. Composers of featured works are identified, as are featured performes. The collection is linked to the larger Lawrence and Lee collection of which it is a part. Once again, site information (finding aid, etc.) is included in the notes.

Example 36

> Field recordings of Southwest American Indians [sound recording], [1920?-1939?].
> 34 sound discs : analog ; 10 in.
> Arranged alphabetically by song title.
> Preservation tape copy available in *LT-10 4985-4986.
> Field recordings made in the 1920s or 1930s of Southwest American Indian songs. The collection contains 47 songs of Hopi, Zuni, Comanche, and Navajo tribes.
> Access to discs restricted; advance notification required.
> Finding aid available in repository: *L(Special) 90-17.
> Location: Rodgers & Hammerstein Archives of Recorded Sound, The New York Public Library, 111 Amsterdam Avenue, New York, NY, 10023.

The dates have been supplied rather than transcribed, so note that they are in square brackets, and that they utilize uncertain formulations (i.e., using question marks to indicate uncertainty, APPM rule 1.1B5 footnote 7). This is a somewhat smaller collection of recordings than those above, so less information is included in the scope note. Notice, too, that access to these recordings is restricted and the user is directed to notify the repository in advance if research requires actual use of the disc recordings.

SUMMARY

Archival practice may be used to advantage in music collections for providing access to collections that are kept together to preserve the intellectual integrity of the collective entity. Such collections can be described effectively using guidelines found in *Archives, Personal Papers, and Manuscripts*.

Description of the collection will rely heavily on the provision of notes. Titles generally are supplied by the cataloger, together with inclusive dates. A physical description details the gross extent of the collection.

Notes then are used to define the scope of the collection and to place the collection in its proper historical context. Other notes will be made to describe the organization of subunits within the collection (series and subseries) and to identify the repository.

CHAPTER 6: CHOICE AND FORM OF ENTRY

Access points are the means by which users retrieve bibliographic records. They are the doorways to the process of becoming informed. As such, the creation of access points is probably the most critical part of descriptive cataloging.

Access points are created to identify the intellectual entities—the works—contained in the items represented in a bibliographic description. Access points will serve as index entries in the catalog for those works, primarily by providing access to the names of creators (composers, performers, authors, etc.) and titles. Works themselves are accessed using name-title access points. AACR 2 instructs the cataloger first to prepare the item description, then subsequently to identify the work (and amend the description if necessary to make certain the work is identifiable), to ascertain attribution for its creation, and to determine the title by which it is called. This process is called "choice of access points." Once it has been determined for which entities access should be provided, the specific headings must be formulated. This process is called "form of access points." Finally, the access points and description will be assembled into a unified bibliographic record that represents the bibliographic entity in hand.

The next two chapters are devoted to these several aspects of providing access to works. Chapter 6 includes instructions for selecting main entry and added entries for works and for formulation of headings for persons and corporate bodies. Chapter 7 covers the specific problem of creating uniform titles for musical works. Examples of completed bibliographic records, with access points, appear at the end of chapter 7.

The steps in creating access to works are as follows:

1. Identify the work for which access is to be provided.

2. Determine whether the work is a work of personal or multiple authorship, or that it emanates from a corporate body.

3. Select the person, title, or corporate body that will serve as main entry for the work.

4. Select the persons, titles, or corporate bodies that will serve as added entries to provide additional access to the work.

5. Formulate headings for persons, corporate bodies, and uniform titles, and provide references from variant forms of headings.

CHOICE OF ACCESS POINTS

The basic rule for choice of entry, AACR 2 rule 21.1A1, "enter ... under the heading for the personal author ... the principal personal author ... or the probable personal author." Composers of music, and in some cases performers as well, are considered to be the authors of the works they create. For this reason the only special rules for music materials in chapter 21 are those for modifications of works (rules 21.18-21.22), sound recordings (rule 21.23), and related works such as cadenzas and librettos (rule 21.28). The rules for modifications of works are all fairly straightforward and require no particular explanation. Library of Congress rule interpretations and cataloging decisions concerning related works are discussed briefly below. The rules for sound recordings, however, are somewhat confusing and receive special attention below. The rules for entering motion pictures and videorecordings are not necessarily complex, but they are controversial in some quarters and thus also receive special attention below.

ADAPTATIONS AND ADDED ACCOMPANIMENTS

21.18C MCD For a musical work adapted by its original composer, see MCD Appendix D "Musical work." (rev. May 1989)(*MCD* 39)

21.21 MCD For uniform titles, subject headings, and classification for works with added accompaniments, etc., see MCD 25.35C. (rev. April 1990)(*MCD* 42)

POPULAR MUSIC FOLIOS

For popular music folios that contain the songs from a record "album" by a group, and that feature that group prominently in the item, apply rule 21.1B(e) and enter the folio under the heading for the performing ensemble, if it qualifies as a corporate body that has a name.

21.23C MCD For popular music folios, apply LCRI 21.23C only when a sound recording exists which has essentially the same title and content as the printed folio being cataloged. (rev. June 1994)(*MCB* 25:8:2)

CADENZAS AND LIBRETTOS

A cadenza is a passage inserted near the end of a concerto movement that is intended to display the technical accomplishments of the solo performer. Though sometimes improvised, cadenzas also are composed and published, sometimes by the concerto's composer, sometimes by a virtuoso performer. The difficulty in choice of entry is that the cadenza almost always will be used in conjunction with another composition, so it might or might not commonly be sought under its own heading.

In keeping with the basic rule 21.1, rule 21.28 directs entry of a related work under its own heading. A Library of Congress Music Cataloging Decision reminds us that a cadenza is always a related work:

21.28A MCD Treat cadenzas as related works under this rule whether they are composed by the composer of the works into which they are to be interpolated or by someone else.

> **Mozart, Wolfgang Amadeus**
> [Cadenzas, piano. Selections]
> Trente-cinq points d'orgue pour le piano-forté / composés par W.A. Mozart et se rapportant à ses concertos ...
> *Added entry*: Mozart ... Concertos, piano, orchestra. Selections

Backhaus, Wilhelm
　　Kadenz zum Rondo des C-Dur Konzerts von Beethoven / von Wilhelm Backhaus ...
Added entry: Beethoven, Ludwig van. Concertos, piano, orchestra, no. 1, op. 15, C major.
Rondo

(rev. September 1983)(*MCD* 48)

For librettos the Library of Congress has chosen to apply the alternative rule 21.28, in footnote 7,
entering them under the heading appropriate to the musical work.

21.28A MCD In order for a libretto to qualify for entry "under the heading appropriate to the
musical work" (footnote 7), a reference to the libretto's musical setting must appear in the
chief source of information or in the foreword or other prefatory matter of the publication.
(rev. September 1983)(*MCD* 48)

SOUND RECORDINGS

In choosing the main entry for a sound recording, the process of assigning responsibility for the
intellectual content is somewhat more complex. AACR 2 introduced main entry under performer for
certain recordings. Performers may be designated as the main entry by virtue of their activities as
writers (i.e., composers, etc.), interpreters, or players.

The first consideration in choice of entry for sound recordings is the content of the recording. If
the recording contains works by the same person(s) or body (bodies), then main entry is determined
as it would be for the same works in their printed manifestations. For example, a recording that
contains only a performance of *String quartet no. 13 in G major, op. 106* by Antonín Dvorák, is
entered under the heading for Dvorák because it is a recording of one work by one person (21.23A).
Likewise, a recording that contains performances of *Romeo and Juliet* and *Francesco da Rimini* by
Tchaikovsky is entered under the heading for Tchaikovsky because it is a recording of two works by
the same person (21.23B).

If a sound recording contains works by two or more different persons (do not confuse this with
the provisions for joint authorship, for which apply rules 21.23A-B and 21.6), the choice of main
entry is dependent first upon whether or not a collective title is present in the description. If there is a
collective title, the main entry is under the heading for the principal performer or the first of two or
three principal performers. If there are four or more principal performers, or no principal performers,
main entry is under the collective title. A Library of Congress Rule Interpretation clarifies these
provisions, and includes a variety of examples illustrating the most common situations.

Principal Performer

21.23C LCRI In applying the rules and these interpretations, understand "performer" in
21.23C1 to mean a person or corporate body whose performance is heard on the sound
recording. When a person performs as a member of a corporate body, do not consider him or
her as a separate person to be a performer. Do not consider a conductor or accompanist to be
a member of the body he or she conducts or accompanies. If the person's name appears in
conjunction with the name of a group, determine whether the corporate name includes this
personal name. If the conclusion is that the corporate name does not include the person's
name, do not consider the person a member of the group; if the conclusion is that it does
include the person's name, consider the person to be a member of the group.

For recordings containing musical works by different composers or writers, follow the guidelines below in 1) deciding whether or not there are principal performers and 2) identifying the principal performers, if any.

The use of the term "principal performer" in 21.23C1 and 21.23D1 can lead to confusion since the term implies a performer who is more important (or, in the words of footnote 5 on p. 344, given greater prominence) than other performers. This interpretation, however, would often produce undesirable results: it would make main entry under the heading for a performer impossible under 21.23CI when there is only one performer or when there are only two or three performers who are given equal prominence. To avoid this difficulty, apply the following:

1) When two or more performers are named in the chief source of information, consider to be principal performers those given the greatest prominence there. If all the performers named in the chief source of information are given equal prominence there, consider all of them to be principal performers.

2) When only one performer is named in the chief source of information, consider that performer to be a principal performer.

3) When no performers are named in the chief source of information, consider that there are no principal performers.

In judging relative prominence on the basis of wording, layout, and typography, consider names printed in the same size and style of lettering and in association with one another to have equal prominence. When names appear in the same size and style of lettering but in different areas of the same source of information, consider those in a location implying superiority (e.g., a higher position) to have greater prominence. Do not consider names near the beginning of a list or sequence to have greater prominence than those near the end.

> *Chief source:*
> JESS WALTERS SINGS CLASSIC FOLK SONGS
> Jess Walters, baritone
> Hector Garcia, guitar
> *Main entry under the heading for Walters as principal performer*

> *Chief source:*
> Joan Sutherland
> SONGS MY MOTHER TAUGHT ME
> Songs by Dvorák, Mendelssohn, Massenet, Gounod, Delibes, Grieg, Liszt, and others
> Richard Bonynge
> The New Philharmonia Orchestra
> *Main entry under the heading for Sutherland as principal performer*

> *Chief source:*
> SONATAS OF J.S. BACH & SONS
> JEAN-PIERRE RAMPAL, Flute
> ISAAC STERN, Violin
> JOHN STEELE RITTER,
> Harpsichord and Fortepiano

LESLIE PARNAS, Cello
Main entry under title; Rampal, Stern, Ritter, and Parnas are principal performers

Chief source:
MUSIC OF CHABRIER AND MASSENET
Detroit Symphony Orchestra
Paul Paray
Main entry under the heading for the orchestra
Added entry under the heading for Paray
(The orchestra and Paray are principal performers)

Chief source:
LAS VOCES DE LOS CAMPESINOS
Francisco García and Pablo and Juanita Saludado sing corridos about the farm
workers and their union
Main entry under the heading for García
Added entries under the headings for P. Saludado and J. Saludado
(García and the Saludados are principal performers)

Chief source:
SARAH BERNHARDT & THE COQUELIN BROTHERS
(Dramatic readings performed by Sarah Bernhardt, Constant Coquelin, and Ernest
Coquelin)
Main entry under the heading for Bernhardt
Added entries under the headings for C. Coquelin and E. Coquelin
(Bernhardt, C. Coquelin, and E. Coquelin are principal performers)

Chief source:
SONGS OF THE WOBBLIES
with
Joe Glazer
(Sung by Glazer, with instrumental ensemble)
Main entry under the heading for Glazer as principal performer

Chief source:
Serge Cassel
POESIES ET PROSES FRANÇAISES
(Various poems and prose selections read by Serge Cassel)
Main entry under the heading for Cassel as principal performer

Chief source:
SOUTHERN CLAWHAMMER BANJO
(No performers named)
Main entry under title
(No principal performers)

(*CSB* 45: 28-31)

21.23D LCRI See LCRI 21.23C. (*CSB* 36: 18)

Collective Activity of a Corporate Body

One should also remain aware of the provisions that stipulate main entry under a corporate body for a performing group whose "responsibility goes beyond that of mere performance" (AACR 2 21.1B2(e)). While this provision is offered here as justification for main entry under corporate body, it is unlikely that such a body would not also appear as principal performer. It is germane, though, when a performing corporate body has been transcribed in the statement of responsibility, to consider that body's responsibility for creation of the work recorded to supersede that of any composer or author listed. The scope of this provision is further narrowed by the Library of Congress Rule Interpretation:

> **21.1B2e LCRI** This category emphasizes that the responsibility of a performing group must go beyond "mere performance, execution, etc." This means that the group must be responsible to a major degree for the artistic content of the work being performed. A typical example is an acting group that performs by means of improvisation. The group collectively "plans" the drama, that is, determines the broad outline of the plot, the nature of the characters, etc., in the absence of a written dialogue. The development of the drama proceeds entirely on the basis of improvised dialogue. The performance is recorded and it is the recording that is being cataloged. (*CSB* 25: 54)

VIDEORECORDINGS

Videorecordings are almost always motion pictures. Motion pictures are collaborative projects, usually created by a producer, a director, and writers in conjunction with one another. Thus motion pictures almost always are entered under their titles proper, as works of multiple authorship.

There is no exception for motion pictures or videorecordings that contain musical works. Main entry will be under title proper, with added entries for the musical work as well as for any performers who are prominently featured in the videorecording.

INTERACTIVE MULTIMEDIA PACKAGES

Interactive multimedia packages will need to be considered on two levels. First, what should be the access points for the entire package? And second, what access points are needed to identify musical works and performances that are contained as part of the interactive package?

The *Guidelines for Bibliographic Description of Interactive Multimedia* include brief instructions, referring the cataloger to Part II of AACR 2. Access points for the entire work should be chosen accordingly, and often, if the work is collaborative, main entry will be under title proper with added entries for developers, authors of text, designers, etc.

Once access points have been chosen for the interactive work, the music cataloger then should assign appropriate access points for any musical works contained within the package, and for the performances of those works, as appropriate.

MUSICAL ARCHIVAL COLLECTIONS

The basic rule for the choice of entry for archival collections (APPM 2.1) stipulates that entry should be made on the basis of provenance, under the name of the person or body chiefly responsible for the creation of the materials. Title entry is preferred for collections when the creator is unknown or when the provenance and origin are mixed.

ADDED ENTRIES

In general, the rules in chapters 21 and 25 specify added entries as required. Further, the cataloger of music materials should exercise judgment in applying rule 21.29C, which provides guidance for making added entries under additional headings the cataloger thinks users might seek.

ORDER OF ADDED ENTRIES

21.29 LCRI Give added entries in the following order:

1) Personal name;
2) Personal name/title;
3) Corporate name;
4) Corporate name/title;
5) Uniform title (all instances of works entered under title);
6) Title traced as Title-period;
7) Title traced as Title-colon, followed by a title;
8) Series.

For arrangement within any one of these groupings, generally follow the order in which the justifying data appear in the bibliographic description. If such a criterion is not applicable, use judgment. (*CSB* 12: 24)

The rule interpretations and cataloging decisions that follow in this section outline the Library of Congress policy in three particularly complex areas. First are special rules for added entries that might be required in cataloging sound recordings (performers, joint composer, etc.); second are the LC policy decisions on analytical added entries for collections, both printed and recorded; and third are the LC policies on added entries for musical titles.

SPECIAL PROVISIONS FOR SOUND RECORDINGS

Joint Author, Arranger, Librettist

21.23 LCRI For a sound recording covered by 21.23A or 21.23B, make whatever added entries are prescribed by the rules under which the choice of main entry for the work or works recorded was made (e.g., for a joint author or composer under 21.6C1; for an arranger under 21.18B1; for a librettist under 21.19A1) as well as any others provided for under LCRI 21.29.

Chief source: L'ELISIR D'AMORE -- Highlights (Donizetti; Romani)
(Music by Donizetti; libretto by Romani, based on Le philtre by Eugene Scribe)
Main entry under the heading for Donizetti as composer (21.23A1, 21.29A1); added entries under the headings for Romani and for Scribe's Le philtre (21.19A1).

(*CSB* 44: 37)

Performers Named on a Sound Recording

21.29D LCRI Make added entries for all performers named on a sound recording (persons or corporate bodies) with the following exceptions:

1) Do not make an added entry for a person who functions entirely or primarily on the item being cataloged as a member of a corporate body represented by a main or added entry. Do not consider a conductor or accompanist to be a member of the body he or she conducts or accompanies. If a person's name appears in conjunction with the name of a group, determine whether the corporate name includes this personal name. If the conclusion is that the corporate name does not include the person's name, do not consider the person a member of the group; if the conclusion is that it does include the person's name, consider the person to be a member of the group.

2) If both the chorus and orchestra of an opera company, opera house, etc., participate in a performance and both are named, along with the name of the parent body, make only a single added entry under the heading for the parent body.

> *source*: Bolshoi Theater Orchestra and Chorus
> *added entry under the heading for the theater*

3) When a featured performer is accompanied by an unnamed group that, if it had a name, would be given an added entry as a corporate body, do not make added entries for the individual members of the group. Do not, however, apply this exception to jazz ensembles, even if one or more of the performers is given greater prominence than the others, i.e., normally make added entries for all the individual performers (except any who are covered by exceptions 4) and 5) below) in such cases.

4) Do not make an added entry for a performer who participates in only a small number of the works in a collection or for a performer whose role is minor (e.g., an announcer on a radio program).

5) Do not make an added entry for a performer who receives main entry heading as principal performer under 21.23C1.

6) If there are many performers performing the same function (e.g., singers in an opera, actors in a drama), make added entries only for those who are given the greatest prominence in the chief source of information. If all are given equal prominence, make added entries only for those who are given prominence over the others in other places on the sound recording (e.g., the container, the program booklet) or, if that criterion does not apply, for those performing the most important functions (e.g., singing the principal roles, acting the principal parts).

Chief source (labels): L'ELISIR D'AMORE -- Highlights (Donizetti; Romani) Spiro Malas, Maria Casula, Joan Sutherland, Luciano Pavarotti, Dominic Cossa with the Ambrosian Opera Chorus and the English Chamber Orchestra conducted by Richard Bonynge

Container: Donizetti L'ELISIR D'AMORE Highlights JOAN SUTHERLAND, LUCIANO PAVAROTTI Dominic Cossa, Spiro Malas, Maria Casula Ambrosian Opera Chorus, English Chamber Orchestra RICHARD BONYNGE
added entries under the headings for Sutherland, Pavarotti, Bonynge, the chorus, and the orchestra

If a performer for whom an added entry would be made according to the guidelines above is also the composer of one or more works on the recording, make an added entry to represent the performing function in addition to any name/title access points (main entry or analytical added entries) made for his or her works. (*CSB* 45: 32-33)

21.29D MCD In determining whether the name of a performing group includes a personal name that appears in conjunction with it (LCRI 21.29D, first paragraph), apply MCD 24.1A. (June 1990)(*MCD* 49)

Popular Performing Groups

21.23D MCD In determining whether the name of a performing group includes a personal name that appears in conjunction with it (LCRI 21.23D, first paragraph), apply MCD 24.1A. (June 1990)(*MCD* 45)

21.30E LCRI If an added entry is needed on a sound recording for both the chorus and orchestra of an opera company, opera house, etc., make the added entry for the parent body alone. If an added entry is needed for the chorus alone or for the orchestra alone, make the added entry specifically for the body involved. (*CSB* 60: 16)

ANALYTICAL ADDED ENTRIES FOR COLLECTIONS

Analytical added entries in name-title form are made by many libraries for all works contained in sound recording anthologies. For most of them this is the only way to achieve full indexing of musical recordings, because most recordings are by nature anthologies and the main entry heading is rarely sufficient to supply access to more than one work or, in some cases, to a collective uniform title such as Selections; arr. The following LC policies apply to both printed music and sound recordings, unless otherwise stated.

Collections With Collective Title

21.7B LCRI If a collection contains no more than three works, make an analytical added entry for each work (cf. LCRI 21.30M [*CSB* 63: 11]).

If a collection contains four or more works that are entered under no more than three different headings, apply the following:

1) If one heading is represented by one work, make an analytical added entry for the work.

2) If one heading is represented by one excerpt from one work, make an analytical added entry for it.

3) If one heading is represented by two or more consecutively numbered excerpts from one work, make one analytical added entry (25.6B1).

4) If one heading is represented by two unnumbered or nonconsecutively numbered excerpts from one work, make an analytical added entry for each excerpt (25.6B2).

5) If one heading is represented by three or more unnumbered or nonconsecutively numbered excerpts from one work, make one analytical added entry (25.6B3).

6) If one name heading is represented by two works, make an added entry for the name heading alone.

7) If one personal name heading is represented by three or more works, make an analytical added entry using an appropriate collective uniform title (e.g., "Selections").

If a collection contains four or more works that are entered under four or more different headings, make an added entry for the person or body named first in the chief source.

Sound recordings

If a sound recording collection contains twenty-five or fewer musical works entered under two or more different headings, normally make up to fifteen entries according to the following instructions:

1) If one heading is represented by one work, make an analytical added entry for the work.

2) If one heading is represented by one excerpt from one work, make an analytical added entry for it (25.32A).

3) If one heading is represented by two or more consecutively numbered excerpts from one work, make one analytical added entry (25.32 B).

4) If one heading is represented by two unnumbered or nonconsecutively numbered excerpts from one work, make one analytical added entry for each excerpt (25.32B).

5) If one heading is represented by three or more unnumbered or nonconsecutively numbered excerpts from one work, make one analytical added entry (25.32B).

6) If one name heading is represented by two works, make an analytical added entry for each work (25.33).

7) If one personal name heading is represented by three or more works, make an analytical added entry using an appropriate collective uniform title (e.g., "Selections," "Piano music. Selections") (25.34).

Do not make analytical added entries for sound recording collections

1) containing twenty-five or fewer works that would require more than fifteen analytical added entries;

2) containing pop, folk, ethnic, or jazz music;
3) containing recitals with an orientation towards performer(s) or instrument(s) rather than musical repertoire;

4) that are multipart items but incomplete at the time the collection is cataloged.

(*CSB* 65: 11-12)

Collections Without Collective Title

21.7C LCRI If a collection contains no more than three works, enter under the heading appropriate to the first and make analytical added entries for the second and third works.

If a collection contains four or more works that are entered under no more than three different headings, apply the following:

1) If one heading is represented by one work, enter the collection under the first work or make an analytical added entry for it, as appropriate.

2) If one heading is represented by one excerpt from one work, apply 1) above.

3) If one heading is represented by two or more consecutively numbered excerpts from one work, enter the collection under the uniform title for the excerpts (25.6B1) or make an analytical added entry for them, as appropriate.

4) If one heading is represented by two unnumbered or nonconsecutively numbered excerpts from one work, enter the collection under the first excerpt (25.6B2) and make an analytical added entry for the other excerpt; or, make an analytical added entry for each excerpt, as appropriate.

5) If one heading is represented by three or more unnumbered or nonconsecutively numbered excerpts from one work, enter the collection under the uniform title for the excerpts (25.6B3) or make an analytical added entry for them [as appropriate].

6) If one heading is represented by two works, enter the collection under the first work and make an analytical added entry for the other work; or, make an analytical added entry for each work, as appropriate.

7) If one heading is represented by excerpts from two works, apply 2)-5) above to each work.

8) If one personal name heading is represented by three or more works, enter the collection under an appropriate collective uniform title (e.g., "Selections") or make an analytical added entry under this uniform title, as appropriate.

9) If one corporate name heading is represented by three or more works, enter the collection under the heading appropriate to the first work, but do not make any analytical added entries for the others; or, make an added entry for the name heading alone, as appropriate.

If a collection contains four or more works that are entered under four or more different headings, enter the collection under the heading for the work named first in the chief source. Generally do not make added entries for the other works.

Sound recordings

If a sound recording collection contains no more than fifteen musical works entered under two or more different headings, enter the collection under the first work and make analytical added entries for the other works. Do not make analytical added entries for sound recording collections that are covered by the excluded categories in LCRI 21.7B [above]. (*CSB* 65: 12)

COLLECTIVE UNIFORM TITLES AND ANALYTICAL ADDED ENTRIES

25.34B-25.34C MCD Do not apply the following provisions to collections of the types listed in LCRI 25.34B-25.34C. For excerpts from one work, treat each excerpt the same as a separate work unless there are two or more excerpts numbered consecutively (25.6B1) or three or more unnumbered or nonconsecutively numbered excerpts (25.6B3).

Printed and manuscript music

If a music publication or manuscript contains three or more works entered under a single personal name heading, enter the collection under the collective uniform title appropriate to the item as a whole. Make name-title added entries only in the following situations:

1) If the item contains four or more works, and all the works but one form a group for which a collective uniform title naming a type (25.34C2-25.34C3) would be appropriate, make a name-title analytical added entry for the group and one for the single work..

> **Chopin, Frédéric**
> [Piano music. Selections]
> Scherzi ; und, Phantasie f Moll ...
> *Added entries:* Chopin ... Scherzos, piano ; Chopin ... Fantasia, piano, op. 49, F minor

2) If the item contains six or more works, and the works may be divided into two groups of three or more works, for each of which a collective uniform title naming a type (25.34C2-25.34C3) would be appropriate, make a name-title analytical added entry for each group.

Scriabin, Aleksandr Nikolayevich
[Piano music. Selections]
The complete preludes & etudes : for pianoforte solo ...
Added entries: Scriabin ... Preludes, piano; Scriabin ... Etudes, piano

Sound recordings

For sound recording collections containing three, four, or five works entered under a single personal name heading, see LCRI 25.34B-25.34C.

If a sound recording collection contains six or more works entered under a single personal name heading, enter the collection under the collective uniform title appropriate to the item as a whole. Make name-title analytical added entries as follows:

1) If the works may be divided into no more than five groups of three or more works, for each of which a collective uniform title naming a type (25.34C2-25.34C3) would be appropriate, make an analytical added entry for each group .

Chopin, Frédéric
[Piano music. Selections]
Waltzes ; and, Scherzos ...
Added entries: Chopin ... Waltzes, [piano]; Chopin ... Scherzos, piano

2) If some of the works can be grouped as in (1) above and others cannot, and the groups and the remaining individual works together add up to five or less, make an analytical added entry for each group and for each of the remaining works.

Saint-Saëns, Camille
[Orchestra music. Selections]
Symphonies ; & Tone poems [sound recording] ...
Added entries: Saint-Saëns ... Symphonies, no. 1-3; Saint-Saëns ... Symphonic poems; Saint-Saëns ... Marche héroïque

3) If neither (1) nor (2) above can be applied but one of the works is featured, make an analytical added entry for that work; in addition, make an analytical added entry under the collective uniform title appropriate to the remaining works if it is different from that used in the main entry.

Glinka, Mikhail Ivanovich
[Instrumental music. Selections]
Trio pathétique : in D minor for clarinet, bassoon, and piano ; Selected piano works [sound recording] ...
Added entries: Glinka ... Trio pathétique; Glinka ... Piano music. Selections

Reger, Max
    [Chamber music. Selections]
    Chamber music [sound recording] ...
(Contains the String quartet, op. 109 (55 min.), and various short works for clarinet
and piano or violoncello and piano (10 min. total))
Added entry: Reger ... Quartets, strings, op. 109, E♭ major

For references for collections without a collective title, see MCD 26.4B4.

Collections of Works all Having the Same Title

If all the works in a collection entered under a personal name heading have the same title and
this title is not the name of a type of composition, assign a collective uniform title according
to 25.34B, 25.34C1, or 25.34C2, using the most specific uniform title that will cover all the
works in the collection. If appropriate, add "Selections" according to the first paragraph of
25.34C3. If the collection is a sound recording, make name-title analytic added entries
according to LCRI 25.34B-25.34C and MCD 25.34B-25.34C(1-2). For references for
collections without a collective title, see MCD 26.4B4.

    [Selections]
    (*Contains* Antiphony I *for unaccompanied chorus,* Antiphony III *for piano, and*
    Antiphony V *for orchestra*)

    [Instrumental music. Selections]
    (*Contains* Antiphony III *for piano,* Antiphony V *for orchestra, and* Antiphony VII
    for string quartet)

    [String quartet music]
    (*Contains* Antiphony VII, Antiphony IX, and Antiphony XI, *all for string quartet and
    the composer's only works in that medium*)

If, however, the works are consecutively numbered, apply the second paragraph of 25.34C3,
adding the consecutive numbering to the title of the individual works (in the singular). Do
this even if the collection contains all of the composer's works with that title.

    [Antiphony, no. 2-4]
    [Kammermusik, no. 1-7]

(rev. June 1994)(*MCB* 25:8:2-3)

25.34B-25.34C LCRI If a sound recording collection contains three, four, or five musical
works entered under a single personal name heading, enter the collection under the collective
uniform title appropriate to the whole item. Make name-title analytical added entries for each
work in the collection. For excerpts from one work, make a separate analytical added entry
for each excerpt unless there are two or more excerpts numbered consecutively (25.6B1) or
three or more unnumbered or nonconsecutively numbered excerpts (25.6B3).

Do not apply these provisions to the following sound recording collections:

1) a collection whose contents consist of all of a composer's works of a particular type or of a particular type for a particular medium of performance (25.34C2);

2) a collection made up of a consecutively numbered group of works (25:34C3);

3) collections of pop, folk, ethnic, or jazz music;

4) multipart collections that are not yet complete.

(*CSB* 46: 54)

TITLE ADDED ENTRIES

21.30J MCD Follow the instructions in LCRI 21.30J [cf. *CSB* 66: 11-19] in making title added entries for music publications and music sound recordings, disregarding the restriction in rule 21.30J1(d). *Exception*: For items entered under the heading for a composer, do not make an added entry under a title that is not sufficiently distinctive by itself to be a useful access point (e.g., Piano music; Symphony no. 3 in F major).

For collections without a collective title, follow the instructions in LCRI 21.30J, subject to the exception above.

Transcription: Die kleine Kammermusik [GMD] ; Sonata in A minor ; L'hiver ; Naise ; Napolitana ; Air trompette ...
Title added entries: I. Title. II. Title: Kleine Kammermusik ; Sonata in A minor ; L'hiver ; Naise ; Napolitana ; Air trompette.

Transcription: Flos campi [GMD] : for viola, voices, and orchestra (six movements segue) ; Suite for viola and orchestra ...
Title added entry: I. Title.

Transcription: Balorosa soldatesca ; Gradevole assemblea ; Partite...
Title added entries: I. Title. II. Title: Gradevole assemblea. III. Title: Balorosa soldatesca ; Gradevole assemblea ; Partite.

When a title that is to be traced contains a number, follow the instructions in LCRI 21.30J. When such a title begins with a cardinal number that is not an integral part of the title, also make an added entry under the title with the number omitted.

Title proper: 5 romances sans paroles
Title added entries: I. Title. II. Title: Cinq romances sans paroles. III. Title: Romances sans paroles.

When such a title begins with an ordinal number that is not an integral part of the title, make only one title added entry under the title with the number omitted.

> *Title proper:* Third Brazilian suite.
> *Title added entry:* I. Title: Brazilian suite.

(rev. June 1994)(*MCB* 25:8:2)

21.30L1 MCD For special provisions for analyzed volumes of collected works of composers (Gesamtausgaben) see MCD 1.5H. (January 1991)(*MCD* 52).

RELATED PERSONS AND WORKS

21.30F MCD
Related Persons
Make an added entry for any person mentioned in the title proper or other title information of a bibliographic record for a musical work or collection. *Exception:* do not make an added entry if the person's relationship to the item is purely a subject relationship.

> **Liszt, Franz**
> Präludium und Fuge über den Namen Bach ...
> *Added entry:* Bach, Johann Sebastian

Electronic or Computer Music Studios
For recordings of electronic or computer music, make an added entry for the studio or studios where the music was realized, when the item being cataloged identifies the studio or studios. If more than three studios were involved, however, make no such added entries.

Many studios are (or can be assumed to be) corporate bodies and can be established as such, if not already established. For studios [that] are [not] corporate bodies and are not already established, follow the procedures outlined in *Subject cataloging manual* H 405, "Procedures for Group Two headings. Heading requested by descriptive cataloger for use as descriptive access point." For further guidance see DCM Z11.3

Library of Congress Foundations and Funds
If the work being cataloged was commissioned by a Library of Congress foundation or fund (e.g., Elizabeth Sprague Coolidge Foundation, McKim Fund), make an added entry under the corporate heading for the foundation or fund. Justify the added entry by naming the foundation or fund in a note (see 21.29F). (Rev. June 1994)(*MCB* 25:8:2)

21.30G MCD When an instrumental work or collection is based on, inspired by, etc., one or two individual literary works, make a simple added entry or entries (cf. LCRI 21.30M [*CSB* 63: 11-12]) for the literary work or works. (For vocal works based on literary works, see 21.19A.)

Tchaikovsky, Peter Ilich
    [Romeo et Juliette (Fantasy-overture)]
    Romeo und Julia : Fantasie-Ouvertüre nach Shakespeare ...
Added entry: Shakespeare, William. Romeo and Juliet.

When an instrumental work or collection is based on, inspired by, etc., three or more literary works by the same author, or an author's oeuvre in general, make an added entry for the author.

Henze, Hans Werner
    [Royal winter music. No. 1]
    Royal winter music. First sonata on Shakespearean characters ...
Added entry: Shakespeare, William

When a musical work is based on, inspired by, etc., one or more works by an artist, or an artist's oeuvre in general, make an added entry of the artist.

Mussorgsky, Modest Petrovich
    [Kartinki s vystavki]
    Pictures at an exhibition ...
Note: Suite, based on paintings and drawings by Victor Hartmann.
Added entry: Gartman, Viktor Aleksandrovich

(rev. May 1989)(*MCD* 51-52)

21.30H MCD For electronic or computer music studios, see MCD 21.30F. (July 1986)(*MCD* 52)

REFERENCES

Follow the instructions in chapters 21 through 26 and exercise judgment in making references, particularly from forms of titles not used as uniform titles. In general, refer from any variant form of a name or uniform title that has appeared on an item being cataloged (and therefore that might be the form sought by a user who has seen it). Previously, Library of Congress policy provided for the making of references from the name of an individual whose name is contained in the name of a performing ensemble (e.g., Crosby Stills & Nash) to the name of the corporate body. The following limited policy is now applicable (i.e., LC no longer makes the references).

26.2C LCRI When the name of a performing group contains the name of one or more of its members, make a *see also* reference from the heading for each person to the heading for the group (but not from the group to the person). The Library of Congress is limiting this practice to collections of special materials in lieu of making multiple added entries on individual bibliographic records. (*CSB* 67: 20)

DIFFERENT TITLES OR VARIANTS OF THE TITLE

For the same reasons that make uniform titles so critically important in organizing access to musical works, the potential for multiple manifestations of a given work appearing under different titles proper makes references between the titles not chosen and the authorized uniform title equally critical. The following Library of Congress Music Cataloging Decisions provide detailed instructions for constructing references in such cases. Important principles to bear in mind are: 1) references should be made in the form in which they would appear had they been used as the uniform title; and, 2) because of the frequent use in music publications of titles that include names of types of composition, additions will sometimes be required to distinguish a reference under a composer heading from another work with a similar title that has been used as an authorized uniform title.

26.4B1 MCD
Introduction
The following instructions deal with the choice and form of the title portion of name-title see references to headings for musical works. They apply also to the name-title references for parts of works prescribed in rule 25.32A1. When references not in conformity with these instructions are encountered in a name authority record, they should be changed to conform if the record is being changed for another reason.

Generally, the heading referred to should include only the basic uniform title of the work, without additions such as "arr." (25.35C), "Vocal score" (25.35D), "Libretto" (25.35E), language (25.35F), etc., even if such additions are used in the uniform title in the bibliographic record for item being cataloged. If, however, the title being referred from is specific to the arrangement, format, language, etc., brought out by an addition to the uniform title, and the title would not logically be used for a different manifestation of the work, refer to the uniform title with the addition.

> **Bartók, Béla**
> Duke Bluebeard's castle
> *search under:*
> **Bartók, Béla**
> Kékszakállu herceg vára

not:

> **Bartók, Béla**
> Duke Bluebeard's castle
> *search under:*
> **Bartók, Béla**
> Kékszakállu herceg vára. English

but:

> **John, Elton**
> Words of Elton's smash hit "Crocodile Rock"
> *search under:*
> **John, Elton**
> Crocodile rock. Text

For further information regarding arrangements, see below under NON-DISTINCTIVE TITLES (section 4).

Underlying these instructions is the principle that each reference should, to the extent possible, be constructed "in the same form in which it would be constructed if used as the heading" (LCRI 26.1 [*CSB* 47: 57]). Thus, for example, it is understood that if a title being referred from begins with an article, the article should be omitted in accordance with 25.2C.

The instructions are divided into two parts: the first for references from distinctive titles and the second for references from non-distinctive titles. Essentially, consider a title to be non-distinctive if it fits the description in the first paragraph of rule 5.1B1. Consider other titles to be distinctive.

Distinctive Titles
When the title proper of a work (or the principal title if a secondary entry is being made for the work in question) is distinctive and is significantly different from the work's uniform title, make a reference from it to the uniform title. Generally do not include other title information in the title referred from.

Similarly, refer from any other distinctive and significantly different title under which catalog users are likely to search for the work: e.g., a parallel title, especially one in English; an alternative title or a subtitle that has the nature of an alternative title; a nickname; the original title. Such titles may appear in the item being cataloged or may be found in a reference source; generally, however, do not do research solely for the purpose of identifying titles from which references should be made.

> **Sullivan, Arthur, Sir**
> Bunthorne's bride
> *search under:*
> **Sullivan, Arthur, Sir**
> Patience

> **Mendelssohn-Bartholdy, Felix**
> Italian symphony
> *search under:*
> **Mendelssohn-Bartholdy, Felix**
> Symphonies, no. 4, op. 90, A major

> **Schubert, Franz**
> Momens musicals
> *search under:*
> **Schubert, Franz**
> Moments musicaux
> (Preface of the item being cataloged indicates the work was originally published under the title "Momens musicals")

Conflicts

When a distinctive title to be referred from is the same as the uniform title of another work entered under the same composer (apart from any additions made to that uniform title under rule 25.31B), resolve the conflict by making an addition or additions to the reference according to 25.31B. Change the existing uniform title by making a corresponding addition or additions to it, if it does not already include them.

Bach, Johann Sebastian
 Nun danket alle Gott (Chorale), BWV 79, no. 3
search under:
Bach, Johann Sebastian
 Gott, der Herr, is Sonn' und Schild. Nun danket alle Gott
(Established uniform title: [Nun danket alle gott (Cantata)])
(The index to Schmeider lists six works or parts of works with the title "Nun danket alle Gott": one cantata, three chorales, one chorale prelude, and one motet)

Schubert, Franz
 Tod und das Mädchen (String quartet)
search under:
Schubert, Franz
 Quartets, strings, D. 810, D minor
(Established uniform title, [Tod und das Mädchen], to be changed to [Tod und das Mädchen (Song)])

When a distinctive title to be referred from is the same as the title in a name-title reference to another work by the same composer, resolve the conflict by making additions to both references according to rule 25.31B.

Beethoven, Ludwig van
 Leonore overture, no. 1
search under:
Beethoven, Ludwig van
 Ouvertüre zur Oper Leonore, no. 1

Beethoven, Ludwig van
 Leonore overture, no. 3
search under:
Beethoven, Ludwig van
 Fidelio (1806). Ouverture

Glière, Reinhold Morits[ligature]evich
 Valse triste, clarinet, piano
search under:
Glière, Reinhold Morits[ligature]evich
 P'esy, op. 35. Grustnyi´ val's

Glière, Reinhold Morits[ligature]evich
 Valse triste, pianos (2)
search under:
Glière, Reinhold Morits[ligature]evich
 P'esy, pianos (2), op. 41. Grustnyĭ val's

Debussy, Claude
 Obrazy, orchestra
search under:
Debussy, Claude
 Images, orchestra

Debussy, Claude
 Obrazy, piano, 1st ser.
search under:
Debussy, Claude
 Images, piano, 1st ser.

Debussy, Claude
 Obrazy, piano, 2nd ser.
search under:
Debussy, Claude
 Images, piano, 2nd ser.

Variant Forms of Titles

1. **Ampersand**. When an ampersand (or other symbol, e.g., +, representing the word "and") occurs as one of the first five words filed on in a distinctive uniform title or in a distinctive title being referred from, make a reference (or an additional reference) substituting the word "and" in the language of the title.

Green, David Llewellyn
 Allegro moderato and three metamorphoses
search under:
Green, David Llewellyn
 Allegro moderato & three metamorphoses

Green, David Llewellyn
 Allegro moderato & drei Metamorphosen
search under:
Green, David Llewellyn
 Allegro moderato & three metamorphoses

Green, David Llewellyn
 Allegro moderato und drei Metamorphosen
search under:
Green, David Llewellyn
 Allegro moderato & three metamorphoses

2. **Numbers**. When a cardinal number occurs as one of the first five words filed on in a distinctive uniform title or in a distinctive title being referred from, make references [(or additional references)] according to the principles governing the making of added entries set forth in LCRI 21.30J (7-11) [*CSB* 66: 15-18]. In addition, when a distinctive title being referred from begins with a number that is not an integral part of the title, make a reference from the title with the number omitted (unless the resulting title is the same as the uniform title).

> **Bach, Johann Sebastian**
>   6 concerti brandesburghesi
> *search under:*
> **Bach, Johann Sebastian**
>   Brandenburgische Konzerte

> **Bach, Johann Sebastian**
>   Sei concerti brandesburghesi
> *search under:*
> **Bach, Johann Sebastian**
>   Brandenburgische Konzerte

> **Bach, Johann Sebastian**
>   Concerti brandesburghesi
> *search under:*
> **Bach, Johann Sebastian**
>   Brandenburgische Konzerte

3. **Other**. If a distinctive title proper or a distinctive title being referred from contains data within the first five words filed on for which there could be an alternative form that would be filed differently, make a reference (or an additional reference) from that form if it is thought that some users of the catalog might reasonably search under that form, following the guidelines for title added entries in LCRI 21.30J (3-11) [*CSB* 66: 13-18].

> **Finnissy, Michael**
>   Mister Punch
> *search under:*
> **Finnissy, Michael**
>   Mr. Punch

Non-Distinctive Titles

Make references based on non-distinctive titles only when the uniform title that would result from the application of 25.30 to such a title is different from the actual uniform title. Then make a reference only in the form that the uniform title would take if the title in question had been selected as the basis for the uniform title. The following examples illustrate the most typical situations in which references based on non-distinctive titles are needed.

1. The title selected as the basis for the uniform title is distinctive but the work is also known by a non-distinctive title.

Hovhaness, Alan
Concertos, horn, string orchestra, op. 78
search under:
Hovhaness, Alan
Artik

Routh, Francis
Concertos, violin, violoncello, orchestra, op. 19
search under:
Routh, Francis
Double concerto[1]

2. The work is also known by the name of a type of composition different from that selected as the basis for the uniform title.

Pleyel, Ignaz
Trios, piano, strings, B. 465-467
search under:
Pleyel, Ignaz
Sonatas, piano trio, B. 465-467

3. The work is identified in the item being cataloged by a number from a numbering system different from that used in the uniform title.

Dvořák, Antonín
Symphonies, no. 4, op. 88, G major
search under:
Dvořák, Antonín
Symphonies, no. 8, op. 88, G major

Haydn, Joseph
Symphonies, no. 6, D major
search under:
Haydn, Joseph
Symphonies, H. I, 6, D major

Vivaldi, Antonio
Concertos, oboes (2), continuo, op. 42, no. 2, D minor
search under:
Vivaldi, Antonio
Concertos, oboes (2), continuo, RV 535, D minor

---

[1] For works with such titles as "Double concerto," "Triple concerto," etc., make a reference based on the non-distinctive title "Concerto" even if there is no evidence that the work actually is also known by the non-distinctive title, if such a reference would provide useful access to the work.

Vivaldi, Antonio
> Concertos, oboes (2), continuo, P. 302, D minor
search under:
Vivaldi, Antonio
> Concertos, oboes (2), continuo, RV 535, D minor
> (*Title on item being cataloged*: Concerto for two oboes and bassoon in D minor, op. 42, no. 2, P. 302)

(Generally do not refer from titles using numbers not found in the item being cataloged unless such numbers originated with the composer.)

4. The item being cataloged is published for a medium of performance other than the original, and a statement of medium of performance would be required in the uniform title if the version being cataloged were the original version.

Boccherini, Luigi
> Quintets, oboe, violins, viola, violoncello, G. 436, D minor
search under:
Boccherini, Luigi
> Quintets, flute, violins, viola, violoncello, G. 436, D minor

Pleyel, Ignaz
> Trios, clarinets, bassoon, op. 20. No. 1
search under:
Pleyel, Ignaz
> Quartets, flute, violin, viola, violoncello, B. 386, C major; arr.

Conflicts

When a title in a reference formulated in uniform-title format according to these instructions is the same as the uniform title of another work entered under the same composer, resolve the conflict by making an addition or additions to the reference according to rule 25.30E1. Also change the existing uniform title by making a corresponding addition or additions.

Hindemith, Paul
> Sonatas, horn, piano (1943)
search under:
Hindemith, Paul
> Sonatas, alto horn, piano
> (*For alto horn, horn, or saxophone and piano; established uniform title,* [Sonatas, horn, piano], *to be changed to* [Sonatas, horn, piano (1939)])

If the application of these instructions results in two identical references to different uniform titles entered under the same composer, resolve the conflict by making an addition or additions to each reference according to rule 25.30E1. (rev. June 1994)(*MCB* 25:8:2)

PARTS OF A WORK

26.4B3 MCD For references from titles of parts of music works, see MCD 25.32A1. (rec. May 1989)(*MCD:* 95)

COLLECTIVE UNIFORM TITLES

26.4B4 MCD
Collections Without Collective Title
For a collection without a collective title entered under a personal name heading with a collective uniform title, make a name-title "see" reference from the title proper to the uniform title, if no analytic added entry is made for the first work. (If an analytic added entry is made for the first work, sufficient access to the bibliographic record is provided by that analytical added entry and associated references.)

See LCRI 21.30J (1) [*CSB* 66: 11] for guidance as to what constitutes the title proper of a collection without a collective title. If the title proper contains more than three titles separated by semicolons, terminate the reference after the third title, following it with the mark of omission (...). If the title proper contains only one title, and that title is identical with a uniform title that has been used under the heading for the composer in a bibliographic record or name authority record in the catalog, make the reference a "see also" reference (see "CONFLICTS" below).

> **Debussy, Claude**
>   Cathédrale engloutie ; Ondine ; Estampes ...
> search under:
> **Debussy, Claude**
>   Piano music. Selections
> (*Title proper:* La cathédrale engloutie ; Ondine ; Estampes ; Etude pour les arpèges composés ; Children's corner ; L'isle joyeuse)

> **Chopin, Frédéric**
>   Allegro de concert
> *search also under:*
> **Chopin, Frédéric**
>   Instrumental music. Selections
> (*Title transcription:* Allegro de concert : A-dur = A major, op. 46 ; Fuga a-moll = Fugue in A minor, op. post. ; Preludium As-dur = Prelude in A flat major, op. post. ; Wariacje B-dur na temat Je vends des scapulaires = Variations in B flat major, op. 12 ; [etc.] ; established uniform title: [Allegro de concert])

Follow the above instructions also when three or more parts of a single work are published together without an overall title.

> **Ugolini, Vincenzo**
>   Exultate omnes ; Beata es, Virgo Maria ; and, Quae est ista
> *search under:*
> **Ugolini, Vincenzo**
>   Motecta et Missae. Selections

Conflicts

When the title proper (or other title being referred from) of a collection of, or selection from, a composer's works is identical with a uniform title that has been used under the heading for that composer in a bibliographic record or name authority record in the catalog, trace the name-title reference from the bibliographic title to the collective uniform title as a "see-also" reference.

> **Schubert, Franz**
>   An die Musik
> *search also under:*
> **Schubert, Franz**
>   Songs. Selections
> (*Established uniform title:* [An die Musik])

> **Boyce, William**
>   Concerti grossi
> *search also under:*
> **Boyce, William**
>   Instrumental music. Selections
> (*Established uniform title:* [Concerti grossi])

In all other cases, trace the reference as a "see" reference.

> **Ellington, Duke**
>   Sophisticated lady
> *search under:*
> **Ellington, Duke**
>   Songs. Selections
> (*Uniform title* [Sophisticated lady] *not established*)

> **Baksa, Robert F.**
>   Chamber music
> *search under:*
> **Baksa, Robert F.**
>   Instrumental music. Selections
> (*Uniform title* [Chamber music] *not established*)

When a uniform title is established (i.e., used in a heading in a name authority record or an access point in a bibliographic record) which is identical with the title portion of a name-title "see" reference under the same composer, change the reference to a "see also" reference.

Variant Forms of Collective Titles

1. Ampersand. When an ampersand (or other symbol, e.g., +, representing the word "and") occurs as one of the first five words filed on in a collective title being referred from, make an additional reference substituting the word "and" in the language of the title.

Bloch, Ernest
    Gesamtwerk für Violoncello & Orchester
search under:
Bloch, Ernest
    Instrumental music. Selections

Bloch, Ernest
    Gesamtwerk für Violoncello und Orchester
search under:
Bloch, Ernest
    Instrumental music. Selections

2. Numbers. When a cardinal number ocurs as one of the first five words filed on in a collective title being referred from, make references according to the principles governing the making of added entries set forth in LCRI 21.30J (6-9) [*CSB* 66: 15-18]. In addition, when a distinctive collective title being referred from begins with a number that is not an integral part of the title, make a reference from the title with the number omitted.

Brahms, Johannes
    Vier Symphonien
search under:
Brahms, Johannes
    Symphonies

Brahms, Johannes
    4 Symphonien
search under:
Brahms, Johannes
    Symphonies

Mozart, Wolfgang Amadeus
    Six last symphonies
search under:
Mozart, Wolfgang Amadeus
    Symphonies. Selections

Mozart, Wolfgang Amadeus
    6 last symphonies
search under:
Mozart, Wolfgang Amadeus
    Symphonies. Selections

Mozart, Wolfgang Amadeus
    Last symphonies
search under:
Mozart, Wolfgang Amadeus
    Symphonies. Selections

3. Other If a distinctive collective title being referred from contains data within the first five words filed on for which there could be an alternative form that would be filed differently, make an additional reference from that form if it is thought that some users of the catalog might reasonably search under that form, following the guidelines for title added entries in LCRI 21.30J (3-10) [*CSB 66:* 14-18].

> **Bach, Johann Sebastian**
>   Orgelmusik in St. Blasius Münden
> *search under:*
> **Bach, Johann Sebastian**
>   Organ music. Selections
>
> **Bach, Johann Sebastian**
>   Orgelmusik in Sankt Blasius Münden
> *search under:*
> **Bach, Johann Sebastian**
>   Organ music. Selections

(rev. June 1994)(*MCB* 25:8:2)

FORM OF ENTRY

There are no rules for forms of entry specifically for use with music materials. However, because forms of entry are based on the forms found in chief sources of information, there are a few extra considerations.

COMPOSERS

Composers should be treated as authors.

> **22.1B LCRI** ... Treat music composers as authors and determine the name from the form found in the chief sources of information in publications of the printed music. If no form in these chief sources of information is in the composer's language, determine the name from reference sources of the composer's country of residence or activity. If the name is not listed there, use the form found in the chief sources of information. (*CSB* 44: 39)

PERFORMERS

For a performer, apply the second sentence of rule 22.1B and determine the name from reference sources in his or her language, or issued in his or her country of residence or activity. Consider a performer's recordings among the "reference sources."

When a performer is also known as a composer, a determination should be made about whether he or she is known primarily as a composer or as a performer. If the person is primarily known as a performer, establish the name from chief sources of information on recordings. Otherwise, or in the case of doubt, prefer the form found on chief sources of information in the published music.

BIRTH DATES

22.17 MCD When an item being cataloged is accompanied by a dealer's order slip that gives a date for the composer, and the date does not appear in the item itself and has not otherwise come to light, record the date in the composer's name authority record in the 670 :"sources found" field for the item being cataloged, giving "Harrassowitz slip," ["Blackwell slip," etc.] as the location.

Do not include in the heading for a composer a date whose only source is a dealer's slip, unless the date is needed to resolve a conflict and an unsuccessful attempt has been made to find confirmation of the date in reference sources. (rev. May 1989)(*MCD* 53)

IDENTICAL NAMES

22.19B MCD When no other means (including changing the existing heading) is available for distinguishing between a musician and another person with the same name for whom a heading is already established, a word designating a musician's occupation, such as "violinist," "soprano," etc., may be used as a qualifier under this rule when such a term appears with the person's name in the item being cataloged or in a reference source. If the term appears only in a foreign language, substitute the English equivalent. If only the name of the instrument a person plays appears, substitute the corresponding agent noun, e.g., "pianist" for "piano."

If a musician is established with an undifferentiated heading according to 22.20, and a qualifier as described above is available to distinguish him or her, establish the name separately according to the last paragraph of LCRI 22.17-22.20.

If a musician is established with a qualifier according to the above instructions and at a later time it appears that the qualifier gives an inaccurate or misleading characterization of the person, change the heading. Add a date (22.17) and/or the full form of a name represented by an initial (22.18) if either is available; otherwise substitute as a qualifier a more appropriate term that has appeared with the person's name. (rev. May 1989)(*MCD* 56).

NAMES NOT CONVEYING THE IDEA OF A CORPORATE BODY

24.4B LCRI
Surnames
Generally, do not add a general designation as a qualifier to a corporate name containing two or more surnames (without forename or without forename initials).

    Morgan and Morgan
  not Morgan and Morgan (Firm)
  but **B. Morgan and D. Morgan (Firm)**

Performing Duets
For performing duets, also do not add a general designation as a qualifier if the name contains two surnames (with or without forenames or forename initials) or if the name contains two forenames.

Performing Groups
In dealing with performing groups, apply the following:

> 1) If the name contains a word that specifically designates a performing group or a corporate body in general (e.g., band, consort, society) or contains a collective or plural noun (e.g., Ramblers, Boys, Hot Seven) do not add a designation to the name.
>
> 2) If the name is extremely vague, consisting primarily of single common words (e.g., Circle, Who, Jets) or the name has the appearance of a personal name (e.g., Jethro Tull), add a designation to the name.
>
> 3) If the name falls between the above categories (e.g., Led Zeppelin, Jefferson Airplane, Road Apple, L.A. Contempo), add a designation to the name.
>
> 4) If there is doubt whether a designation should be added, add it.

Use the designation "(Musical group)" unless special circumstances (such as a conflict) require a more specific term. (CSB 49: 30-32)

POPULAR PERFORMING GROUPS

21.23D MCD In determining whether the name of a performing group includes a personal name that appears in conjunction with it (LCRI 21.23D, first paragraph), apply MCD 24.1A. (June 1990)(*MCD* 45)

24.1A MCD When the name of an individual performer appears in conjunction with the name of a performing group, ordinarily do not consider the person's name to be part of the name of the group, in the absence of evidence to the contrary.

> *On item:* J.D. Crowe and the New South
> *Corporate heading*: New South (Musical group)
> *On item:* Artie Shaw and his orchestra
> *No corporate heading (body is unnamed; cf. 21.1B1).*

(June 1990)(*MCD* 58).

SERIES ENTERED UNDER TITLE

For series on music or sound recordings apply Library of Congress Rule Interpretation 25.5B (*CSB* 66: 19-21). Generally, qualifying terms are added to the uniform title for a series only when the series conflicts with another work with the same title proper. In most cases the place of publication is considered the appropriate addition to a uniform title for a series.

Example 37

Edition Eulenburg

SYMPHONY No. 1

C minor
for Orchestra

by

JOHANNES BRAHMS
Op. 68

Foreword by Wilh. Altmann

Ernst Eulenburg Ltd., London © Ernst Eulenburg & Co. GmbH, Mainz
Edition Eulenburg GmbH, Zürich © Edition Eulenburg Inc., New York

---

At foot of p. 1: No. 425

At foot of every page: E.E. 4558

On p. [i]: facsimile of autograph of opening theme in 4th movement

vii, 166 pages; 19 cm.

```
Brahms, Johannes, 1833-1897.
  [Symphonies, no. 1, op. 68, C minor]
  Symphony no. 1, C minor, for orchestra, op. 68 / by
Johannes Brahms ; foreword by Wilh. Altmann. -- London :
Eulenburg ; New York : Edition Eulenburg, [19-]
  1 miniature score (vii, 166 p.) : facsim. ; 19 cm.

  Publisher's no.: Edition Eulenburg no. 425.
  Pl. no.: E.E. 4558.
```

Main entry is under the heading for Brahms as composer using the general rule for choice of entry for a work of personal authorship (21.1A2). An added entry could be made for Altmann if desired (21.30D1), although because he contributed nothing to the musical work it is unlikely that most catalogers would do so.

Example 38

ÉDITION CLASSIQUE A. DURAND & FILS
*************************************☆************************************

I. MOSCHELÈS

———

C A D E N C E S
pour les concertos de piano
de BEETHOVEN

———

Doigtées et révisées
par
I. PHILIPP
Professeur au Conservatoire National de Paris

No. 10473 — DEUX CADENCES POUR LE CONCERTO EN UT MAJEUR (op. 15)   net : 1.50
No. 10474 — CADENCE POUR LE CONCERTO EN SI BÉMOL (op. 19)   — 1.50
No. 10475 — CADENCE POUR LE CONCERTO EN UT MINEUR (op. 37)   — 1.50
No. <u>10476</u> — DEUX CADENCES POUR LE CONCERTO EN SOL (op. 58)   — 1.50

Paris, A. DURAND & FILS, Éditeurs
DURAND & Cie
4, Place de la Madeleine

On caption:

DEUX CADENCES
pour le 4<u>e</u> Concerto, Op. 58
de BEETHOVEN

I. MOSCHELÈS

At foot of first page: Copyright by Durand et Cie 1924

At foot of each page: D. & F. 10,476

7 pages; 32 cm.

Example 38

```
Moscheles, Ignaz, 1794-1870.
Deux cadences pour le 4e concerto, op. 58 de Beethoven
/ I. Moschelès. -- Paris : Durand, c1924.
   7 p. of music ; 32 cm. -- (Cadences pour les concertos
de piano de Beethoven / I. Moschelès) (Edition classique
A. Durand & fils)

   Caption title.
   Revised and fingered by I. Philipp.
   Pl. no.: D. & F. 10, 476.

   I. Philipp, Isidore, 1863-1958.  II. Beethoven, Ludwig
van, 1770-1827. Concertos, piano, orchestra, no. 4, op.
58, G major.  III Series: Moscheles, Ignaz, 1794-1870.
Cadenzen zu Beethoven'schen Klavierkonzerten (1924).
```

This work is a cadenza, which is intended to be interpolated into a performance of Beethoven's fourth piano concerto. This is the sort of "related work" referred to in rule 21.28—that is, the cadenza is related to the concerto. The main entry will be under the heading for the work itself—Moschelès' cadenza—with an added entry for the related Beethoven concerto (21.28B1). Added entries are required for Philipp, whose editorial contribution was substantial (21.30D1), and for the Beethoven concerto (21.28B1).

The Moschelès series was originally published in four volumes by B. Senff, Leipzig, with the title *Cadenzen zu Beethoven'schen Klavierkonzerten*; consequently a uniform title must be formulated for the series entered under the heading for Moschelès. The other series is disregarded because of 21.30L(1).

Example 39

Neil Young
Hawks & Doves

©1981 SILVER FIDDLE
All rights reserved

Table of contents, p. [3]:

CAPT. KENNEDY ★ 25
COASTLINE ★ 34
COMIN' APART AT EVERY NAIL ★ 44
HAWKS & DOVES ★ 50
LITLE WING ★ 5
LOST IN SPACE ★ 18
THE OLD HOMESTEAD ★ 10
STAYIN' POWER ★ 30
UNION MAN ★ 37

First page of music:

LITTLE WING
Words and Music by NEIL YOUNG
[guitar chord diagrams and symbols above a score for voice and piano]

Facing page:

Little Wing
All her friends call her Little Wing
But she flies rings around them all
She comes to town when the children sing
And leaves them feathers if they fall
She leaves her feathers if they fall

Little Wing, don't fly away
When the summer turns to fall
Don't you know some people say
The winter is the best time of them all
Winter is the best of all

Words and Music by NEIL YOUNG
© 1975 SILVER FIDDLE

Verso of back cover:

Exclusive Selling Agent for
the United States and Canada
WARNER BROS. PUBLICATIONS INC.
75 Rockefeller Plaza (New York, NY 10019   SILVER FIDDLE

$7.95
in U.S.A.

VF0842

55 pages; no illustrations; 30 cm.

Phonolog lists an album; *Hawks & Doves* (Reprise HS 2297)

Example 39

```
Young, Neil.
   Hawks & doves / Neil Young. -- [United States] :
Silver Fiddle ; New York, NY : exclusive selling agent
for the United States and Canada, Warner Bros.
Publications, c1981.
   1 score (55 p.) ; 30 cm.

   Songs from the record album of the same title; for
voice and piano with chord symbols and guitar chord
diagrams; words printed also as text.
   Contents: Little wing -- The old homestead -- Lost in
space -- Capt. Kennedy -- Stayin' power -- Coastline --
Union man -- Comin' apart at every nail -- Hawks & doves.
   Publisher's no.: VF0842.

   I. Title.
```

This is what is referred to as a "pop-folio," a printed transcription of the music found on a sound recording.

Main entry is under the heading for Young, the composer of this music, using the general rule for works of personal authorship (21.1A2).

The sound recording would also be entered under the heading for Young as composer (21.23B). In a library that collects both folios and recordings these entries will collocate in a name index under the heading for Young. Because the Library of Congress normally would not add a uniform title for a pop-folio vocal score, elements of the description (such as the GMD) will be relied upon to distinguish the entries.

Example 40

Label side 1:

Side 1 Stereo
VICS 1265 (UVRS-1467)

Strauss

Also sprach Zarathustra, Op. 30
Part 1

Chicago Symphony Orchestra
Fritz Reiner, Conductor

TMK(s) ® REGISTERED • MARCA(s) REGISTRADA(s)
RADIO CORPORATION OF AMERICA — MADE IN U.S.A.

Label side 2:

Side 2 Stereo
VICS 1265 (UVRS-1468)

Strauss

Also sprach Zarathustra, Op. 30
Concluded

Chicago Symphony Orchestra
Fritz Reiner, Conductor
John Weicher, *Violinist*

TMK(s) ® REGISTERED • MARCA(s) REGISTRADA(s)
RADIO CORPORATION OF AMERICA — MADE IN U.S.A.

On container:

STEREO

Immortal Performances

RCA
VICTROLA

On container verso:

TMK(s) ® by RCA Corporation
©1967, RCA Records, New York, NY • Printed in USA

Timings: Side 1 - 16:06 • Side 2 - 15:43
Library of Congress card number: R67-3339
Cover painting by Barron Storey

(Recorded March 8, 1954)

Program notes on container verso.

Example 40

```
Strauss, Richard, 1864-1949.
    Also sprach Zarathustra [sound recording] : op. 30 /
Strauss. -- New York, NY : RCA Victrola, c1967.
    1 sound disc (32 min.) : analog, 33 1/3 rpm, stereo. ;
12 in. -- (Immortal performances)

    RCA Victrola: VICS 1265.
    Symphonic poem.
    Chicago Symphony Orchestra ; Fritz Reiner, conductor.
    Recorded Mar. 8, 1954.

    I. Reiner, Fritz, 1888-1963.  II. Chicago Symphony
Orchestra.  III. Title.  IV. Series.
```

This is a sound recording of a single work. Main entry is under the heading for Strauss, the composer (21.23A1). Added entries will be made for the principal performers named on the item, the orchestra and conductor (21.23A1). There will be an added entry for the title proper (21.30J1) because this title is distinctive. A series added entry is also made (21.30L1).

Example 41

Label side 1:

AMERICA
Produced by Ian Samwell with Jeff Dexter
and America
Engineered by Ken Scott

BS 2576   **SIDE 1**
(S39997)REI

1. RIVERSIDE (Bunnell) 3:02
2. SANDMAN (Bunnell) 5:03
3. THREE ROSES (Bunnel) 3:54
4. CHILDREN (Bunnell) 3:07)
5. A HORSE WITH NO NAME (Bunnell) (4:10)
6. HERE (Beckley) 5:30

STEREO

Label side 2:

AMERICA
Produced by Ian Samwell with Jeff Dexter
and America
Engineered by Ken Scare

BS 2576   **SIDE 2**
(S39998)

1. I NEED YOU (Beckley) 3:04
2. RAINY DAY (Peek) 3:00
3. NEVER FOUND THE TIME (Peek) 3:50
4. CLARICE (Beckley) 4:00
5. DONKEY JAW (Peek) 5:17
6. PIGEON SONG (Bunnell) 2:17

STEREO

Around perimeter of label: **BURBANK, HOME OF WARNER BROS. RECORDS**

On container verso:

All selections Warner Bros. Music Corp. (ASCAP)
AMERICA is Dewey Bunnell, Gerry Beckley and Dan Peek
Produced by Ian Samwell with Jeff Dexter and AMERICA
Engineered by Ken Scott
Recorded at Trident Studios, London, Englad
"A Horse with No Name" recorded at Morgan Studios, London
Cover Photos and Design by Nigel Waymouth
Logo Flash Fox

Warner Bros. Records Inc., a Subsidiary & Licensee of Warner Bros. Inc., 4000 Warner Blvd., Burbank, California
44 East 50th Street, New York, New York 10022 • Made in U.S.A. ©1971 Warner Bros. Records Inc.

On edge of container: ℗1972

Example 41

```
America (Musical group).
    America [sound recording]. -- Burbank, Calif. : Warner
Bros. Records, p1972.
    1 sound disc (51 min.) : analog, 33 1/3 rpm, stereo. ;
12 in.

    Warner Bros. Records: BS 2576.
    Songs written and performed by America.
    Recorded in London.
    Contents:  Riverside (3:02) ; Sandman (5:03) ; Three
roses (3:54) ; Children (3:07) ; A horse with no name
(4:10) / Bunnell -- Here (5:30) ; I need you (3:04) /
Beckley -- Rainy day (3:00) ; Never found the time (3:50)
/ Peek -- Clarice / Beckley (4:00) -- Donkey jaw / Peek
(5:17) -- Pigeon song / Bunnell (2:17).

    I. Bunnell, Dewey.  II. Beckley, Gerry.  III. Peek,
Dan.  IV. Title.
```

Because the songs are composed individually by the three members of the performing group, this recording is considered a collection. Main entry is under the heading for America, the group, as principal performer (21.23C1). Added entries may be made under the headings for each of the named composers (21.30C1). In a library that collects popular music for research purposes, these would be considered useful entries; it is unlikely, however, that these added entries would be made in most libraries. Analytical added entries are not made by the Library of Congress for collections of popular music (LCRI 21.7B).

Example 42

Label side 1:

MOTHER
MAYBELLE CARTER

KG 32436
C 32437
STEREO

SIDE 1
AL 32437
Ⓟ1973 CBS, Inc.

1. DIALOGUE - 1st record 1927 - Original Carter Family 2:00
2. GOOD OLD MOUNTAIN DEW 1:59 - S. Wiseman - B Lunsford -
3. STILL 3:17 - B. Anderson -
4. ARKANSAS TRAVELLER 4:52
- Arr. M. Carter - With Dialogue
5. WATERLOO 2:00
- M. Wilkin - J. Loudermilk -
6. BLACK MOUNTAIN RAG 1:48 - Arr. M. Carter -

Label side 2:

MOTHER
MAYBELLE CARTER

KG 32436
C 32437
STEREO

SIDE 2
BL 32437
Ⓟ1973 CBS, Inc.

1. DIALOGUE - JIMMY RODGERS & TRAIN 1:29
2. WABASH CANNONBALL 2:06 - A.P. Carter -
3. ROCKY TOP 3:04 - F. Bryant - B. Bryant -
4. RELEASE ME 2:37
- E. Miller - W.S. Stevenson - R. Yount -
5. HEY LIBERTY 2:17 - Arr. M. Carter -
6. CHINESE BREAKDOWN 5:32
- Arr. M. Carter -
With Dialogue

Example 42

Label side 3:

**MOTHER
MAYBELLE CARTER**

KG 32436
C 32438
STEREO

SIDE 3
AL 32438
℗1973 CBS, Inc.

1. THE BELLS OF ST. MARY 3:17 - E. Adams -
D. Furber - With Dialogue
2. THE WORLD NEEDS A MELODY 3:11
- R. Lane - L. Henley - J. Slate -
3. NEVER ON SUNDAY 3:39 - B. Towne - M. Hadjidakis -
4. TENNESSEE WALTZ 3:20
- P. King - R. Stewart -
5. RED WING 3:41
- Arr. M. Carter -
With Dialogue

Label side 4:

**MOTHER
MAYBELLE CARTER**

KG 32436
C 32438
STEREO

SIDE 4
BL 32438
℗1973 CBS, Inc.

1. WILDWOOD FLOWER 5:46 - A.P. Carter -
With Dialogue
2. RUNNING BEAR 3:06 - J.T. Richardson
3. DRUNKARD'S HELL 4:05 - Arr. M. Carter
4. SWEET ALLIE LEE 3:33
- Arr. M. Carter -

On notes in center of album cover:

This album ... is Mother Maybelle Carter ... playing guitar and autoharp ... Larry Butler, Producer.

Example 42

```
Carter, Maybelle, 1909-1978.
    Mother Maybelle Carter [sound recording]. -- New York
: Columbia, p1973.
    2 sound discs (67 min.) : analog, 33 1/3 rpm, stereo.
; 12 in.

    Columbia: KG 32346 (32437-32438).
    Mother Maybelle Carter, guitar or autoharp with
instrumental ensemble; with spoken reminiscences.
    Contents: Dialogue : 1st record 1927 / original Carter
family (2:00) -- Good old mountain dew / S. Wiseman, B.
Lunsford (1:59) -- Still / B. Anderson (3:17) -- Arkansas
traveller / arr. M. Carter ; with dialogue (4:52) --
Waterloo / M. Wilkin, J. Loudermilk (2:00) -- Black
Mountain rag / arr. M. Carter (1:48) -- Dialogue / Jimmy
Rogers & Train (1:29) -- Wabash Canonball / A.P. Carter
(2:06) -- Rocky Top / F. Bryant, B. Bryant (3:04) --
Release me / E. Miller, W.S. Stevenson, R. Yount (2:37)
-- Hey Liberty / arr. M. Carter (2:17) -- Chinese
breakdown / arr. M. Carter ; with dialogue (5:32) -- The
bells of St. Mary / E. Adams, D. Furber ; with dialogue
(3:17) -- The world needs a melody / R. Lane, L. Henley,
J. Slate (3:11) -- Never on Sunday / B. Towne, M.
Hadjidakis (3:39) -- Tennessee waltz / P. King, R.
Stewart (3:20) -- Red Wing / arr. M. Carter ; with
dialogue (3:41) -- Wildwood flower / A.P. Carter ; with
dialogue (5:46) -- Running bear / J.T. Richardson (3:06)
-- Drunkard's hell / arr. M. Carter (4:05) -- Sweet Allie
Lee / arr. M. Carter (3:33).

    I.  Title.
```

This recording features Mother Maybelle Carter playing folk tunes—music in a popular idiom—some composed and some traditional. Mother Maybelle's personal reminiscences are interspersed with the music. The main entry is under the heading for Carter as principal performer because the recording contains many works of diverse origin (21.23C1). Analysis is not provided because this is not art music (LCRI 21.7B). An added entry is made for the title proper (21.30J1).

Example 43

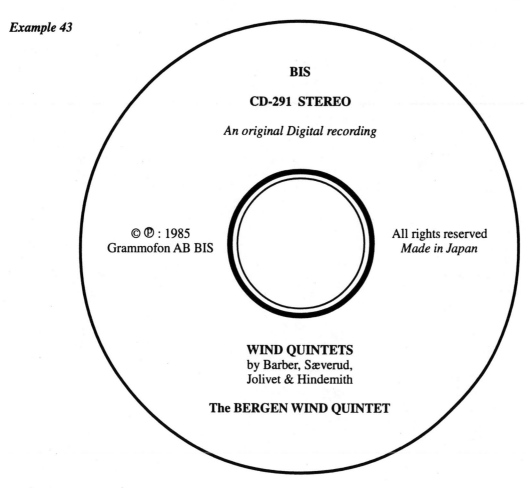

Inside rear cover of booklet:

Recording Data: 1984-12-13/15 in the Petrus Church, Stocksund, Sweden
Recording Engineer & Digital Editing: Robert von Bahr
Sony PCM-F1 Digital Recording Equipment, 2 Schoeps CMC 541 U & 2 Neumann U-89 Mics., SAM 82
Mixer, Sony Tape
Producer: Robert von Bahr
Cover Text: Lorenz Reitan
English Translation: John Skinner
German Translation: Per Skans
French Translation: Arlette Chené-Wiklander
Cover Photos: Hans Jørgen Brun, Bergen, Norway
Album Design: Robert von Bahr
Type-Setting: Marianne von Bahr
Lay-Out: William Jewson
Repro: KåPe Grafiska, Stockholm
Print: Offizin Paul Hartung, Hamburg, W. Germany 1985
CD-Production: Sanyo, Japan

© ℗ : 1985: Grammofon AB BIS

This record can be ordered from Gramofon AB BIS Väringavägen 6 S-182 63 Djursholm Sweden
Phone: Stockholm (08) (*Int.*: +468) - 755 41 00 Telex: 13880 bis s
or from BIS' agents all over the world

Example 43

On container verso:

BARBER, SAMUEL (1910-1981):
1. Summer Music for Woodwind Quintet Op. 31   *(Schirmer)* 11'26

SÆVERUD, HARALD (1897-):
Slåtter og stev fra "Siljustøl" Op. 21 a   *(M/s)*   13'00
2. *Kristi-blodsdråper (Fucsia) 1'32 -*
3. *Dvergmålslått (Canzone dell'Eco) 1'26 -*
4. *Bå'nlåt (Ninnarella) 1'58 -*
5. *Kvellingsull og Lokk (Voci ed ombre nel vespero d'estate) 2'55 -*
6. *Marcia Silijuana 4'53*

JOLIVET, ANDRÉ (1905-1974):
Sérénade pour Quintette à vent
avec Hautbois principal (1945)   *(Billaudot)* 16'36
7. *Cantilène 4'18 -*
8. *Caprice 3'14 -*
9. *Intermède 4' -*
10. *Marche Burlesque 4'53*

HINDEMITH, PAUL (1895-1963):
Kleine Kamermusik für fünf Bläser Op. 24:2   13'40
11. *Lustig, Mäßig schnelle Viertel 2'51 -*
12. *Walzer, Durchweg sehr leise 2'06 -*
13. *Ruhig und einfach 4'48 -*
14. *Schnelle Viertel 0'49 -*
15. *Sehr lebhaft 2'52*

THE BERGEN WIND QUINTET

Example 43

```
Bergen blåsekvintett (Norway)
     Wind quintets [sound recording] / by Barber, Saeverud,
Jolivet & Hindemith. -- Djursholm, Sweden : Bis, p1985.
     1 sound disc (55 min.) : digital, stereo. ; 4 3/4 in.

     Bis: CD-291.
     The 2nd work originally for piano.
     Bergen Wind Quintet.
     Recorded Dec. 13-15, 1984, in the Petrus Church,
Stocksund, Sweden.
     Compact disc (indexed); digital recording.
     Notes in English, Swedish, German, and French ([12]
p.) in container.
     Also issued as analog disc: Bis LP-291.
     Contents: Summer music : for woodwind quintet, op. 31
/ Barber, Samuel (11:26) -- Slåtter og stev fra
"Siljustøl" : op. 21a / Saeverud, Harald (13:00) --
Sérénade pour quintette à vent avec hautbois principal :
1945 / Jolivet, André (16:36) -- Kleine Kammermusik : für
fünf Bläser, Op. 24:2 / Hindemith, Paul (13:40).

     I. Barber Samuel, 1910-     Summer music. II.
Sæverud, Harald, 1897-     Slåtter og stev fra Siljustøl;
arr. III. Jolivet, André, 1905-1974.  Serenades, wind
quintet (1945).  IV. Hindemith, Paul, 1895-1963.  Kleine
Kammermusik.
```

This compact disc contains works for wind quintet—music composed in the Western art tradition.

Main entry is under the heading for the principal performer—the performing ensemble Bergen Blaserkvintett (21.23C1). Analytical added entries (composer-uniform title) are made for each of the works (LCRI 21.7B).

Example 44

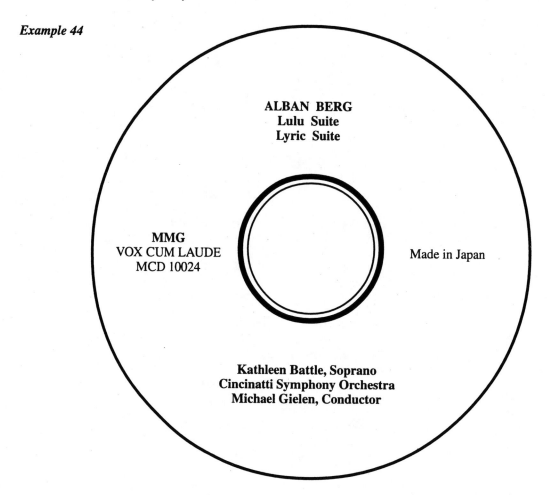

ALBAN BERG
Lulu Suite
Lyric Suite

MMG
VOX CUM LAUDE
MCD 10024

Made in Japan

Kathleen Battle, Soprano
Cincinatti Symphony Orchestra
Michael Gielen, Conductor

Along perimeter of disc: ℗ 1983 THE MOSS MUSIC GROUP, INC.

On container verso:

AN ORIGINAL DIGITAL RECORDING

ALBAN BERG
Kathleen Battle, Soprano
Cincinatti Symphony Orchestra
Michael Gielen, Conductor

Lulu Suite (34:33)
Rondo: Andante und Hymne (Tr. 1-15:37)
Ostinato: Allegro (tr. 2-3:31)
Lied der Lulu: Comodo* (Tr. 3-2:33)
Variationen: Moderato (Tr. 4-3:34)
Adagio: Sostenuto; Lento; Grave* (Tr. 5-8:54)
*with Kathleen Battle, Soprano

Lyric Suite (16:06)
Andante amoroso (Tr. 6-6:00)
Allegro misterioso (Tr. 7-3:44)
Adagio appassionato (Tr. 8-6:10)

℗1983 The Moss Music Group, Inc., New York • Los Angeles • Toronto • London • Amsterdam

Example 44

On booklet verso:

Recorded September 2-4, 1981 • Produced by Marc Aubort & Joanna Nickrenz
Engineering: ELITE RECORDINGS INC., N.Y.C. • Digital Engineer: Frank Dickinson
Cover Painting: EGON SCHIELE—Portrait of Gerta Schiele (1909)
TMK(s) ® MMG • Marca(s) Registrada(s) • Printed in USA
℗ & © 1983 THE MOSS MUSIC GROUP, INC
48 West 38th Street, New York, NY 10018 • Avenue de Floreal 126, Bruxelles, Belgium
Distribué au Canada par/Distributed in Canada by The Moss Music Group (Canada) Inc.
510 Coronation Drive, West Hill, Ontario, Canada M1E 4X6

DIDX 363

```
    Berg, Alban, 1885-1935.
    [Lulu.  Suite]
    Lulu suite [sound recording] ; Lyric suite / Alban
Berg. -- New York, N.Y. : Vox Cum Laude, p1983.
    1 sound disc (51 min.) : digital ; 4 3/4 in.

    Vox Cum Laude: MCD 10024.
    The 2nd work originally for string quartet.
    Kathleen Battle, soprano (1st work) ; Cincinnati
Symphony Orchestra ; Michael Gielen, conductor.
    Recorded Sept. 2-4, 1981.
    Compact disc.
    Durations: 34:33 ; 16:06.
    Program notes, including German text of 1st work with
English translation (11 p.), in container.

    I. Battle, Kathleen.  II. Gielen, Michael, 1927-
III.  Berg, Alban, 1885-1935.  Lyrische Suite.
Selections; arr.  IV. Cincinnati Symphony Orchestra.  V.
Title.  VI. Title: Lyric suite.
```

This compact disc recording contains two works by one composer. The main entry is under the heading for Berg, who composed both works (21.23B1). Added entries are made for the principal performers (21.23B1).

An analytical added entry (composer-uniform title) is made for the second work (LCRI 21.7B).

Two title added entries are formulated to create unique access points for both titles included in area 1 of the description (LCRI 21.30J).

SUMMARY

Access points are created to identify the intellectual entities—the works—contained by the items represented in a bibliographic description.

The basic rule for choice of entry is to "enter ... under the heading for the personal author ... the principal personal author ... or the probable personal author." (AACR 2 21.1A1) Composers of music, and in some cases performers as well, are considered to be the authors of the works they create. Related works (cadenzas, librettos, etc.) are entered under their own headings.

For a sound recording, the content of the recording is central to the decision about choice of main entry. If the recording contains works by the same person(s) or body (bodies), main entry is determined as it would be for the same works in their printed manifestations. If a sound recording contains works by two or more different persons, the choice of main entry is dependent, first, upon whether or not a collective title is present in the description. If there is a collective title, the main entry is under the heading for the principal performer or the first of two or three principal performers. If there are four or more principal performers, or no principal performers, main entry is under the collective title.

Videorecordings almost always are representations of motion pictures, which are usually collaborative projects. Motion pictures almost always are entered under their titles proper, as works of multiple authorship. Main entry for musical videorecordings usually will be under title proper, with an added entry for the musical work as well as for any performers who are prominently featured in the videorecording.

Added entries are made as required under headings for writers of words, performers, and arrangers, and under distinctive titles proper following the rules in chapters 21 and 25. Analytical added entries are made for the works in collections under certain, limited circumstances. The LCRIs are complex and must be consulted in individual cases. In general an attempt is made to provide composer-uniform title access to works that would otherwise be inaccessible.

Forms of entry are based on the forms of names found in chief sources of information. Composers are treated as authors; forms are determined from the chief sources of information in their printed musical works. Forms of entry for performers are determined from reference sources in their languages.

CHAPTER 7: UNIFORM TITLES

INTRODUCTION

Uniform titles are unique identifiers for works. Uniform titles are employed whenever manifestations of a work have appeared with differing titles proper. For musical works, the composer-uniform title combination provides the key citation for the work in the catalog. Because of the nature of music collections, the typical disc or score is more likely to represent another manifestation of a particular work than it is to contain a new work altogether.

Uniform titles will be used for almost all music materials. We know from experience and from research that musical publications are very likely to present musical works with varying titles proper. That is, it is likely that titles proper found on chief sources of information will differ from manifestation to manifestation of a work. Also, so-called "generic" titles routinely contain elements that can be presented in differing languages, styles, or order from one publication to the next, so it is likely that the title will not be constant from one edition to another. By virtue of all these reasons, at least one or more of the typical functions for uniform titles is likely to come into play for any musical works cataloged. These functions are:

1) to draw together in the catalog bibliographic descriptions of various physical manifestations of a particular work;

2) to identify a work when the title by which the work is commonly known differs from the title given on the item that contains it;

3) to distinguish different works that have similar or like titles; and,

4) to draw together in the catalog bibliographic descriptions of items that contain like types of works (i.e., all collective uniform titles). (Cf. AACR 2 rule 25.1)

Application at the Library of Congress is determined as follows:

25.25 MCD When the uniform title assigned to a particular manifestation of a musical work is identical (except for the deletion of an initial article) to the title proper of the item, do not include the uniform title in the bibliographic record for the item, even though a name authority record must be generated in order to trace references to the uniform title, unless one or more of the following exceptions applies:

1) If the uniform title contains any of the elements prescribed as additions in 25.30-25.32 and 25.35, include the uniform title in the bibliographic record.

2) If the uniform title is for one or more parts of a musical work (25.32), include it in the bibliographic record.

3) If the uniform title is a collective one (25.34), include it in the bibliographic record.

4) If a uniform title is required for a work entered under title and a qualifier must be added to the uniform title to distinguish the work from others with the same title, include the uniform title in the bibliographic records for all manifestations of the work (LCRI 25.5B, p. 8).

Note that an alternative title is part of the title proper (1.1B1). Therefore when the title proper contains an alternative title, the uniform title, which will not include the alternative title (MCD 25.27) will be different from the title proper and must be included in the bibliographic record.

Note also that for collections without a collective title the title proper is the first title in the title statement of responsibility area, inclusive of part title and alternative titles but exclusive of parallel titles and other title information. (cf. 1.1C2 and LCRI 21.30J). (rev. June 1994)(*MCB* 25:8:2)

This decision requires the cataloger to know (or at least to have an educated idea about) the form a uniform title for a musical work would take if it were assigned. Thus the uniform title should be formulated whether it is to be applied or not.

Whatever the rationale, the formulation of a uniform title can seem puzzling to the uninitiated. Rules governing all uniform titles are contained in AACR 2 chapter 25. Rules that are music-specific appear in rules 25.25-25.35. General instruction on which rules to apply is contained in rule 25.25.

While the specific formulation of any uniform title is a unique process that blends elements of research, precedent, and interpretation, the following general pattern is always applicable and will govern the specific discussion that follows.

1) Choose the title of the work in the original language (the initial title element).

2) Manipulate the initial title element (i.e., drop superfluous words, pluralize and/or render into English, etc.).

3) If the initial title element is "generic," make additions to it to make it distinctive or unique.

4) Add further identifying elements to the formulated uniform title (whether its origin is distinctive or generic) to resolve conflicts among different works with like uniform titles.

5) If the work represented is an excerpt, add a designation to represent the part of the work.

6) Add terms that indicate the manifestation in hand.

SELECTION OF TITLES

The first step in the formulation of a uniform title is the selection of the initial title element. What really must be done at this stage is to identify the work(s) contained in the item being cataloged, then to select the version of the title for that work. This is the initial title element that then will then be used to formulate the uniform title.

Next is the choice among different language forms of the initial title element. In following the concept of entry under the heading most likely to be sought and commonly identified by the user, rule 25.27A1 specifies use of "the composer's original title in the language in which it was presented ...

[unless] another title in the same language has become better known ..." (AACR 2 p. 518). That is to say, the basis of the uniform title must be determined based on knowledge of the variant titles under which a work might have appeared *and* then selected from among those variants that are in the composer's language.

> **25.27A MCD** If the title of the first edition of a work is not known to be different in wording or language from the composer's original title, use the first edition title as the basis for the uniform title unless a later title in the same language is better known. (September 1981)(*MCD* 63)

The initial formulation of a uniform title might require significant research on the part of the cataloger. The experienced music cataloger will, of course, garner clues from the form, style, and period of composition, knowledge of other works by the same composer or by others of the composer's contemporaries, the reputation of a particular publisher, etc. These clues will help shorten the amount of time spent searching in reference sources. Nevertheless, there are a few shortcuts.

Ideally, each title should be verified in a biobibliographical source (for a list of sources see Chapter 8). Usually a thematic index is the best place to verify the composer's original title, as well as the title of the first edition, and to determine the language in which they were formulated. It is also helpful for determining in one step the title of a whole work and of all of its parts, should the work in question actually constitute an excerpt.

Once the language is determined, standard music encyclopedias in that language can be checked to determine whether another, better-known title in the original language should be preferred. Ideally at least three modern sources should be checked to determine whether a particular form of title is really better known (the sources should all agree).

Practically speaking, there are shortcuts that can reduce much of this work. The practicality of any particular approach depends to a large degree upon the particulars of the work being verified, but the following are general guidelines:

> 1) Works composed to about 1800, and works by prolific composers, should be verified first in thematic indexes and then in encyclopedias that include lists of works.

> 2) Works composed after 1800 can be dealt with more efficiently by first checking standard encyclopedias in the composer's language. In the event that a later, better-known title exists, it will be found in this manner, regardless of the composer's original title.

> 3) A recently composed work might exist in no other manifestation than that in hand, so one can use the titles as they appear on the item as long as they appear to be formulated in the composer's language or in the language of the country of his or her principal residence or activity. A quick search of one of the online bibliographic utilities can confirm this.

In each case, the amount of verification required will depend upon the results of the initial check. If the title in hand is the same as that in a standard list, less verification will be necessary than is the case when inconsistency results. In all cases the cataloger should remain aware of the dual functions the uniform title will serve, identification and differentiation. During the verification process one must check not only for information to identify the work in hand, but also for information about other works by the same composer in the event that distinguishing elements will be required.

GENERIC TITLES

Music catalogers use the term "generic title" to mean a title that consists of the name of a type of composition (or in some cases names of more tan one type of composition). Footnote 9 to rule 25.27A (p. 518 in AACR 2 (1988)) gives an explanation of what constitutes the name of a type of composition—musical form, genre, liturgical titles such as Mass, Requiem, etc. Catalogers may consult standard musical reference sources (e.g., *The New Harvard Dictionary of Music*) to see which terms are there defined as types of composition, forms, or genres.

WORKS IN A NUMBERED SEQUENCE

25.27D MCD Note that 25.27D does not apply if a work is cited as one of a numbered sequence of compositions of a particular type but the title selected according to 25.27A-25.27C does not include the name of the type.

Kelterborn, Rudolf
Espansioni : Sinfonie III ...
(*Uniform title*, [Espansioni], *not included in bibliographic record*; cf. MCD 25.25)
but
Hovhaness, Alan
[Symphonies, no. 21, op. 234]
Symphony Etchmiadzin : Symphony no. 21 ...

The word "cited" in 25.27D1 means that the work in question must be explicitly identified as one of a numbered sequence of compositions in at least one reference source or manifestation. (rev. May 1989)(*MCD* 64)

MANIPULATION OF THE INITIAL TITLE ELEMENT

Once an initial title element has been chosen, it must be manipulated to make it "uniform." The first step is to apply the list at rule 25.28A to strip away excess words. This is very much the same decision-making process that was encountered earlier in formulating the description. If the remaining title element is distinctive, it will be used virtually unaltered.

25.3B LCRI Omit alternative titles from uniform titles when basing the uniform title on a title proper than includes an alternative title. (*CSB* 44)

25.28 MCD For alternative titles, see MCD 25.27.
For pre-twentieth century works, normally consider phrases such as "a due," "a cinque," etc., to be statements of medium of performance and not part of the title as defined in this rule.

For pre-twentieth century works with titles such as *Duo concertant, Quartetto concertante*, etc. (but not titles naming a form, such as *Sinfonia concertante* (cf. rule 25.29A), *Rondeau concertant,* etc.), consider the word "concertant" or its equivalent to be an adjective or epithet not part of the original title of the work, and omit it from the uniform title.

Vanhal, Johann Baptist
　　[Quartets, flute, violin, viola, violoncello, op. 14]
　　Sei quartetti concertantte : a flauto o violino, violino, alto e basso, op. 14 ...

Vanhal, Johann Baptist
　　[Quartets, strings, op. 1]
　　Six quatuors concertantes : à 2 violons, alto et basse, oeuvre 1 ...

Vanhal, Johann Baptist
　　[Quartets, strings, op. 13]
　　Sei quartetti a due violini, alto et basso, opera 13a ...

(rev. December 1990)(*MCD* 64)

No further manipulation of the title element takes place in distinctive uniform titles, unless required to resolve conflicts.

Other initial title elements fall into two categories:

　　1) titles consisting solely of the name of one type of composition (Quartet, Symphonie, Concerto, Requiem); or,

　　2) titles consisting of more than one name of one type of composition (Prelude and fugue, Introduction and allegro, Rondo with fugato).

Titles that fall into the first category must be regularized and given in English if the name is the same or cognate in English, French, German, and Italian. If the composer wrote more than one work of the type, the term is given in the plural form.

Titles that fall into the second category (i.e., those consisting of the names of two or more types of composition) are used unaltered.

　　Introduction und Allegro appassionato
　　Preludium und Fuge
　　Variationen und Fuge über ein Originalthema

25.29A LCRI *Initial title elements consisting solely of the name of one type of composition.*

One Work of One Type

When cataloging the first occurrence of a work of a particular type by a composer, apply the following:

1) If the composer is deceased, search reference sources to determine whether the composer wrote more than one work of the type, and use the singular or plural form in the uniform title according to the information found.

2) If the composer is living, use the singular form in the uniform title unless the work being cataloged bears a serial number (including 1); in that case use the plural form on the assumption that the composer has written or intends to write more works of the type.

When cataloging the second occurrence of a work of a particular type by a composer, if the singular form has been used in the uniform title for the first work of the type, revise that uniform title to use the plural form.

Note that the medium of performance is not a criterion in the application of this provision of the rule; if the composer wrote one piano sonata and one violin sonata, he or she wrote two sonatas and the plural form must be used.

Mélodie/Melody

When a French work for solo voice and keyboard stringed instrument has the title *Mélodie* or *Mélodies*, do not translate the title into English, since the cognate words in English and other languages do not have the specific meaning of the French word. Consider the medium of performance to be implied by the title and do not include it in the uniform title (25.30B1a).

When a French work for solo voice without accompaniment or with accompaniment other than a keyboard stringed instrument alone has the title *Mélodie* or *Mélodies*, do not translate the title into English. Include the medium of accompaniment or a statement of the absence of accompaniment (25.30B10).

When the word *Melody* or *Melodies,* or its cognate in another language (including French), is the title of any other work, consider it the name of a type of composition. Use the English form in the uniform title and include the medium of performance (25.30B1).

Liturgical Titles

Give Latin liturgical titles (e.g., "Gloria," "Salve Regina," "Te Deum") in the singular. *Exception*: Use "Magnificats" and "Requiems" when appropriate. Apply 25.30B1a, and do not normally include a statement of medium of performance.

(*CSB* 44: 6)

ADDITIONS TO THE INITIAL TITLE ELEMENT

Initial title elements that consist of the unmodified name(s) of a type or types of composition are likely to conflict in an author file unless distinguishing elements are added. Those elements are: 1) the medium of performance; 2) serial, opus, or thematic index numbering; 3) key or tonal center; and, when all else fails to produce a unique uniform title, 4) date of composition or original publication, or place of composition, or name of first publisher. This fourth category is used only rarely.

MEDIUM OF PERFORMANCE

In four cases, the medium of performance should not be added to the initial title element of a uniform title. The first case in which medium of performance should *not* be added is titles that consist of names of types of composition that imply a medium of performance. "Chorale prelude" (organ is implied) and "overture and symphony" (orchestra is implied) are the most obvious examples listed in AACR 2. In case of doubt the cataloger should check a standard reference source for a definition of the type of composition. This criterion works both ways. That is, in cases where the work in question is composed for a medium of performance other than that implied by its title, a statement of medium of performance is added to the uniform title.

```
[Symphonies, organ ...]
[Symphonies, band ...]
[Symphonies, string orchestra ...]
```

The second case is when the work in question is a set of works (e.g., Handel's opus 1, which contains fifteen sonatas for diverse solo instruments) or a series of works (e.g., Monteverdi's madrigal sets, which are numbered serially, but comprise varying performance media) for which there is no single medium of performance.

The third case is when no medium of performance is designated by the composer.

Vinci, Pietro
[Motetti i ricercari]
(For 3 voices)

The fourth case is when the medium is judged too complex or not useful in file organization. Mozart's Divertimenti are a notorious example and are used as illustrations in AACR 2. Because there are so many Divertimenti (somewhere between 20 and 30, depending upon the source), all for varying instrumental combinations, the file would be difficult to understand were medium statements added to each. A considerably more convenient arrangement results from using Köchel thematic index numbers:

Mozart, Wolfgang Amadeus
[Divertimenti, K. 131, D major]
(For orchestra)

[Divertimenti, K. 136, D major]
(For string quartet)

[Divertimenti, K. 137, B major]
(For string quartet)

[Divertimenti, K. 186, B major]
(For wind ensemble)

25.30 MCD Do not apply this rule to titles consisting of two words each of which alone would be the name of a type of composition, when the combination of the two words produces a distinctive title (cf. LCRI 25.27A).

[Humoreske-bagateller]

not   [Humoreske-bagateller, piano ...]

Note, however, that "trio sonata" (cf. 25.29C1) and "chorale prelude" are each the name of *one* type of composition. (rev. May 1989)(*MCD* 66)

25.30B1(a) MCD Although section a) of 25.30B1 seems to prohibit the use of statements of medium of performance in uniform titles whose initial title element (as formulated under 25.27-25.29) is "Mass(es)" or "Requiem(s)," add the medium of performance to such uniform titles when no other information is available to distinguish between two or more works by the same composer.

> **Byrd, William**
> [Masses, voices (3)]

> **Byrd, William**
> [Masses, voices (5)]

For the title *Melody* or *Melodies* and its cognates in other languages, and for commonly used liturgical titles such as *Requiem, Te Deum, Salve Regino, Dixit Dominus*, etc., see LCRI 25.29A. (rev. February 1991)(*MCD* 67)

When the medium of performance is stated, generally the statement is limited to three elements, to be listed in a combination of score and featured instrument/accompaniment order. List voices first:

```
[Canons, women's voice, piano ...]
```

List the keyboard instrument first if there are no voices and there is more than one non-keyboard instrument:

```
[Trios, piano, clarinet, violoncello ...]
```

but

```
[Sonatas, violin, piano ...]
```

Other instruments should be listed in score order. Traditional practice has been to arrange instruments and/or voices in order of descending pitch within groups:

flutes}
oboes}
clarinets} woodwinds
bassoons}

horns}
trumpets}
trombones} brasses
tubas}

percussion} percussion

violins}
violas}
violoncellos} strings
double basses}

When cataloging a recording without benefit of a printed score, this traditional order may be used. When continuo is an element of the medium of performance, it is always stated last.

The final condition involves the number of parts for a particular instrument or voice. In general the number is given in parentheses following the name of the instrument or voice, unless the number is implied by other elements of the uniform title.

Constructing The Statement of Medium

The rules in this section of AACR 2 are sufficiently explicit. General advice about constructing a statement of medium of performance would include an admonition that the segments of rule 25.30 are not necessarily hierarchical, and that they are in many instances interdependent. For example, the accompanying ensemble required by rule 25.30B7 might be one of those specified in rule 25.30B3 or rule 25.30B5. There are, however, a number of Rule Interpretations and Music Cataloging Decisions from the Library of Congress that will help elucidate or expand provisions of the various segments.

For guidance in the use of standard chamber combinations in uniform titles, see 25.30B3.

If the uniform title begins with the word "Trio", "Quartet", or "Quintet", use the form given in the column on the right.

If the uniform title begins with a name of a type of composition other than "Trio", "Quartet", or "Quintet", use the form in the column on the left.

If the uniform title begins with the word "Trio", "Quartet", or "Quintet", but the instrumentation differs from the seven combinations specified, record the full statement of medium, even if this requires the use of more than three elements:

```
[Quartets, violins, violas, ...]
[Quartets, oboe, saxophones, bassoon ...]
[Quintets, piano, violins, violas ...]
[Quintets, flutes, clarinet, oboe, bassoon ...]
```

25.30B4 LCRI Use the following instrument names: violoncello, English horn, contrabassoon, and timpani.

If the application of 25.30B4 results in the separation of a composer's works between harpsichord or clavichord on the one hand and piano on the other, choose the instrument for which the major portion of the works of a given type was intended and use that instrument name for all works of the type. If the "major" instrument is not apparent, use "keyboard instrument." (*CSB* 64: 38)

25.30B4 MCD The list of terms for keyboard instruments in this rule is illustrative, not restrictive. Other terms may be used as necessary.

clavichord, 3 hands
harpsichords (3)
player-piano

(rev. January 1990)(*MCD* 69)

Use the term "continuo" whether the bass line is figured or not.

25.30B5 LCRI *Groups of Instruments*
Use the phrase "instrumental ensemble" as a statement of medium that is added to a title in a uniform title only if the medium is a group of diverse instruments not already provided for by other terms in the list. (*CSB* 44: 70)

25.30B5 MCD Use "winds" in uniform titles for chamber music combinations only when it is either not possible (e.g. because of the three-element limitation in 25.30B1) or not more informative to use "woodwinds" or "brasses" together with the names of individual instruments. Specifically:

1) For works for two different woodwind instruments and two different brass instruments, state the medium of performance simply as "winds." Do not list the woodwind instruments individually and group the brass instruments (e.g., "flute, oboe, brasses") or group the woodwind instruments and list the brass instruments individually (e.g., "woodwinds, trumpets (2), horn") since the choice of which to list and which to group is arbitrary; do not use "woodwinds, brasses," since this would convey no additional information.

2) For works for two different woodwind instruments and three or more different brass instruments or for two different brass instruments and three or more different woodwind instruments, list the two and group the others.

> [Serenade, woodwinds, horn, trombone ...]
> [Suite, flutes (2), oboe, brasses ...]

3) For works for two or more different woodwind instruments, two or more different brass instruments, and one other instrument or group of instruments, use "winds," not "woodwinds, brasses."

> [Suite, piano, winds]
> *(For piano, flute, oboe, trumpet, and trombone)*

Do not use the phrases "string ensemble," "wind ensemble," etc., under this rule. For groups of four or more different instruments from a single family, use "strings," "winds," etc., as in the first example in the rule. (rev. June 1989)(*MCD* 70)

25.30B7 LCRI *Solo instrument(s) and accompanying ensemble.*
For an accompanying ensemble that has only one performer to a part, use the work "ensemble" preceded by the appropriate qualifying term (e.g., "string ensemble," "jazz ensemble," "wind ensemble") as a statement of medium that follows the statement for solo instruments in a uniform title. (*CSB* 44: 70)

25.30B7 MCD The phrase "jazz ensemble" may be used, when appropriate, for either the accompanying ensemble or the group of solo instruments.

> [Concertos, violin, jazz ensemble ...]
> [Concertos, jazz ensemble, orchestra ...]

(rev. May 1989)(*MCD* 71)

Note that the initial title element of the uniform title must be "Songs," "Lieder," "Chansons," etc., and the work must not be in a popular idiom, before this rule applies. This rule is not applicable to collective uniform titles formulated under rule 25.36B. While it is extremely unlikely that any work in the popular idiom would be titled "Song," or "Lieder," should this occur, the provisions of this rule would not apply.

OTHER IDENTIFYING ELEMENTS

The serial number, opus number, and key should be added to titles consisting of the unmodified name(s) of a type or types of composition, following the statement of medium of performance (if any). In the absence of a serial or opus number, or in certain cases in preference to them, a thematic index number is used.

Do not confuse the instruction in rule 25.31A3 to include "any number within the opus" with the somewhat different provisons for excerpts. This instruction is intended to apply to individually published works that are serially numbered sequentially, but that also bear inclusive opus numbering. Such cases are rare.

Authorized Thematic Indexes

The following list, updated regularly in *Music Cataloging Bulletin*, comprises those "certain composers" referred to in rule 25.30C4) for whom thematic index numbers are to be preferred. (For complete citations see Chapter 8)

Composer	*Abbrev.*	*Compiler, etc.*
Albinoni, Tomaso	G.	Giazotto
Bach, Carl Philipp Emanuel	H.	Helm
Bach, Johann Christoph Friedrich	W.	Wohlfarth
Bach, Johann Sebastian	BWV	Schmieder
Bach, Wilhelm Friedemann	F.	Falck
Beethoven, Ludwig van	WoO	Kinsky[1]
Benda, Franz	L.	Lee
Boccherini, Luigi	G.	Gerard
Brahms, Johannes	WoO*	McCorkle
Brunetti, Gaetano	J.	Jenkins
Bull, John	MB	Musica Brittanica[2]
Buxtehude, Dietrich	BuxWV	Karstadt
Charpentier, Marc Antoine	H.	Hitchcock[3]
Clementi, Muzio	T.	Tyson
Coperario, John	RC	Charteris
Donizetti, Gaetano	In.	Inzaghi
Eckhardt-Gramatté, S. C.	E.	Eckhardt, Ferdinand
Eybler, Joseph, Edler von	H.	Herrmann
Frederick II, King of Prussia	S.	Spitta
Gabrieli, Giovanni	K.	Kenton
García, Jose Mauricio Nunes	M.	Mattos
Gassmann, Florian Leopold	H.	Hill

Composer	Abbrev.	Compiler, etc.
Griffes, Charles Tomlinson	A.	Anderson[1]
Handel, George Frideric	HWV	Hallische-Handel
Haydn, Joseph	H.	Hoboken
Hoffmeister, Franz Anton	H	Hickman
Mozart, Wolfgang Amadeus	K	Köchel 6[4]
Novotny, Ferenc	S.	Somorjay
Oxinaga, Joaquín de	L.	Lavilla
Paganini, Nicolo	M.S.	Moretti & Sorrento
Pleyel, Ignaz	B.	Benton
Purcell, Henry	Z.	Zimmerman
Quantz, Johann Joachim	QV	Augsbach
Rust, Friedrich Wilhelm	C.	Czach
Ryba, Jakub Jan	N.	Nemecek
Scarlatti, Domenico	K..	Kirkpatrick
Schneider, Franz	F.	Freeman
Schubert, Franz	D.	Deutsch
Soler, Antonio	M.	Marvin
Sperger, Johann Mathias	M.	Meier
Stamitz, Anton	S.	Sandberger
Stamitz, Johann	W.	Wolf
Strauss, Richard	AV	Mueller von Asow[1]
Tartini, Giuseppe	D.	Dounias[5]
	B.	Brainard
Telemann, Georg Philipp	TWV	Telemann werke Verzeichnis
Torelli, Giuseppe	G.	Giegling
Tye, Christopher	W.	Weidner
Viotti, Giovanni Battista	W.	White[6]
Vivaldi, Antonio	RV	Ryom
Vogler, Georg Joseph	S.	Schafhautl
Wagenseil, Georg Christoph	WV	Scholz-Michelitsch
Ward, John	MB	Musica Britannica
Weiss, Silvius Leopold	K.	Klima[7]
Zelenka, Johann Dismas	ZWV	Reich

---

1   Abbreviation used only for works without opus no.
2   Volumes 14 and 19 (keyboard music)
3   In New Grove
4   Use boldfaced nos.; or nos. from earliest ed. of Köchel
5   Violin concertos
6   Instrumental works
7   Roman numerals translated into Arabic

25.30C4 MCD For works by Franz Schubert, use numbers from Deutsch's thematic index in preference to opus numbers. As a corollary to this decision, enter a song which is not part of a cycle (such as *Die schöne Müllerin, Schwanengesang*, etc.) directly under its own title (with the Deutsch number added where necessary to distinguish between songs having the same title), even if it was originally published as part of an opus, since Deutsch does not group songs by opus. When cataloging a publication of one of the original opera, apply 25.34C3 and use the uniform title [Songs. Selections] unless the original opus contained only two songs (e.g., op. 36), in which case apply 25.33.

For works by Antonio Vivaldi, use numbers from Ryom's thematic index preceded by the abbreviation RV (without a period). Exception: for works in Vivaldi's op. 1-12, use the opus numbers instead of RV numbers. (rev. May 1989)(*MCD* 73)

Key

Add the key as the last element in the uniform title when the initial title element is the name of one or more types of composition. Give the key in the form of an upper case letter followed by the mode (major or minor).

> **Brahms, Johannes**
> [Symphonies, no. 4, op. 98, E minor]

For twentieth-century works, include the key or upper case letter designating the tonal center if it has been designated by the composer.

25.30D LCRI *Key*
Use English terms in stating the key in a uniform title. (*CSB* 44: 70)

25.30D2 MCD For post-nineteenth-century works, include the key in the uniform title if it is part of the composer's original title (25.27A) or the first-edition title used as a substitute for the composer's original title (MCD 25.27A) (before the deletion of elements such as key under 25.28). (rev. May 1989)(*MCD* 74)

> **Hindemith, Paul**
> [Symphonies, band, B♭]

Occasionally these elements will not be sufficient to distinguish among works with otherwise identical characteristics, or they will be unavailable altogether. In these rare cases, other additions, in the order of preference stated in the rule, may be made.

> **Caix d'Hervelois, Louis de, ca. 1670-1760.**
> [Pièces (1708)]
> [Pièces (1731)]

As before, the best source for this information is a thematic index or a comprehensive bio-bibliographical dictionary. Notes on such sources used by the Library of Congress will appear in name authority records. Sometimes the Library of Congress Music Section will issue an "operational decision" in the *Music Cataloging Bulletin* that will more fully explain their sources of information.

RESOLVING DISTINCTIVE TITLE CONFLICTS

Often titles that would otherwise remain unmodified because they do not consist solely of the name(s) of a type of composition will conflict if the composer has used the title more than once for completely different works. Many of J.S. Bach's works bear the same titles, due to various thematic or liturgical relationships. A vogue among twentieth-century composers has been to write a series of compositions that have some loose intellectual relationship to one another and to give them all the same title plus a sequential serial number. When such a conflict occurs, there are three ways to resolve it:

1) add a statement of medium of performance;

2) add a descriptive word or phrase enclosed in parentheses; or,

3) add one of the elements specified in rule 25.30.

When resolving such a conflict it is necessary to be aware of all compositions with the same title by that composer, because only statements of medium of performance or descriptive phrases (but not both) may be used. Identifying-elements from rule 25.30C-25.30E are used to resolve conflicts that remain despite the addition of one of the two specified elements.

Debussy's works titled "Images ... " are the first example given in the rule. His "Images pour orchestre" and "Images pour piano" are entirely different works, but when the initial title elements are isolated according to rule 25.28A, "Images" is the resulting uniform title for each work. In this case the additon of the medium of performance is sufficient to distinguish between the two works.

```
[Images, orchestra ...]
[Images, piano ...]
```

Works by twentieth-century composers are treated in a Library of Congress Music Cataloging Decision.

25.31B1. MCD
NUMBERED WORKS
Read the second paragraph of this rule to mean that the medium of performance or descriptive phrase is to be omitted when this element would be the same for all titles that conflict.

[Fantasie-sonate, no. 1]
[Fantasie-sonate, no. 2]
[Fantasie-sonate, no. 3]
[Fantasie-sonate, no. 4]
(All are for organ)

(This is based on a statement published in *Music Cataloging Bulletin*, v. 12, no. 11 (November 1981), p. 4.)

For works with titles not consisting of the name of a type of compositon which have serial numbers associated with them (whether the numbers appear as arabic or roman numerals or spelled out, and whether or not they are preceded by the designation "no." or its equivalent), apply 25.30B1(d) to 25.31B1 and omit the medium of performance when a better file arrangement would result.

> [Antiphony, no. 2]
> Antiphony II : variations on a theme of Cavafy ...

When cataloging the first work received in such a sequence, it may, however, be advisable to defer the use of a uniform title until another work in the sequence is received, since it will then be easier to see what numbering pattern is being followed. When the second work is cataloged, the bibliographic record(s) for the first will have to be revised to add the uniform title.

Singular vs. Plural

Consider that a conflict exists under this rule when two works by the same composer have titles which are identical except that one is in the singular and the other is in the plural.

> [Fantasistykke, clarinet, piano]
> [Fantasistykker, oboe, piano]

(rev. May 1989)(*MCD* 74)

> **Berio, Luciano**
> [Sequenza, no. 6]
> Sequenza VI : for viola ...

Luciano Berio has written at least nine works titled "Sequenza", all of which are sometimes considered elaborations of the first, but which are ultimately different works for different performance media. Arranged by medium of performance, they fall out of order both sequentially and chronologically:

> Sequenza, flute (Sequenza I)
> Sequenza, harp (Sequenza II)
> Sequenza, oboe (Sequenza VII)
> Sequenza, percussion (Sequenza VIII)
> Sequenza, piano (Sequenza IV)
> Sequenza, soprano (Sequenza III)
> Sequenza, trombone (Sequenza V)
> Sequenza, viola (Sequenza VI)
> Sequenza, violin (Sequenza IX)

By adding serial enumeration instead of statements of medium of performance a better file arrangement is achieved:

> [Sequenza, no. 1]
> Sequenza I : für Flote ...

```
[Sequenza, no. 2]
Sequenza II : für Harfe ...

[Sequenza, no. 3]
Sequenza III : für Frauenstimme ...
```

Note that in order to establish the uniform title for "Sequenza VI" it was necessary to have knowledge of the existence and instrumentation of all the works by Berio with the title "Sequenza". This is the problem addressed by the Music Cataloging Decision above. However, if the cataloger is working with a network such as OCLC, WLN, or RLIN, it is likely that other works in the sequence will have been entered in the bibliographic data base, thus obviating the need to wait to establish the uniform title. Also, it may be possible to check sources such as catalogs of the publisher of the work being cataloged or, for older works, sources such as Vinton's Dictionary of Contemporary Music or Anderson's Contemporary American Composers, to ascertain the numbering pattern.

The "Goyescas" by Granados are also different works, but a statement of medium of performance would be too complex for the operatic work, so a distinguishing term is used to resolve the conflict.

```
[Goyescas (Opera)]
[Goyescas (Piano work)]
```

J.S. Bach's works include nine different works with the title "Christ Lag in Todesbanden". One work is a cantata, three are chorales, and five are chorale preludes. Rule 25.30B rules out statements of medium of performance as too complex for the cantata and chorales and not sufficiently distinguishing for the chorale preludes. Descriptive terms are employed initially to resolve the conflict, although even this yields only three unique titles for the nine works. Thematic index numbers are added as the distinguishing element provided in rule 25.31A.

```
[Christ lag in Todesbanden (Cantata), BWV 4]
[Christ lag in Todesbanden (Chorale), BWV 277]
[Christ lag in Todesbanden (Chorale), BWV 278]
[Christ lag in Todesbanden (Chorale), BWV 279]
[Christ lag in Todesbanden (Chorale prelude), BWV 625]
[Christ lag in Todesbanden (Chorale prelude), BWV 695]
[Christ lag in Todesbanden (Chorale prelude), BWV 695a]
[Christ lag in Todesbanden (Chorale prelude), BWV 718]
[Christ lag in Todesbanden (Chorale prelude), BWV Anh.
171]
```

Be careful to apply this provision only to different works. Do not confuse this situation with suites that comprise excerpts from a larger work, variant manifestations (e.g., libretto, vocal score, sketches), or modifications (revisions, adaptations, arrangements).

EXCERPTS

A separately published, performed, recorded, etc., part of a musical work is entered under the heading for the whole work. This provision is different from that for nonmusical works, which are entered under the name of the part. Uniform titles for excerpts will be common in libraries with large collections of chamber music. If analytical added entries are provided for sound recordings, uniform titles for excerpts will also be necessary. Remember that the first step is to identify the larger work from which the excerpt is drawn and establish the complete uniform title for it. The exact configuration of the uniform title for an excerpt is dependent upon the nature of the entire original work. The cataloger must know whether all the parts of the original work are numbered, titled, or both, and if they are not numbered whether the titles or verbal designations (such as tempo markings of movements, e.g., "Allegro") are unique. Uniform titles for excerpts, therefore, should be established from authoritative editions (e.g., manuscripts, first editions, "Urtext" editions, complete works, etc.). Lacking these sources, thematic indexes or, as a last resort, comprehensive biobibliographical dictionaries are sometimes useful. The title and/or numerical designation of the part of the work should be used as it appears in the source.

Vivaldi, Antonio
    [Estro armonico. N. 8]

Mendelssohn-Bartholdy, Felix
    [Präludien und Fugen, organ, op. 37. Nr. 1]

Clementi, Muzio
    [Sonatas, piano, op. 24. No. 2]

25.32A2 LCRI When the number of the part is used as an addition for the purpose of distinguishing between two or more parts with the same title, precede it by the English abbreviation "No." in all cases. (*CSB* 33: 50)

Another caveat is encountered with suites drawn from larger works.

Tchaikovsky, Peter Ilich
[Shchelkunchik. Suite]

Shchelkunchik is the uniform title for the work known in English as The Nutcracker. The suite represented by this uniform title comprises excerpts from the ballet Shchelkunchik. Do not apply this provision to suites that were originally composed as suites.

Tchaikovsky, Peter Ilich
[Suites, orchestra, no.1, op. 43, D minor]

ADDITIONS THAT INDICATE THE MANIFESTATION OF THE WORK

There are three kinds of additions to uniform titles that can be made to indicate the present physical manifestation of the work. They are: 1) "(Sketches);" 2) "Vocal score" or "Chorus score;" and 3) "Libretto" or "Text."

25.35A1 LCRI As 25.25A makes clear, the additions set forth in 25.35B-25.35F may be added as appropriate to any music uniform title, whether collective or for an individual work. The wording of the first sentence of 25.35A1, which implies that these additions may be used only in uniform titles for single works, is incorrect. The first sentence of 25.35A1 should read as follows:

As appropriate, make other additions to individual or collective uniform titles as instructed in 25.35B-25.35F.

(A rule revision proposal to correct this language has been initiated.) (*CSB* 46: 54)

SKETCHES

Sketches (composer's preliminary manuscript jottings) are collocated with editions of the completed works by use of the addition "Sketches" to the uniform title for the work.

Beethoven, Ludwig van
[Quartets, strings, no. 1-6, op. 18 (Sketches)]

Stravinsky, Igor
[Vesna sviashchennaia (Sketches)]

VOCAL AND CHORUS SCORES

25.35D1 MCD   Note that the rule says that "vocal score" or "chorus score" is to be added to the uniform title if the item being cataloged is a vocal score or chorus score, i.e., if it has been described as such in the physical description area (cf. 5.5B1 and MCD 5.5B1). Therefore, whenever either of these terms is used in the physical description area to describe the item as a whole, the term must also be included in the uniform title. The use of such terms in uniform titles is no longer limited to "works in the larger vocal forms" as was the case under AACR 1.

This does not apply if the chorus score or vocal score is part of a set which also includes a full score, parts, etc., since the item being cataloged in such cases cannot be said to "be" a chorus score or vocal score. (rev. May 1989)(*MCD* 84)

```
Handel, George Frideric
    [Messiah.  Vocal score ...]

Bizet, Georges
    [Carmen.  Vocal score ...]
```

LIBRETTOS AND SONG TEXTS

```
Verdi, Giuseppe
    [Forza del destino.  Libretto ...]

John, Elton
    [Crocodile rock.  Text ...]
```

ADDITIONS THAT INDICATE MODIFICATION OF A WORK

It can be difficult to determine whether a work that appears to be a new version of another work is in fact a modification of it or an entirely new work. In general, modification must be extensive before the new version can be considered to be an entirely new work. In making such decisions, consult the LCRI for rule 25.26B above.

ARRANGEMENTS OR OTHER ALTERATIONS OF MUSICAL WORKS

The glossary of AACR 2 defines an arrangement as "a musical work, or a portion thereof, rewritten for a medium of performance different from that for which the work was originally intended ..." (*AACR* 2 (1988), p. 615). This definition should be kept in mind when applying rule 25.35C1. The addition of the abbreviation "arr." to a uniform title is contingent upon the amount of change a work has undergone. Arrangement can be either by the original composer or by another person.

Do not use the abbreviation "arr." to describe a work in a popular idiom that describes itself as an arrangement without evidence that an original fixed instrumentation has undergone considerable revision. It is common in popular music for one person to compose a melody and another person to provide an orchestration or other instrumentation to accompany it. This process is referred to idiomatically as arrangement. The abbreviation "arr." should not be used in the uniform title for such works.

Likewise, when a work is revised by the composer and it does not carry a new title or opus number, it is not considered to be an arrangement because the aural iteration of the intellectual entity has not changed substantially.

25.35C MCD
REVISIONS BY THE ORIGINAL COMPOSER (Cf. MCD Appendix D. "Musical Work") [*MCB* 25:7:5 If a composer revises a work, retaining the original title and opus number, and the revision is one of different instrumentation within the same broad medium (e.g., orchestra, instrumental ensemble, band) rather than extensive overall revision and the introduction of new material, do not consider the revised version an arrangement, etc. Use the same uniform title for the original and revised versions.

> **Schoenberg, Arnold**
> [Stücke, orchestra, op. 16]
> Fünf Orchesterstücke, op. 16 : Originalfassung ...

> **Schoenberg, Arnold**
> [Stücke, orchestra, op. 16]
> Five pieces for orchestra, op. 16 : new version = Fünf Orchesterstücke ...
> (*"Revised edition, reduced for normal-sized orchestra by the composer."*)

> **Stravinsky, Igor**
> Petrushka : complete original 1911 version ...

> **Stravinky, Igor**
> [Petrushka]
> Petrouchka : burleske in four scenes (revised 1947 version) ...

Added Accompaniments, Etc.

Do not add *arr.* to the uniform title for a musical work to which an additional accompaniment or additional parts have been added with no alteration of the original music (21.21). [Further access is provided by subject headings and classification.]

Bach, Johann Sebastian
    [Sonaten und Partiten, violin, BWV 1001-1006]
    Sechs Sonaten für Violine solo / von Joh. Seb. Bach ; herausgegeben von J. Hellmesberger ; Klavierbegleitung von Robert Schumann ...
    (*Contains the 3 sonatas and 3 partitas*)

Alternative Instruments

Do not consider to be an arrangement

1) a work composed before 1800 for a baroque, renaissance, or other early instrument (viola da gamba, recorder, etc.) which is edited for or performed on a contemporary instrument;

2) a work for a melody instrument which is edited for or performed on an alternative instrument specified by the composer or in early editions, preferably the first

—provided the key is unchanged and the notation has not been significantly changed.

Bach, Johann Sebastian
    [Sonatas, viola da gamba, harpsichord, BWV 1027-1029]
    Sonatas for cello and piano, BWV 1027, 1028, 1029 [sound recording] ...

Kuhlau, Friedrich
    [Sonatas, violin, piano, op. 79. No.1]
    Sonate en fa majeur pour flute & piano, op. 79, no. 1 ...
    (*Originally for violin or flute and piano*) ...

Song Transpositions

When a song or a set or collection of songs is published or performed at a pitch other than the original to accomodate a voice range different from the one for which it was composed, do not consider this transcription to constitute an arrangement.

Schubert, Franz
    [Songs]
    Lieder, Gesange und Klavier / Franz Schubert. — Neue. Ausg. ... tiefe Stimme
    (*Originally for high voice*)

(rev. January 1993)(*MCB* 24:2:6)

ALTERATIONS OF MUSICO-DRAMATIC WORKS

When the non-musical portions of a dramatic work have been substantially altered or entirely replaced (not including translations, however), and the title has changed, the title of the new dramatic work is added in parentheses following the uniform title of the original musical work, as instructed in 25.31C1.

> **Bizet, Georges**
>   [Carmen (Carmen Jones)]
>   Carmen Jones / by Oscar Hammerstein II ...
>   *(Hammerstein updated the libretto)*

TRANSLATIONS AND OTHER LANGUAGE EDITIONS

According to rule 25.35F, if the text of a work is a translation, add the language(s) following the title element. Language names are formulated according to a Library of Congress Rule Interpretation:

> **25.5C LCRI** When naming a language in a uniform title, use the name found in the latest edition of *USMARC Code List for Languages* .... (*CSB* 44: 66)

Liturgical texts formerly were considered exceptions to this rule, but that no longer holds true. A Music Cataloging Decision clarifies the issue:

> **25.35F MCD** Under rule 25.35F2, which was cancelled in 1993, the language was added to the uniform title for a liturgical work even if the text was in the original language only. When adding to the catalog an access point for a musical setting of a liturgical text, delete such language designations from any existing access points for the same work. (rev. June 1994)(*MCB* 25:8:2)

COLLECTIONS

There are four categories of collections, each of which receives a slightly different treatment in the application and formulation of uniform titles. While special rules and examples are present in rules 25.35-25.36, these provisions are heavily dependent upon the rules for non-musical materials in rules 25.7-25.10. The four categories are: 1) two works published together; 2) complete works; 3) selections (or incomplete works); 4) works in a single form (either works of various types in one medium, or works in various media but of one type).

Follow the instructions in rule 25.8 for collections that consist of two individual works published together. Make the main entry under the heading for the first work, and make a composer-title analytical added entry under the heading for the second work.

> **Tchaikovsky, Peter Ilich**
>   [Suites, orchestra, no. 1, op. 43, D minor]
>   Two orchestral suites [sound recording] ...
> *(Added entry under* Tchaikovsky, Peter Ilich ...
> Suites, orchestra, no. 3, op. 55, G major)

```
Feldman, Morton
     [Spring of Chosroes]
Spring of Chosroes / Morton Feldman. Sonata for
violin and piano / Artur Schnabel [sound recording]
...
(Added entry under Schnabel, Artur ... Sonatas,
violin, piano)
```

COLLECTIVE UNIFORM TITLES

Complete Works

Follow the instructions in rule 25.8. For a collection that comprises (or purports to comprise) the complete works of a person, including collections that were complete at the time of publication, use "Works."

25.8 LCRI The collective uniform title "Works" is used frequently enough to make it advisable to use additions for the purposes of making these collective titles distinct, of insuring that translations file after editions in the original language, and of distinguishing between two or more editions published in the same year. To achieve these objectives, apply the following when using "Works":

1) When an item is first cataloged, add the date of publication of the edition at the end of the uniform title. (If a multipart item is incomplete, give the earliest date known. If an item being added to the set was published earlier than the date given in the uniform title, do not change the date in the uniform title until the set is complete.) Reduce the publication date to a simple four digit form that most nearly represents the publication date (of the first volume or part if more than one) given in the publication, distribution, etc., area. Convert a hyphen to a zero.

Form in publication, distribution, etc., area	Form in analytical added entry
1978	1978
c1978	1978
[1978?]	1978
[ca.1978]	1978
1978, c1970	1978
1966 [i.e., 1968]	1965
[1966 or 1967]	1966
1978/1979	1978
1969 (1971 printing)	1969
c1942, 1973 printing	1942
[between 1906 and 1912]	1906
1934 [1974]	1974
anno XVIII [1939]	1939
1969-<1973>	1969
1970-1978	1970
<1975>-	1975
[18—]	1800
[197-]	1970
[197-?]	1970

Add the date in all cases, including translations. When making a reference from the title proper of the item (25.5E2), add the date at the end of the title proper in all cases.

2) If two editions bear the same publication date *and* it becomes necessary to refer to a particular edition in a secondary entry, add the publisher's name after the publication date in the most succinct but intelligible form. Make this addition to the uniform title of the edition(s) needing to be distinguished for secondary entry. ... If different editions are published in the same year by the same publisher, add an appropriate qualification to the publisher's name .... (*CSB* 63: 17-18)

> **Handel, George Frideric**
>   [Works. 1787]
>   The works of Handel ... under the inspection and
> direction of Dr. Arnold ...

> **Sheppard, John**
>   [Works. 1978]
>   Collected works ...

Composers and Writers

25.8 LCRI If a person has written both musical and literary works, apply the following:

    1) If the person is primarily a composer, use the uniform title "Works"

    a) for editions containing the complete musical and literary works and

    b) for editions containing the complete musical works.

(For complete collections of the literary works alone, use the uniform title "Literary works." For partial collections of the literary works, see LCRI 25.10 [below].)

    2) If the person is primarily a writer, use the uniform title "Works"

    a) for editions containing the complete literary and musical works and

    b) for editions containing the complete literary works.

(For complete collections of the musical works [alone], use the uniform title "Musical works." For partial collections of the musical works, see LCRI 25.10 [below]. (*CSB* 63: 18-19)

Selections

Use the collective title "Selections" for collections that consist of three or more selections from the works of one composer, originally composed for various performance media and in various types of composition.

25.34B1 LCRI Do not add a date of publication, etc., to the uniform title "Selections" when this is used for collections of musical works by one composer (*CSB* 64: 38).

Works of One Type of Composition or for One Medium of Performance

If all the works in a collection are by one composer and are composed in one broad medium of performance, use the designation of that medium as the uniform title.

```
[Chamber music]
[Instrumental music]
```

Use "Vocal music" or "Choral music" whether or not the selections are accompanied.

If all the works in a collection are by one composer and are composed for one specific medium of performance, use the statement of that medium of performance as the uniform title.

```
[String quartet music]
(All selections for 2 violins, viola, and violon-
cello; not all titled "String quartet")
[Piano music]
```

If all the works in a collection are by one composer and are made up of one type of composition, use the name of the type of composition as the uniform title. Add a statement of medium of performance (cf. rule 25.30B above) if all the selections are composed for the same medium of performance, unless the medium is implicit (e.g., Operas) (cf. rule 25.30B1).

```
[Concertos]
(All selections are concertos, for various media)

[Concertos, piano, orchestra]
(All selections are piano concertos)

[Operas]

[Quartets, strings]
(All selections are titled "String quartet" and
are for 2 violins, viola, and violoncello)

[Songs]
```

25.34C2 LCRI For collections of music by a single composer for various motion pictures, use the uniform title "Motion picture music" or "Motion picture music. Selections" (without a statement of medium) instead of such uniform titles as "Orchestra music. Selections." (*CSB* 44: 71)

Composers and Writers

25.10 LCRI If a person has written both musical and literary works, apply the following:

1) If the person is primarily a composer, use the uniform title "Literary works" for editions containing the complete literary works. (For collections containing the complete musical and

literary works, apply LCRI 25.8.) For partial collections of the literary works containing one particular form, use one of the uniform titles specified in 25.10. For partial collections of the literary works containing more than one particular form, use the uniform title "Literary works. Selections" *not* "Selections."

2) If the person is primarily a writer, use the uniform title "Musical works" for editions containing the complete musical works. (For collections containing the complete literary and musical works, apply LCRI 25.8.) For partial collections of the musical works containing various types of compositions in one broad or specific medium or containing one type, use one of the uniform titles specified in 25.34C. For partial collections of the musical works containing various types of compositions in various media, use the uniform title "Musical works. Selections" *not* "Selections." (*CSB:* 61: 9-10)

Selections

For incomplete collections with collective uniform titles add "Selections" to the uniform title. If the selections are a consecutively numbered group, use the inclusive numbering instead of the term "Selections."

> **Tchaikovsky, Peter Ilich**
>   [Symphonies, no. 1-3]
>   The early Tchaikovsky symphonies [sound
> recording] ...

Arrangements

Add "arr." to any collective uniform title if the works contained in the collection have undergone arrangement (cf. rule 25.31B2)

> **Bach, Johann Sebastian**
>   [Selections; arr.]
>   Brandenburg boogie [sound recording] / J.S. Bach
> ; arr. Laurie Holloway ...
>
> **Satie, Erik**
>   [Piano music. Selections; arr.]
>   Transcriptions for guitar [sound recording] /
> Satie ...
>
> **Williams, John**
>   [Motion-picture music. Selections; arr.]
>   Pops in space [sound recording] / John Williams
>   ...

Works with the Same Title that is Not The Name of a Type of Composition

25.34B-25.34C MCD If all the works in a collection entered under a personal name heading have the same title and this title is not the name of a type of composition, assign a collective uniform title according to 25.34B, 25.34C1, or 25.34C2, using the most specific uniform title that will cover all the works in the collection. If appropriate, add "Selections" according to the first paragraph of 25.34C3. If the collection is a sound recording, make name-title analytic added entries acording to LCRI 25.34B-25.34C and MCD 25.34B-25.34C (1-2). For references for collections without a collective title, see MCD 26.4B4.

> [Selections]
> (*Contains* Antiphony I *for unaccompanied chorus*, Antiphony III *for piano, and* Antiphony V *for orchestra*)

> [Instrumental music. Selections]
> (*Contains* Antiphony III *for piano*, Antiphony V *for orchestra, and* Antiphony VII *for string quartet*)

> [String quartet music]
> (*Contains* Antiphony VII, Antiphony IX, *and* Antiphony XI, *all for string quartet and the composer's only works in that medium*)

If, however, the works are consecutively numbered, apply the second paragraph of 25.34C3, adding the consecutive numbering to the title of the individual works (in the singular). Do this even if the collection contains all of the composer's works with that title.

> [Antiphony, no. 2-4]

> [Kammermusik, no. 1-7]

> (rev. June 1994)(*MCB* 25:8:2)

SERIES ENTERED UNDER A NAME HEADING

Most series of this type are multipart collections entered under the heading for the composer, and an appropriate uniform title should be assigned according to the provisions of 25.35-25.36. Because these series uniform titles almost always will conflict with the collective uniform titles assigned to monographic publications that are collections, qualifiers must be added. The cataloger first applies LCRI 25.5B ("Serials/Including Series," *CSB* 66: 19-29) and is instructed to add a qualifying term that will distinguish the work. Such qualifiers are created according to the provisions of LCRI 25.8-25.11 ("Collective Uniform Titles," *CSB* 46: 52-53.). When the collective uniform title is "Works," a date always is chosen as the qualifying term. In other cases, LCRI 25.5B suggests the title proper as the element most likely to provide a unique heading, though the cataloger is allowed leeway in providing a qualifier. A thorough discussion of techniques that have been used by the Library of Congress appears in Richard H. Hunter's article "Uniform Titles for Series: A Summary of Library of Congress Practice as it Relates to Music" (*MCB* 15:12:1-5).

WORKS ENTERED UNDER TITLE PROPER (MOTION PICTURES AND VIDEORECORDINGS)

Videorecordings, as motion pictures essentially, will almost always be entered under title proper, which given the ubiquity of manifestations almost certainly will require the use of a uniform title to distinguish the work from others of the same title. The uniform title should be the title proper of the first manifestation of the work (rule 25.3). If this title is not unique, additions will be required to distinguish manifestations from one another.

25.5B LCRI *Radio and Television Programs*
Add the qualifier "(Radio program)" or "(Television program)" to the title of a radio or television program whenever the program is needed in a secondary entry and the title is the same as a Library of Congress subject heading or the title has been used as the title of another work. (It does not matter if the other work is entereed under title or under a name heading.) This same uniform title for the radio or television program must be used in all entries for the particular work. (Exisiting records in which the radio or television program has been used as a main or added entry must be adjusted).

Motion Pictures
If a motion picture is entered under a title proper that is the same as the title proper of another motion picture (or other work), do not assign a uniform title to either to distinguish them, even if there are multiple editions of either work. However, if a motion picture is needed in a secondary entry and the title of the motion picture is the same as a Library of Congress subject heading or the title is the same as the title of another work, add the qualifier "(Motion picture)" to the title of the motion picture. This same uniform title must be used in all entries for the particular work. (Exisiting records in which the motion picture is used as a main or secondary entry must be adjusted.)

> *New work*
> **Copland, Aaron, 1900-**
>> The red pony ...
>> (*Music for the motion picture of the same title*)

> *Existing works*
> **Steinbeck, John, 1902-1968.**
>> The red pony ...
>> (*A book*)
> **The Red pony** [motion picture] ...

> *Added entry on the new work*
>> I. Red pony (Motion picture)

> *Revised record for the motion picture*
> **Red pony (Motion picture)**
>> The red pony [motion picture] ...

(*CSB* 66: 25-26)

Example 45

Gitarre - Kamermusik
Herausgegeben von KARL SCHEIT

GEORG FRIEDRICH HÄNDEL
SONATE A - DUR
für Violine und Basso continuo
(Gitarre-Continuo : Erwin Schaller)

V E R L A G   D O B L I N G E R
Wien   München

On caption:

Sonate in A-Dur

Herausgegeben von
KARL SCHEIT
G K M   Nr. 95

GEORG FRIEDR. HÄNDEL
Gitarre - Continuo: Erwin Schaller

At foot of page 1:

© Copyright 1971 by Ludwig Doblinger (Bernard Herzmansky) K. G., Wien, München

At foot of each page: D. 14.000

Includes 1 score for violin and continuo, one part for violin, and one part for basso continuo. The score is 7 pages long. All three are 30 cm. in height.

Example 45

```
Handel, George Frideric, 1685-1759.
    [Sonatas, violin, continuo, HWV 361, A major]
    Sonate A-dur, für Violine und Basso continuo / Georg
Friedrich Händel ; Gitarre-Continuo, Erwin Schaller. --
Wien : Doblinger, c1971.
    1 score (7 p.) + 2 parts ; 30 cm. -- (Gitarre-
Kammermusik ; Nr. 95)

    Unfigured bass realized for guitar; includes part for
bass instrument.
    Edited by Karl Scheit.
    Pl. no.: D. 14.000.

    I. Schaller, Erwin, 1904-     II. Scheit, Karl, 1909-
III. Series.
```

Handel wrote many sonatas for treble instruments and continuo, and this publication fails to specifically identify the sonata. A search through the authorized thematic catalog comparing musical incipits, shows us that this is actually the third of a set of fifteen sonatas originally published as opus 1. In the thematic catalog the first editions (and most modern editions, as well) were titled *Sonates*, though Handel's original title was *Solos*. *Sonatas* is used because it is a better known title in the same language as the composer's original (25.27A1).

Because "sonata" is a type of composition, and is cognate in English, French, German, and Italian, and because Handel wrote more than one work of this type, the uniform title is based on the English plural form "Sonatas" (25.29A1)

The medium of performance is given as "violin, continuo" according to rule 25.30B4. The thematic index number is included as a distinguishing element (25.30C4).

"Arr." is not used because the music has not been altered (25.35C1). That is, although the piece identifies itself as being for "guitar continuo," no change has been made to the music—the "realized" notes that could be played on the guitar have been *added* to the original continuo, which could itself be realized by an accomplished musician.

Example 46

SECHS DUETTE
aus Opern Georg Friedrich Händels

Ausgabe für zwei Singstimme und Klavier

VEB Deutscher Verlag für Musik Leipzig

On title page verso:

2. Auflage
VEB Deutscher Verlag für Musik Leipzig © 1976
Lizenznummer 418-515/C 826/76
Umschlagentwurf: Joachim Thamm, Leipzig
Printed in the German Democratic Republic
Druck und Bindarbeit: III/18/299
Bestellnummer DVfM 9071

On page following title page:

1. „Bramo haver mille vite".....................................5
Duett für Sopran und Tenor, aus „Ariodante"
3. Akt, Sz. X/XI, Nr. 40

2. „Troppo oltraggi la mia fede".........................13
Duett für Sopran und Tenor, aus „Xerxes"
3. Akt, Sz. IX, Nr. 46

3. „Dite spera"..19
Duett für Sopran und Tenor, aus „Ariodante"
3. Akt, Sz. IX, Nr. 38

4. „Se mai turbo il tuo riposa"...........................29
Duett für Sopran und Baß, aus „Poros"
1. Akt, Sz. XII, Nr. 11

5. „Caro amico amplesso!"..................................36
Duett für Sopran und Baß, aus „Poros"
2. Akt, Sz. II/III, Nr. 13

6. „Caro! Bella!"...38
Duett für Sopran und Baß, aus „Julius Caesar"
3. Akt, Letzte Sz., Nr. 39

The caption for each selection contains only the quoted portion of the contents list.
Each selection has German and Italian words writen under the music.

At the foot of page 1:

DVfM 9071   © VEB Deutscher Verlag für Musik Leipzig • 1974

44 pages ; 27 cm.

The number DVfM 9071 appears only on page 1.

Example 46

```
Handel, George Frideric, 1685-1759.
   [Operas.  Vocal scores.  Italian & German.
Selections]
   Sechs Duette : aus Opern Georg Friedrich Händels /
Ausgabe für zwei Singstimme und Klavier. -- 2. Aufl. --
Leipzig : Deutscher Verlag für Musik, 1976, c1974.
   1 vocal score (44 p.) ; 27 cm.

   For solo voices (ST or SB) and piano.
   Contents: Bramo haver mille vite : aus "Ariodante" --
Troppo oltraggi la mia fede : aus "Xerxes" -- Dite spera
: aus "Ariodante" -- Se mai turbo il tuo riposo : aus
"Poros" -- Caro amico amplesso : aus "Poros" -- Caro!
Bella! : aus "Julius Caesar."
   Publisher's no.: DVfM 9071.
```

Because this item contains excerpts from several works, the uniform title is based on the uniform title for the original works themselves. In this case all of the works are operas, so the first element of the unifom title is "Operas" (25.34C2).

The term "Vocal score" is added to indicate the physical manifestation (25.35D1).

Because the words are presented in both the original Italian as well as in German translation, the languages are indicated in the uniform title (25.35F1).

Finally "Selections" is added to show that the item contains three or more diverse excerpts (25.34B1).

Example 47

FIDELIO

OR
WEDDED LOVE

AN OPERA IN TWO ACTS

Words adapted from the French of
J. N. BOUILLY
by
J. F. SONNLEITHNER
and
F. TREITSCHKE

Music by
LUDWIG VAN BEETHOVEN

English version by
EDWARD J. DENT

OXFORD UNIVERSITY PRESS
London   New York   Toronto
1938

On back cover:

OPERA LIBRETTI
English Versions by EDWARD J. DENT

THE MAGIC FLUTE
THE MARRIAGE OF FIGARO
DON GIOVANNI
FIDELIO

Price 2s. net each
Other operas in preparation

xvi, 37 pages; 19 cm.

(Kinsky lists this work as "Opus 72 Fidelio (Leonore)." The first edition of the score of the first version ("Erste Fassung (1805)") was titled *Leonore*. The work was revised twice ("Zweite Fassung (1806)," "Dritte Fassung (1814)"). The 1814 version is the one that is usually performed today. Original editions, as well as the autograph, were titled *Fidelio*. Riemann lists the work as "Fidelio (Leonore)." This libretto contains the text for the 1814 version, translated into English. There is no music.)

Example 47

```
Beethoven, Ludwig van, 1770-1827.
   [Fidelio (1814).  Libretto.  English]
   Fidelio, or, Wedded love : an opera in two acts /
words adapted from the French of J.N. Bouilly by J.F.
Sonnleithner and F. Treitschke ; music by Ludwig van
Beethoven ; English version by Edward J. Dent. -- London
; New York : Oxford University Press, 1938.
   xvi, 37 p. : 19 cm. -- (Opera libretti / English
versions by Edward J. Dent)

   Translation of: Fidelio, oder, Die eheliche Liebe,
adapted by Sonnleithner and rev. by Treitschke from
Bouilly's Léonore, ou, L'amour conjugal.

   I. Sonnleithner, Joseph Ferdinand, 1766-1835.  II.
Treitschke, Georg Friedrich, 1776-1842.  III. Dent,
Edward Joseph, 1876-1957.  IV. Bouilly, Jean Nicolas,
1763-1842.  Léonore.  V. Title.  VI. Title: Fidelio.
```

This item is a libretto for Beethoven's opera *Fidelio*. According to the rules for librettos in the alternative rule at 21.28A, this is entered under the heading (composer-uniform title) for the opera itself.

The uniform title is based on the title *Fidelio* because it was Beethoven's original title, and because it is the title by which the work is best known today (25.27A1).

The qualifying date "(1814)" is added to indicate the particular version because Beethoven's revisions were extensive (25.30E1).

The manifestation "Libretto" and the language of translation "English" are also indicated in the uniform title (25.35E-F).

Example 48

Label side 1:

angel

Bizet: Carmen Suite No. 1
Jeux d'enfants

1
S-1-36955
(2YLA-9128)
STEREO 33 1/3

ORCHESTRE DE PARIS
DANIEL BARENBOIM cond.

Recorded in France
℗ 1973 E.M.I. Records Limited

Label side 2:

angel

Bizet: L'Arlésienne Suite No. 1
Prelude–Minuetto–Adagietto–Carillon

2
S-2-36955
(2YLA-9129)
STEREO 33 1/3

ORCHESTRE DE PARIS
DANIEL BARENBOIM cond.

Recorded in France
℗ 1973 E.M.I. Records Limited

Biobibliographical program notes on container verso.

Example 48

```
Bizet, Georges, 1838-1875.
   [Selections]
   Carmen suite [sound recording] : no. 1 ; Jeux
d'enfants ; L'Arlésienne : suite no. 1 / Bizet. -- [Los
Angeles, Calif.] : Angel, p1973.
   1 sound disc (44 min.) : analog, 33 1/3 rpm, stereo. ;
12 in.

   Angel: S-36955.
   Opera excerpts (1st work); the 2nd work originally for
piano, 4 hands, orchestrated by the composer; the 3rd
work taken from the incidental music for the play by
Alphonse Daudet, arr. by the composer.
   Orchestre de Paris ; Daniel Barenboim, conductor.
   Recorded in France.
   Program notes on container.
   Durations: 11:45; 11:57; 19:35.

   I. Barenboim, Daniel, 1942-     II. Orchestre de
Paris.  III. Bizet, Georges, 1838-1875.  Carmen.
Selections.  IV.  Bizet, Georges, 1838-1875.  Jeux
d'enfants.  Selections; arr.  V. Bizet, Georges, 1838-
1875.  Arlésienne.  Suite.  VI.  Title.  VII.  Title: Jeux
d'enfants.  VIII.  Title: Arlésienne.
```

This recording contains several works by Bizet. The collective uniform title "Selections" is chosen to represent the diversity of the works contained on this recording (25.34B1).

Example 49

Label side 1:

COMPOSERS RECORDINGS INC.
CRI
DA CAPO CHAMBER PLAYERS'
10TH ANNIVERSARY
JOSEPH SCHWANTNER
WIND, WILLOW, WHISPER...
The Players

SIDE 1   CRI SD 441-A
                                stereophonic

SHULAMIT RAN
PRIVATE GAME
LAURA FLAX, clarinetist; ANDRE EMELIANOFF, cellist
JOAN TOWER
PETROUSHSKATES
The Players
℗ 1981 Composers Recordings, Inc.

Label side 2:

COMPOSERS RECORDINGS INC.
CRI
DA CAPO CHAMBER PLAYERS'
10TH ANNIVERSARY
CHARLES WUORINEN
JOAN'S
The Players

SIDE 2   CRI SD 441-B
                                stereophonic

GEORGE PERLE
SCHERZO
PATRICIA SPENCER, flutist; LAURA FLAX, clarinetist;
JOEL LESTER, violinist; ANDRE EMELIANOFF, cellist
PHILIP GLASS (arr. Robert Moran)
MODERN LOVE WALTZ
The Players
℗ 1981 Composers Recordings, Inc.

Example 49

On container:

american contemporary

THE DA CAPO PLAYERS
CELEBRATE THEIR TENTH ANNIVERSARY

On container verso:

THE DA CAPO PLAYERS' 10TH ANNIVERSARY CELEBRATION
Patricia Spencer, flutist; Laura Flax, clarinetist; Joel Lester, violinist; André Emelianoff, cellist;
Joan Tower, pianist

WIND, WILLOW, WHISPER... – Theodore Presser (ASCAP): 3'58"
PETROUSHSKATES – AMP (BMI): 5'32"
JOAN'S – C.F. Peters (BMI): 6'27"
MODERN LOVE WALTZ – Dunvagen Music Publishers - arr. Robert Moran (BMI): 4'05"
Recorded by David Hancock, New York, February and March 1981
Produced by Carter Harman and Carolyn Sachs
Cover © Judith Lerner 1981
THIS IS A COMPOSER-SUPERVISED RECORDING

Example 49

> Da Capo Chamber Players.
>   Da Capo Chamber Players' 10th anniversary [sound recording]. -- [New York, N.Y.] : Composers Recordings, p1981.
>   1 sound disc (31 min.) : analog, 33 1/3 rpm, stereo. ; 12 in. -- (American contemporary)
>
>   Composers Recordings: CRI SD 441.
>   Titles on container: The Da Capo Chamber Players celebrate their tenth anniversary ; The Da Capo Chamber Players' 10th anniversary celebration.
>   Editions recorded: Helicon Music; T. Presser; AMP; C.F. Peters; ms.; Dunvagen.
>   Recorded by David Hancock, New York, Feb. and Mar. 1981.
>   Contents: Wind, willow, whisper / Jospeh Schwantner (6:20) -- Private game / Shulamit Ran (3:58) -- Petroushskates / Joan Tower (5:32) -- Joan's / Charles Wuorinen (6:27) -- Scherzo / George Perle (4:05) -- Modern love waltz / Philip Glass ; arr. Robert Moran (4:05).
>
>   I. Schwantner, Joseph C. Wind, willow, whisper. II. Ran, Shulamit, 1949-   Private game. III. Tower, Joan, 1938- Petroushskates. IV. Wuorinen, Charles. Joan's. V. Perle, George, 1915-   Scherzo, instrumental ensemble. VI. Glass, Philip. Modern love waltz; arr. VII. Title. VIII. Title: Da Capo Chamber Players celebrate their 10th anniversary. IX. Title: Da Capo Chamber Players' tenth anniversary. X. Series.

Analytical added entries are provided for each of the compositions. Title added entries are made for each of the alternative collective titles.

Example 50

Label side 1

MUSICAL HERITAGE SOCIETY
GENEVAN ORGAN MUSIC

MHS 3873   STEREO
Side 1   33 1/3 RPM

OTTO BARBLAN
Pasacille, Op. 6
ALEXANDRE MOTTU
Pour un jour de Contrition
Pour la fête de Paques
BERNARD REICHEL
Prelude grave

Prelude in E Minor
François RABOT
Great Organ of St. Peters Cathedral Geneva
Recorded by Phonotec
Licensed by Group Genevois des Amis de L'Orgue

Label side 2

MUSICAL HERITAGE SOCIETY
GENEVAN ORGAN MUSIC

MHS 3873   STEREO
Side 2   33 1/3 RPM

HENRI GAGNEBIN
Psalm 150 - Bourdons, musettes
Dialogue et Pasacaille
Psalm XXIII
ERIC SCHMIDT
First Toccata
ROGER VUATAZ Flutes de joie
PIERRE SEGOND Psalm 92

François RABOT
Great Organ of St. Peters Cathedral Geneva
Recorded by Phonotec
Licensed by Group Genevois
des Amis de l'Orgue

Example 50

On container verso:

Side 1: **OTTO BARBLAN**
Passacille, Op. 6
[Edition Peters, No. 576]
ALEXANDRE MOTTU
Pour un jour de Contrition (for a day of contrition)
Pour la fête de Paques (for Easter)
(excerpts from Twelve Liturgical Pieces for Organ; Editions Salabert)
BERNARD REICHEL
Prelude Grave
Prelude in E Minor
(excerpts from Pieces for Organ; Editions Cantate Domino Monthey)
Side 2: **HENRI GAGNEBIN**
Psalm 150 - Bourdons, musettes
Dialogue et Pasacaille
Psalm XXIII
(Editions Henn-Chapuis; Dialogue et Passacaile, unpublished)
ERIC SCHMIDT
First Toccata
(excerpt from Triptyque for Organ; Editions Hen-Chapuis)
ROGER VUATEZ
Flutes de joie
(excerpt from Diptyque de Concert, Op. 13; Editions Cantate Domino)
PIERRE SEGOND
Psalm 92
(Editions Scola Cantorum, Paris)

Francois Rabot, *Great Organ* of St. Peters Cathedral, Geneva

Timings:
Side 1: 11:08, 2:25. 2:25, 4:35, 2:42 / 23:35
Side 2: 3:33, 9:53, 1:34, 4:44, 3:42, 3:21/ 27:10

MUSICAL HERITAGE SOCIETY
Musical Heritage Society Building
14 Park Road
Tinton Falls, New Jersey 07724

Example 50

```
Rabot, François.
    Genevan organ music [sound recording]. -- Tinton
Falls, N.J. : Musical Heritage Society, [1978].
    1 sound disc (51 min.) : analog, 33 1/3 rpm, stereo. ;
12 in.

    Musical Heritage Society: MHS 3873.
    François Rabot, playing the great organ of St. Peter's
Cathedral, Geneva.
    Editions recorded: Edition Peters no. 576; Editions
Salabert; Editions Cantate Domino Monthey; Editions Henn-
Chapuis; ms.; Editions Henn-Chapuis; Editions Cantate
Domino; Editions Schola Cantorum.
    Contents: Passac[a]ille, op. 6 / Otto Barblan (11:08)
-- Pour un jour de contrition ; Pour la fête de Paques /
Alexandre Mottu (2:25 ; 2:25) -- Prelude grave ; Prelude
in E minor / Bernard Reichel (4:35 ; 2:42) -- Psalm 150 ;
Dialogues et pa[s]sacaille ; Psalm XXIII / Henri Gagnebin
(3:33 ; 9:53 ; 1:34 ) -- First toccata / Eric Schmidt
(4:44) -- Flûtes de joie / Roger Vuataz (3:42) -- Psalm
92 / Pierre Segond (3:21).

    I. Barblan, Otto, 1860-1943.  Passacaglia, organ, op.
6, F minor.  II.  Mottu, Alexandre.  Pièces liturgiques.
Pour un jour de contrition.  III.  Mottu, Alexandre.
Pièces liturgiques.  Pour la fête de Paques.  IV.
Reichel, Bernard, 1901-    Pièces, organ.  Prelude
grave.  V. Reichel, Bernard, 1901-    Pièces, organ.
Prelude, E minor.  VI. Gagnebin, Henri, 1886-1977.  Psalm
150.  VII. Gagnebin, Henri, 1886-1977.  Dialogue et
passacaille, organ.  VIII. Gagnebin, Henri, 1886-1977.
Psalm XXIII.  IX. Schmidt, Eric, 1907-    Triptyque.
Toccata, no. 1.  X. Vuataz, Roger, 1898-    Diptyque de
concert.  Flutes de joie.  XI. Segond, Pierre, 1913-
Psalm 92.  XII. Title.
```

Again, this is a recording that would not be analyzed according to the current Library of Congress Rule Interpretation for rule 21.7B. However, many academic libraries would provide the analysis without which these works would probably not be retrievable. Some of the uniform titles (the Schmidt work for example) are based entirely on the data that appear on this recording, because no other information is available in reference sources.

SUMMARY

Uniform titles are employed whenever manifestations of a work have appeared with differing titles proper. Uniform titles will be used for almost all music materials.

The following general pattern is applicable to the formulation of uniform titles for musical works:

    1) Choose the initial title element;

    2) Manipulate the initial title element;

    3) If the initial title element is "generic," make additions to it to make it distinctive or unique;

    4) Add further identifying elements to the formulated uniform title to resolve conflicts among different works with like uniform titles;

    5) If the work represented is an excerpt, add a designation to represent the part of the work.

    6) Add terms that indicate the manifestation in hand.

CHAPTER 8: A MUSIC CATALOGER'S REFERENCE COLLECTION

CATALOGING

Richard P. Smiraglia. *Music Cataloging: The Bibliographic Control of Printed and Recorded Music in Libraries*. Englewood, Colo.: Libraries Unlimited, 1989.

> In this narrative text the author explains the historical and theoretical background of music cataloging and comprehensively covers the techniques and tools used to create bibliographic control for library collections of music and musical sound recordings.

These publications are of major importance to music catalogers because they announce policy and interpretations from the Library of Congress:

Cataloging Service Bulletin. Washington, D.C.: Library of Congress, 1978-
   Available from: Cataloging Distribution Service, Library of Congress, Washington, DC 20541

Music Cataloging Bulletin. Canton, Mass.: Music Library Association, 1970-
   Available from: Music Library Association, P.O. Box 487, Canton, MA 02021

—. *Supplement to Volume 1-5, 1970-1974.* Compiled and edited by Ruth Henderson. Ann Arbor, Mich.: Music Library Association, 1976.
—. *Index/Supplement to Volumes 6-10, 1975-1979.* Compiled and edited by Marguerite Iskenderian. Philadelphia: Music Library Association, 1980.
—. *Index/Supplement to Volumes 11-15, 1980-1984.* Compiled and edited by Marguerite Iskenderian. Canton, Mass.: Music Library Association, 1985.
—. *Index/Supplement to Volumes 16-20, 1985-1989.* Compiled and edited by Betsy Gamble. Canton, Mass.: Music Library Association, 1993.

> The four supplements include cumulations of changes in classification, subject headings, and personal, corporate, and uniform title headings. Also included is a cumulation of the column "New Reference Books in the Music Section." Available from the Music Library Association, as above.

Music Cataloging Decisions: As Issued by the Music Section, Special Materials Cataloging Division, Library of Congress in the Music Cataloging Bulletin Through December 1991. Indexed and edited by Betsy Gamble. Canton, Mass.: Music Library Association, 1992.

ARCHIVAL DESCRIPTION

Hensen, Steven L., comp. *Archives, Personal Papers, and Manuscripts: A Cataloging Manual for Archival Repositories, Historical Societies, and Manuscript Libraries.* 2d ed. Chicago: Society of American Archivists, 1989.

Smiraglia, Richard P., ed. *Describing Archival Materials: The Use of the MARC AMC Format.* New York: Haworth Press, 1990.

Saunders, Richard. "Collection- or Archival-Level Description for Monograph Collections." *Library Resources & Technical Services* 38 (1994): 139-48.

Thomas, David H. *Archival Information Processing for Sound Recordings: The Design of a Database for the Rodgers & Hammerstein Archives of Recorded Sound,* MLA technical report no. 21. Canton, MA: Music Library Assn., 1992.

GENERAL MUSIC REFERENCE

Duckles, Vincent A. , and Michael A. Keller. *Music Reference and Research Materials: An Annotated Bibliography.* 4th ed., rev. New York: Schirmer Books, 1994

General guide to major music reference tools, this is the "Mudge" (Winchell/Sheehy) of music librarianship.

Heyer, Anna Harriet. *Historical Sets, Collected Editions, and Monuments of Music: A Guide to their Contents.* 3d ed. Chicago: American Library Association, 1980.

Fast way to locate complete works of composers; useful for locating composers' original titles when no thematic index is available.

Hill, George R., and Norris L. Stephens. *Historical Series & Sets, & Monuments of Music: A Bibliography.* 2 vols. Berkeley: Fallen Leaf Press, in press.

This is the updated, expanded version of Heyer.

Krummel, Donald W. *Guide for Dating Early Published Music: A Manual of Bibliographical Practices.* Hackensack, N.J.: J. Boonin, 1974.

Marco, Guy A. *Information on Music: A Handbook of Reference Sources in European Languages.* Littleton, Colo.: Libraries Unlimited, 1975-1984.

Volume 1: Basic and universal sources. With the assistance of Sharon Paugh Ferris.
Volume 2: The Americas. With Ann M. Garfield and Sharon Paugh Ferris.
Volume 3: Europe. With the assistance of Sharon Paugh Ferris and Ann. G. Olszewski.

Less convenient to use but more detailed in some areas than Duckles.

Randel, Don Michael, ed. *The New Harvard Dictionary of Music.* Cambridge, Mass.: Belknap Press, 1986.

Excellent source for definition of musical terms.

Thorin, Suzanne E., and Carole Franklin Vidali. *The Acquisition and Cataloging of Music and Sound Recordings: A Glossary*, MLA Technical Report no. 11. Canton, Mass.: Music Library Association, 1984.

> Although this pamphlet suffers from some editorial problems, it is a comprehensive glossary of terms encountered frequently by music librarians.

ACCESS TO SOUND RECORDINGS

Billboard's International Buyer's Guide of the Music-Record-Tape Industry. New York: Billboard Publications, 1963-

> Useful for determining which labels are owned by which companies, etc. Reissued (updated) annually.

Phonolog Reporter. Los Angeles: Trade Service Publications, 1948-

> Useful for identifying record labels, manufacturers, distributors, etc. Also handy for determining the origin of printed folios (i.e., those that are printed transcriptions of sound recordings). Also useful for authority work for current recording artists. Looseleaf format with weekly supplements. Usually available for consultation in record stores.

Schwann Opus. Boulder, Colo.: Schwann Publications, 1992-

> Partial successor to *Schwann-1*. Quarterly guide to currently available "classical" sound recordings in the U.S.; includes lists of new releases.

Schwann Spectrum. Boulder, Colo.: Schwann Publications, 1992-

> Partial successor to *Schwann-1*. Quarterly guide to currently available "popular" sound recordings in the U.S.; includes lists of new releases.

BIOBIBLIOGRAPHY

ENGLISH LANGUAGE

Anderson, E. Ruth. *Contemporary American Composers: A Biographical Dictionary.* 2d ed. Boston: G.K. Hall, 1982.

Baker's Biographical Dictionary of Musicians. 8th ed., revised by Nicolas Slonimsky. New York: Schirmer Books; Toronto: Collier Macmillan Canada, 1991.

Cohen, Aaron I. *International Encyclopedia of Women Composers.* 2d ed. New York: Bowker, 1987.

The International Cyclopedia of Music and Musicians. 11th ed., edited by Bruce Bohle. New York: Dodd, Mead, 1985.

The New Grove Dictionary of American Music. 4 vols. Edited by H. Wiley Hitchcock and Stanley Sadie. London: Macmillan; New York: Grove's Dictionaries of Music, 1986.

The New Grove Dictionary of Music and Musicians. 20 vols. Edited by Stanley Sadie. London: Macmillan; Washington: Grove's Dictionaries, 1980.

Southern, Eileen. *Biographical Dictionary of Afro-American and African Musicians.* Westport, Conn.: Greenwood Press, 1982.

Vinton, John. *Dictionary of Contemporary Music.* New York: E. P. Dutton, 1974.

FRENCH LANGUAGE

Encyclopédie de la musique. 3 vols. Paris: Fasquelle, 1958-1961.

Dictionnaire de la musique. Publié sous la direction de Marc Honegger. 2d ed. 2 vols. Paris: Bordas, 1970.

Larousse de la musique. 2d ed. 2 vols. Edited by Antoine Goléa and Marc Vignal. Paris: Larousse, 1982.

GERMAN LANGUAGE

Brockhaus Riemann Musiklexikon. 2 vols. Herausgegeben von Carl Dahlhaus und Hans Heinrich Eggebrecht. Wiesbaden: Brockhaus, 1978-1979.

Die Musik in Geschichte und Gegenwart. 17 vols. Edited by Friedrich Blume. Kassel u. Basel: Bärenreiter, 1949-1986.

Riemann, Hugo. *Musik-Lexikon.* 5 vols. Mainz: B. Schott's Söhne, 1959-1975.

ITALIAN LANGUAGE

Dizionario Ricordi della musica e dei musicisti. Dirretore: Claudio Sartori; redattori, Fausto Broussard, et al. Milano: Ricordi, 1959.

POPULAR MUSIC

Claghorn, Charles Eugene. *Biographical Dictionary of Jazz.* Englewood Cliffs, N. J.: Prentice-Hall, 1982.

The Guinness Encyclopedia of Popular Music . 6 vols. Edited by Colin Larkin. 2d ed. Enfield, Middlesex, England: Guinness; New York: Stockton Press, 1995.

The New Grove Dictionary of Jazz. 2 vols. Edited by Barry Kernfeld. London: Macmillan; New York: Grove's Dictionaries of Music, 1988.

The Rolling Stone Encyclopedia of Rock & Roll. Edited by Jon Pareles and Patty Romanowski. New York: Rolling Stone Press/Summit Books, 1983.

Stambler, Erwin, and Grelun Landon. *Encyclopedia of Folk, Country, and Western Music.* 2d ed. New York: St. Martin's Press, 1984.

The Year in Rock ... From the editors of Musician: Player & Listener. New York: Delilah Books, 1981.

THEMATIC INDEXES

Brook, Barry S. *Thematic Catalogues in Music: An Annotated Bibliography* ... Hillsdale, N.Y.: Pendragon Press, 1972.

> Good source for finding thematic catalogs for most major composers. Should be used in conjunction with the following list of approved thematic indexes, issued for the Library of Congress in Music Cataloging Bulletin, arranged here in alphabetical order by composer indexed. For instructions on the use of thematic index numbers in uniform titles see Chapter 7.

ALBINONI, TOMASO, 1671-1750.

Giazotto, Remo. *Tomaso Albinoni: Musico di violino dilettante veneto.* Milan, Bocca, 1945.

BACH, CARL PHILIPP EMANUEL, 1714-1788.

Helm, E. Eugene. *Thematic Catalogue of the Works of Carl Philipp Emanuel Bach.* New Haven: Yale University Press, 1989.

BACH, JOHANN CHRISTOPH FRIEDRICH, 1732-1795.

Wohlfarth, Hannsdieter. *Johann Christoph Friedrich Bach: Ein Komponist im Vorfeld der Klassik.* Bern: Francke Verlag, 1971.

BACH, JOHANN SEBASTIAN, 1685-1750.

Schmieder, Wolfgang. *Thematisch-systematisches Verzeichnis der Musikalischen Werke von Johann Sebastian Bach, Bach-Werke Verzeichnis (BWV).* Leipzig: Breitkopf & Härtel, 1950.

BACH, WILHELM FRIEDEMAN, 1710-1784.

Falck, Martin. *Wilhelm Friedemann Bach: Sein Leben und seine Werke mit thematischem Verzeichnis seiner Kompositionen.* Leipzig: Kahnt, 1919.

BEETHOVEN, LUDWIG VAN, 1770-1827.

Kinsky, Georg, and Hans Halm. *Das Werk Beethovens: Thematisch-bibliographisches Verzeichnis seiner sämtlichen vollendeten Kompositionen.* München: G. Henle, 1955.

BENDA, FRANZ, 1709-1786.

Lee, Douglas A. *Franz Benda, 1709-1786: A Thematic Catalogue of his Works.* New York: Pendragon Press, 1984.

BOCCHERINI, LUIGI, 1745-1805.

Gerard, Yves. *Catalogue of the Works of Luigi Boccherini.* London: Oxford University Press, 1969.

BRAHMS, JOHANNES, 1833-1897

McCorkle, Margit L. *Johannes Brahms: Thematisch-bibliographisches Werkverzeichnis.* München: Henle, 1984.

BRUNETTI, GAETANO, 1744-1798.

Jenkins, Newell. [in] *The Symphony, 1720-1840.* Reference volume, 1986, p. 96-101.

BULL, JOHN, d. 1628.

Steele, John, Francis Camerin, and Thurston Dart, eds. *John Bull: Keyboard Music.* 2 vols. Musica Britannica, vols. 14 and 19. London: Stainer and Bell, 1960-1963.

BUXTEHUDE, DIETRICH, 1637-1707.

Karstädt, Georg. *Thematisch-systematisch Verzeichnis der musikalischen Werke von Dietrich Buxtehude.* Wiesbaden: Breitkopf & Härtel, 1974.

CHARPENTIER, MARC ANTOINE, 1634-1704.

Hitchcock, H. Wiley. "Charpentier, Marc-Antoine." In *The New Grove Dictionary of Music and Musicians*, 4:162-176. London: Macmillan; Washington: Grove's Dictionaries, 1980.

—. *Les oeuvres de Marc-Antoine Charpentier: Catalogue raisonné.* Paris: Picard, 1982.

CLEMENTI, MUZIO, 1752-1832.

Tyson, Alan. *Thematic Catalogue of the Works of Muzio Clementi*. Tutzing: Hans Schneider, 1967.

COPERARIO, JOHN, 1570 (ca.)-1626.

Charteris, Richard. *John Coprario: A Thematic Catalogue of His Music*. New York: Pendragon Press, 1977.

DONIZETTI, GAETANO, 1797-1848.

Inzaghi, Luigi. "Catalogo generale delle opera." In *Gaetano Donizetti*. Ed. Giampiero Tintori. Milano: Nuove edizioni, 1983.

ECKHARDT-GRAMATTÉ, SOPHIE-CARMEN, 1899-1974.

Eckhardt, Ferdinand. "List of Works." In *Selected Works of S.C. Eckhardt-Gramatté*. Winnipeg, Canada: Estate S.C. Eckhardt-Gramatté, 1980.

EYBLER, JOSEPH, EDLER VON, 1765-1846.

Herrmann, Hildegard. *Thematisches Verzeichnis der Werke von Joseph Eybler*. München: E. Katzbichler, 1976.

FREDERICK II, KING OF PRUSSIA, 1712-1786.

"Thematisches Verzeichniss der Flötensonaten, ed. Spitta." In *Musikalische Werke Friedrichs des Grossen*, vol. 1. Leipzig: Breitkopf & Härtel, 1889.

GABRIELI, GIOVANNI, 1557-1612.
Kenton, Egon. *Life and Works of Giovanni Gabrieli*. N.p.: American Institute of Musicology, 1967.

GARCIA, JOSÉ MAURÍCIO NUNES, 1767-1830.

Mattos, Cleofe Person de. *Catálogo temático das obras do Padre José Maurício Nunes Garcia*. Rio de Janeiro: Ministério da Educação e Cultura, 1970.

GASSMANN, FLORIAN LEOPOLD, 1729-1774.

Hill, George R. *A Thematic Catalog of the Instrumental Music of Florian Leopold Gassmann*. Hackensack, N.J.: J. Boonin, 1976.

GRIFFES, CHARLES TOMLINSON, 1884-1920.

Anderson, Donna K. *The Works of Charles T. Griffes: A Descriptive Catalogue*. Ann Arbor: UMI Research Press, 1983.

HANDEL, GEORGE FRIDERIC, 1685-1759.

Händel-Handbuch. 4 vols. Hrsg. vom Kuratorium d. Georg-Friedrich-Händel-Stiftung von Walter Eisen u. Margret Eisen. Kassel: Bärenreiter, 1978-1986.

HAYDN, JOSEPH, 1732-1809.

Hoboken, Anthony van. *Joseph Haydn: Thematisch-bibliographisches Werkverzeichnis.* 2 vols. Mainz: B. Schott's Söhne, 1957-1971.

HOFFMEISTER, FRANZ ANTON, 1754-1812.

Hoffmeister, Franz Anton. *Two Symphonies, Them. Index D1, G5.* Edited by Roger Hickman. The Symphony, 1720-1840, ser. B, v. 5. New York: Garland, 1984.

MOZART, WOLFGANG AMADEUS, 1756-1791.

Köchel, Ludwig Ritter von. *Chronologisch-thematisches Verzeichniss [sic] sämmtlicher Tonwerke W. A. Mozarts.* 6 Aufl. Wiesbaden: Breitkopf & Härtel, 1964.

NOVOTNY, FERENC, ca. 1749-1806.

Novotny, Ferenc. *The Symphony in Hungary*: Thematic Index 1, 2. Edited by Dorottya Somorjay. *The symphony, 1720-1840*, ser. B, v. 12. New York: Garland, 1984.

OXINAGA, JOAQUÍN DE

Oxinaga, Joaquín de. *Obras Musicales de Joaquin Ojinaga.* Recogidas y publicadas par José López-Calo. San Sebastián, Spain: Eusko Ikaskuntza, 198-?. Use Lavilla numbers.

PAGANINI, NICOLÒ, 1782-1840.

Moretti, Maria Rosa, and Anna Sorrento, editors. *Catalogo tematico delle musiche de Niccolò [sic] Paganini.* Genova: Communa di Genova, 1982.

PLEYEL, IGNAZ, 1757-1831.

Benton, Rita. *Ignace Pleyel: A Thematic Catalogue of His Compositions.* New York: Pendragon Press, 1977.

PURCELL, HENRY, 1659-1795.

Zimmerman, Franklin B. *Henry Purcell, 1659-1695: An Analytical Catalogue of his Music.* London: Macmillan, 1963.

QUANTZ, JOHANN JOACHIM, 1697-1773.

Augsbach, Horst, comp. *Johann Joachim Quantz: Thematisches Verzeichnis der musikalischen Werke* : *Werkgruppen QV2 und QV3.* Dresden: Sächsische Landesbibliothek, 1984.

RUST, FRIEDRICH WILHELM, 1739-1796.

Czach, Rudolf. "Thematisches Verzeichnis der Instrumentalkompositionen Friedrich Wilhelm Rusts," in *Friedrich Wilhelm Rust.* Essen: J. Kauermann, 1927.

RYBA, JAKUB JAN, 1765-1815.

Nemecek, Jan. "Tematicky katalog Rybovych skladeb," in *Jakub Jan Ryba: Zivot a dílo.* Praha: Státní Hudební Vydavatelstvá, 1963.

SCARLATTI, DOMENICO, 1685-1757.

Kirkpatrick, Ralph. *Domenico Scarlatti.* 6th corrected printing. Princeton, N.J.: Princeton University Press, 1970.

Scarlatti, Domenico. *Complete Keyboard Works in Facsimile from the Manuscript and Printed Sources.* 18 vols. Edited by Ralph Kirkpatrick. New York: Johnson Reprint Corp., 1972.

SCHNEIDER, FRANZ, 1737-1812.

Freeman, Robert N. *Franz Schneider, 1737-1812: A Thematic Catalog of his Works.* New York: Pendragon Press, 1979.

SCHUBERT, FRANZ, 1797-1828.

Deutsch, Otto Erich. *Franz Schubert: Thematisches Verzeichnis seiner Werke in chronologischer Folge.* Neuausg. in deutscher Sprache. Kassel: Bärenreiter, 1978.

SOLER, ANTONIO, 1729-1783.

Soler, Antonio. *Sonatas for Piano.* Edited by Frederick Marvin. New York: Continuo Music Press, 1976.

SPERGER, JOHANN MATTHIAS, 1750-1812.

Meier, Adolf, comp. *Thematisches Werkverzeichnis der Kompositionen von Johnannes Sperger, 1750-1812.* Michaelstein: Kultur-und Forschungstätte Michaelstein, 1990.

STAMITZ, ANTON, b. 1750.

Sandberger, Adolf. In *Sinfonien der pfalzbayerischen Schule.* Denkmäler der Tonkunst in Bayern, 3. Jahrg., 1. Bde.

STAMITZ, JOHANN, 1717-1757.
Wolf, Eugene E. *The Symphonies of Johann Stamitz.* Utrecht: Bohn, Scheltema & Holkema; Boston: Martinus Nujhoff, 1981.

STRAUSS, RICHARD, 1864-1949.

Mueller von Asow, E. H. *Richard Strauss: Thematisches Verzeichnis.* 3 vols. Wien: L. Doblinger, 1959-1974.

TARTINI, GIUSEPPE, 1692-1770.

Brainard, Paul. *Le Sonate per Violino di Giuseppe Tartini: Catalogo Tematico.* Padova: Accademia Tartiniana, 1975.

Dounias, Minos. *Die Violinkonzerte G. Tartinis als Ausdruck einer Kunstlerpersönlichkeit und einer Kulturrepoche*: Mit vielen Notenbeispielen und einem thematischen Verzeichnis. Wolfenbüttel: Kallmeyer, 1935. Reprint. Wolfenbüttel: Möseler, 1966.

TELEMANN, GEORG PHILIPP, 1681-1767.

Telemann-Werkverzeichnis, Instrumentalwerke, Bd. 1

Telemann-Werkverzeichnis, Instrumentalwerke, Bd. 2

Hoffmann, Adolf. *Die Orchestersuiten Georg Philipp Telemanns*

Thematisches Verkzeichnis der Vokalwerke von Georg Philip Telemann.

TORELLI, GIUSEPPE, 1658-1709.

Giegling, Franz. *Giuseppe Torelli: Ein Beitrag zur Entwicklungsgeschichte des italienischen Konzerts.* Kassel: Bärenreiter, 1949.

TYE, CHRISTOPHER, 1497?-1572.

Tye, W.C. *The instrumental music.* Edited by Robert Weidner. New Haven: A-R Editions, [1967]

VIOTTI, GIOVANNI BATTISTA, 1755-1824.

White, Chappel. *Giovanni Battista Viotti, 1755-1824: A Thematic Catalogue of his Works.* New York: Pendragon Press, 1985.

VIVALDI, ANTONIO, 1678-1741.

Ryom, Peter. *Verzeichnis der Werke Antonio Vivaldis.* Kleine Ausg.; 2., verb. und erw. Aufl. Leipzig: Deutsche Verlag für Musik, 1977. Reprint, 1985.

— . *Répertoire des oeuvres d'Antonio Vivaldi: les compositions instrumentales.* Copenhagen, Engstrom & Sødring, 1986.

— . *Antonio Vivaldi: table de concordances des oeuvres (RV)*. Copenhagen: Engstrom & sodring, 1973.

> Indispensable for translating numbers from the Pincherle and Fanna catalogs (used with earlier rules) into Ryom numbers.

VOGLER, GEORG JOSEPH, 1749-1814.

Schaufhäutl, Karl Emil von. *Abt Georg Joseph Vogler*. Ausburg: M. Huttler, 1888. Reprint. Hildesheim: Georg Olms, 1979.

WAGENSEIL, GEORG CHRISTOPH, 1715-1777.

Scholz-Michelitsch, Helga. *Das Klavierwerk von Georg Christoph Wagenseil: Thematischer Katalog*. Tabulae musicae Austricae, Bd. 3. Wien: Bohlau, 1966.

—. *Das Orchester- und Kammermusik von Georg Christoph Wagenseil: Thematischer Katalog*. Tabulae musicae Austricae, Bd. 6. Wien: Bohlau, 1972.

WARD, JOHN, 1571-1638.

Musica Britannica, vol. 9.

WEISS, SILVIUS LEOPOLD, 1686-1750.

Klima, Josef. *Silvius Leopold Weiss: Kompositionen für die Laute, Quellen- und Themenverzeichnis*. Wien: J. Klima, 1975.

ZELENKA, JOHANN DISMAS, 1679-1745.

Reich, Wolfgang. *Jan Dismas Zelenka: Thematisch-systematisch Verzeichnis der musikalishen Werke*. 2 vols. Dresden: Sächsische Landesbibliothek, 1985.

USEFUL WORLD WIDE WEB SITES

COMPOSER DATES

Music Library Association Obituary Index. [http://www-sul.stanford.edu/depts/music/mla/necrology/welcome.html]

> On-line version of the annual index of obituary citations published in *Notes*, the quarterly journal of the Music Library Association. Currently contains entries from the 1966 through 1995 issues of *Notes*. Searchable by keywords.

Washington University in Saint Louis. *Gaylord Music Library Necrology*. [http://library.wustl.edu/~music/necro.html]

> Begun as a paper file in the mid-1980's, this is the most up-to-date on-line source of composer dates. Updated monthly.

PUBLISHER INFORMATION

Music Publishers Sales Agency List. [http://www.mpa.org/Welcome.html#2]

Maintained by the Music Publisher's Association (MPA). The list includes a current directory of music publishers and an index of publishers' imprints linked to that directory. Especially useful for contemporary music scores, often "published" in manuscript form without conventional imprint information. Updated annually.

GENERAL MUSIC CATALOGING INFORMATION

Music Library Association (MLA) Clearinghouse. [htttp://www.music.indiana.edu/tech_s/mla/index.htm]

Created and maintained by Ralph Papakhian, the *Clearinghouse* "stores documents of interest to music librarians." Included are sections on the Music Library Association, music librarianship as a vocation, copyright, and reference/collection development, as well as a large section on music cataloging.

GENERAL MUSIC RESOURCES

Indiana University. *William and Gayle Cook Music Library.* [http://www.music.indiana.edu/muslib.html]

Homepages dedicated to music resources are plentiful on the World Wide Web. Indiana University's music library had one of the first, and it is still one of the most thorough. Besides having numerous local resources mounted on the page, there is a tremendous index of links to other sites. It can be considered only an example, however, since the number of sites on the Web, as well as the nature of each one, is constantly changing.

GLOSSARY

This glossary contains definitions of terms that are peculiar to music cataloging or to this text. Terms already defined in AACR 2 are not included here, unless the usage in this manual differs from the definition given in AACR 2. Terms frequently encountered in the practice of music librarianship are defined in The Acquisition and Cataloging of Music and Sound Recordings. Definitions of musical terms can be found in the *Harvard Dictionary of Music* and *The New Grove's Dictionary*. (For complete bibliographical information on these sources, see Chapter 8.)

Accompanying material. (1) For printed music, introductory prose, often biographical or editorial in nature, appearing on pages preceding or (less often) following the music itself. (2) Occasionally, in twentieth century music, a tape recording intended to be used in performance or realization of the composition. (3) For sound recordings, prose (often referred to as "program notes"), printed on the container, usually biographical or historical. Occasionally, a separate pamphlet containing such prose, with or without a libretto or score of the musical work.

Collective title. An inclusive title proper for a sound recording containing recordings of more than one musical work. A collective title may appear on the label(s), the container, or in the accompanying material.

Container (Sound recording). A protective slipcase or box (as opposed to a sleeve) that holds one or more sound recordings, and from which the recordings must be removed to be played.

Cover. For printed music, a folder whether attached or detached, wrapped around the printed music, and made of substantially different material (heavier or different colored paper) than the paper on which the music is printed. See also *Decorative title page*.

Decorative title page. A title page for printed music, made of the same material as the paper on which the music is printed, and bearing a substantial illustration (often in lieu of a cover). See also *Cover*.

Distinctive title. (1) A title proper for a musical work that does not consist of the name of a type of composition, or of one or more names of types of composition and a connector ("and," etc.), (e.g., Lincoln portrait). (2) A title proper for a musical work that consists of the name of a type of composition modified by an adjective (e.g., Little suite). See also *Generic title; Type of composition*.

Duration. The playing time of a musical work.

Excerpts. Separately published and/or recorded segments of a musical work.

Generic title. A title proper for a musical work that consists of the name(s) of one or more types of composition (e.g., fugue, sonata, divertimento, piece, etc.). See also *Distinctive title; Type of composition*.

Gesamtausgabe. German. The complete works of a composer published in one or more volumes, usually edited from authoritative sources.

Identifying elements. Statements appearing with the title proper of a musical work such as serial number, opus or thematic index number, key, and date of composition.

Illustrated title page, see *Decorative title page*.

Initial title element. The basis for a uniform title derived from the title proper of a musical work by deleting statements of medium of performance, identifying elements, and numerals, adjectives, and/or epithets not an integral part of the title.

Label (Sound recording). (1) The paper permanently attached to the center of a sound disc or the case of a sound cassette identifying the works recorded and carrying details of publication. (2) The permanently impressed eye-readable information on the top side of a compact digital audio disc. (3) In popular usage, the label name. See also *Label name*.

Label name. The trade name, appearing on the label, used by a publisher of sound recordings in conjunction with a serial number to identify the particular release.

List title page. A title page for printed music that enumerates several musical works offered by the publisher, often with an asterisk or underscore indicating the work contained within.

Medium of performance. The instruments, voices, etc., used in the realization of a musical work.

Music in the popular idiom. Predominantly twentieth-century musical works composed in a style that requires improvisation in performance. Not to be confused with music that is broadly considered to be popular in the sense that it is "well-loved."

Musical presentation statement. The word or phrase appearing on the chief source of information of printed music indicating the physical format of the item (e.g., Score, Partitur, Stimmen, etc.).

Opus number. A number assigned to a musical composition, generally by the publisher and/or composer, to represent the order of composition.

Parts of works, see *Excerpts*.

Popular idiom, Music in the, see *Music in the popular idiom*.

Popular music, see *Music in the popular idiom*.

Popular music folio. A published collection of songs in the popular idiom, often corresponding to one or more sound recordings by the same performer. See also *Music in the popular idiom*.

Program notes, see *Accompanying material*.

Release (Sound recording). Equivalent to the concept of edition, all the copies of a particular performance issued from a single matter recording at one time.

Sleeve (Sound recording). The paper envelope in which a sound disc is issued. See also *Container (Sound recording).*

Thematic index/catalog. A bibliography of the works by a composer, usually arranged chronologically, usually containing reproductions of the themes or the first few measures of each work, and sometimes including a transcription of the autograph score and a complete listing of published editions of each work.

Thematic index number. A number assigned to each musical work of a composer by the compiler of a thematic index.

Trade name (Sound recording), see *Label name.*

Type of composition. A form of composition (e.g., sonata), a genre (e.g., bagatelle), or a generic term used by many composers (e.g., piece).

Unit description (Sound recording). A bibliographic record for a sound recording lacking a collective title that includes a transcription of the titles and statements of responsibility for each work performed on the recording.

INDEX

(Library of Congress Rule Interpretations are indicated by "LCRI"; Library of Congress Music Cataloging Decisions are indicated by "MCD". Examples were indexed only if a particular situation was illustrated; these are indicated by "ex" preceding the page number.)

publication, distribution, etc., area: interactive multimedia, 103; music videorecordings, 84; printed music, 9-11; sound recordings, 47-49

publisher: printed music, 9

publishers address: printed music, 9-10

publishers' catalogs: dates in, printed music, 11

publisher's name: sound recordings, 47-48

publisher's number: printed music, 7; sound recordings, 52-54

punctuation: prescribed, in performer notes, 54-55

quadraphonic process: in physical description, sound recordings, 51, ex 71

questioned/supplied dates: printed music, ex 21, ex 41

radio programs: uniform titles for, 197

recording sessions notes: sound recordings, 55, ex 61, ex 65

reference works: 213-24

references: 139-50; for ampersand in titles, 143, 148-49; for collections, 147; for non-distinctive titles, 144-46; for numbers in titles, 144, 149; for parts of a work, 147

related persons and works: added entries for, 138-39

reprints: printed music, 19

Research Libraries Information Network: 111

restricted access note: archival collections, ex 120

scope note: archival collections, ex 115, ex 116, ex 117, ex 120

score: 12; types of: 12-13

selections: as collective uniform titles, 193, 195

serial numbers: printed music, 4-5; in uniform titles, 181

series: in archival collections, 112; entered under name headings, uniform titles for, 196

series area: interactive multimedia, 104; music videorecordings, 85; printed music, 15-16, ex 23, ex 24; sound recordings, 51, ex 63

series-level bibliographic records: archival collections, 111

sheet: printed music, 13

short score: 13

size: sound recordings, 51

sketches: uniform titles for, 187, 188

solo instruments: with accompanying ensemble, 180

song texts: uniform titles for, 187, 188

song transpositions: uniform titles for, 190

songs: voice range for, printed music, 8

sound: music videorecordings, 85

sound channels: sound recordings, 51

sound copyright dates: sound recordings, 48-49

sound encoding: sound recordings, 51

sound recording collections: with collective uniform titles, analytic added entries for, 135-37

sound recordings: 43-80; added entries for, 129-31; with collective title, analytic added entries for, 132-33; without collective title, 45, analytic added entries for, 134; descriptive cataloging process, 43; entry of, 125-28; entry under principal performer, 125-27, ex 161, ex 164, ex 167; technical reading of, 43

source of title proper: music videorecordings, 87; printed music, caption, ex 29

source of title proper note: printed music, ex 27, ex 29

span dates: 113

specific material designation: for popular music folios, 14; printed music, 12; sound recordings, 49-50

standard number and terms of availability area: printed music, 22

statement of responsibility: arrangement as, 6; editor in, 27; interactive multimedia, 103; music videorecordings, 83; no name associated with, ex 25; for popular music folios, 6; printed music, 6; sound recordings, 45-46

statement of responsibility note: music videorecordings, 87

subseries: printed music, 15-16

subseries-level bibliographic records: archival collections, 111

subseries note: ex 117

summary note: music videorecordings, 88

supplied dates: archival collections, ex 120

supplied place: music videorecordings, ex 91

supplied title: archival collections, ex 115, ex 117

tactile materials: 15

tape cassettes: playing speed, 51